WOMEN AND EMPOWERMENT

WOMEN AND EMPOWERMENT

APPROACHES AND STRATEGIES

SUSHAMA SAHAY

1998
DISCOVERY PUBLISHING HOUSE
New Delhi-110002.

Published by:

DISCOVERY PUBLISHING HOUSE PVT. LTD.

4383/4B, Ansari Road, Darya Ganj
New Delhi-110 002 (India)
Phone : +91-11-23279245; 23253475; 43596065
E-mail : discoverybooksindia@gmail.com
discoverypublishinghouse@gmail.com
namitwasan9@gmail.com
web : www.discoverypublishinggroup.com

First Published: **1998**

Reprinted: **2022**

ISBN: 978-81-7141-412-3

Women and Empowerment: ***Approaches and Stretegies***

Printed at:
Infinity Imaging Systems
Delhi

PREFACE

Women's empowerment is a global issue, and discussions on women's rights are at the forefront of many formal and informal campaigns worldwide. Empowerment is a word widely used, but seldom defined. Empowerment is an active, multi-dimensional process which enables women to realize their full identity and powers in all spheres of life. Power is not a commodity to be transacted; nor can it be given away as aims. Power has to be acquired and once acquired, it needs to be exercised, sustained and preserved.

Empowerment is a process and is not, therefore, something that can be given to people. The process of empowerment is both individual and collective, since it is through involvement in groups that people most often begin to develop their awareness and the ability to organize to take action and bring about change. Women's empowerment can be viewed as a continuum of several interrelated and mutually reinforcing components. Since empowerment is a necessary part of any intervention to enhance women's income, it is essential to understand some of the critical tenets of empowerment.

Empowerment of women: Approaches and Strategies offers an understanding on the need for empowering women, concept and framework for women's empowerment. Besides, this book also seeks to discuss the various approaches and strategies for empowering women by outlining the, mechanisms and tools that women are using for their empowerment. The overall attempt in assembling and compiling research data on empowerment of women is to advance human rights in the direction of gaining respect, honour, and happiness for all.

I am personally and professionally indebted to many people for the facts presented here. At the outset, I would like to thank Dr. K. K. Misra, Reader, Department of Anthropology, University of Hyderabad for giving me valuable guidance in carrying out this study. I am also profoundly indebted to Prof. Raghav Rao, Head, Department of Anthropology, University of Hyderabad for giving me all necessary support and guidance in writing this book. I shall be failing in my duty if I fail to acknowledge my gratefulness to Prof. Sharma, Dean. School of Social Sciences, and other officials of the cial support from the University Grants commission which awarded me Research Associateship.

I am also very much thankful to my parents, in-laws, husband, and my two daughters who constantly helped and encouraged me to carry out the research study.

SUSHAMA SAHAY
Hyderabad
February, 1998

CONTENTS

CHAPTERT - I
WHY EMPOWER WOMEN ?

Gender and Inequality

Cultural concepts of feminine and masculine, and the ideology of gender, has meant that throughout the world, women continue to occupy disadvantaged positions in production, and are assumed to be primarily responsible for reproduction(biologically, but also in terms of socialization). Not only do men and women allocate labour and receive differently; they also consume, utilize, and receive resources, goods and services quite distinctly **(Moghadam 1990)**.

The persistence of the traditional sexual division of labour within the home has important effects on fertility rates, on female labour force participation rates, on male-female equality in the labour market, and on the effectiveness of government labour, population, social and economic policies. Besides the strain placed on a country's resources and on economic development, high fertility has also been linked to maternal mortality **(Weeks 1988)** and infant mortality **(UNICEF 1989).** Rising fertility rates negatively impact upon women's mobility, especially on educational attainment and labour force participation. Throughout the world, child care and domestic work are considered women's work. A vicious circle is created when the high rates of illiteracy and fertility among women in developing countries keep them tied to child care and domestic work, and perpetuates the sexual division of labour **(Moghadam 1990)**.

Gender asymmetry is a universal fact of life. In many societies around the world, women are discriminated against by law and by custom , rendering them among the vulnerable and disadvantaged social groups. As **Papnek** (1989) puts it: "Gender differences, are based on the social construction of biological sex distinctions, are one of the great 'fault lines' of societies - those marks of difference among categories of persons that govern the allocation of power, authority, and resources." What then is gender? **Gender is a cultural construct of sex roles, a definition of "masculine" and "feminine" and of the prerogatives of male and female. While culturally and historically bound, gender commonly is a function of power relations and the social organisation of inequality**. Feminist scholars define gender as the social organisation of sexual difference, or a system of unequal relationships between the sexes. **De Lauretis** (1987) has elaborated on the concept and the social fact of gender in the following way:

The cultural conceptions of male and female as two complementary yet mutually exclusive categories into which all human beings are placed constitute within each culture a gender system, that correlates sex to cultural contents according to social values and hierarchies. Although the meanings vary with each concept, a sex-gender system is always intimately interconnected with political and economic factors in each society. In this light, the cultural construction of sex into gender and the asymmetry that characterizes all gender systems cross-culturally (though each in its particular ways) are understood as systematically linked to the organisation of social inequality.

What perpetuates gender inequality? Gender distinctions are not accidental or a fact of nature but are reproduced institutionally (**Epstein** 1988). One of the most important institutions is the **family**, a principal site of the reproduction of gender. **Chodorow** (1978) is one of the feminist theorist who links gender inequality to the psychodynamics of **mothering.** Other feminists subscribe to the thesis that women's relative lack of economic power is the most important determinant of inequalities, including those of marriage, parenthood, and sexuality (**Blumberg** 1978). Many feminist scholars use the terms "**sexual division of labour**" or "**gender division of labour**", and these refer to asymmetrical arrangements within the home/family and within the society. In most contemporary societal arrangements, "masculine" and "feminine" are defined by law and custom; men and women have differential access to political power and economic resources, and cultural images and representations of women are fundamentally distinct from those of men. This is the case even in societies formally committed to social (including gender() equality. Inequalities are learned and taught, and " the non-perception of disadvantages of a deprived group helps to perpetuate those disadvantages" (**Kynch** and **Sen** 1983, quoted in **Papnek** 1989). **In addition of being imposed, inequalities are 'internalized"** (**England** and **Brown** 1990). The result (and reflection) of gender inequality is summed up in the now-famous formulation of the United Nations Decade for Women:

While women account for half of the world's population and perform two-thirds of the hours worked (though are recorded as working only one-third of those hours), they receive one-tenth of the world's property registered in their name. These gender inequities are either ignored in development planning and policy formulation, or reinforced

through specific development projects and policies.

Another dimension of gender inequality derives from the excessive work burden women have traditionally been expected to bear. Such expectations continue to shape women's daily lives under changing economic conditions. All across the region in spite of the fact that women's market participation has increased steadily there is no commensurate reduction in the household responsibilities of women. Work outside the home has in most cases been in addition to the domestic chores for which women have always been responsible resulting in excessively long working hours. This is so in both urban and in rural areas where the need for additional cash incomes has been drawing more and more women into the drawing more and more women into the monetized sector adding to their workload. The growing inadequacy of fuel and firewood has exacerbated the problems of rural women. In the families that can afford hired domestic help the load has been shifted to poorer women working as such for whom again the economic contribution they make to the household kitty has not served as a factor in reducing their own domestic workload. The culture of sharing housework by men of the household has not as yet acquired much social acceptability (**Moghadam 1990**).

Critical Areas of Concern

The following critical areas of concern for development of women were identified in the **Jakarta Declaration** for the Advancement of the women in Asia and the Pacific during the Second Asia and Pacific Ministerial Conference on Women in Development, Jakarta, 7-14, June 1994 organised by the Economic and Social Commission for Asia and the Pacific, , United Nations, New York.

"Women represent fifty percent of population, make up thirty percent of the official labour force, perform sixty percent of all working hours, receive ten percent of the world income and own even less than one percent of the world property". This is the lawful economic profile of women in the world. This is also true of Indian women, and very much true of rural women.

Rural women in our country suffer from being both economically and socially **'invisible'**. Economic invisibility stems from the perception that women are not relevant to the wage and market economy. Social invisibility is a result of the general status of second class citizens, usually accorded to women. It is not surprising that development programmes, which do not take into account the aspirations and the participation of women are not effective in achieving their objectives. The growing realization that rural women are not inarticulate, illiterate and ignorant objects of welfare, but are in fact productive, hard working adults, who have coped with the battle for survival from a very young age, makes their participation in the development process increasingly necessary and imperative.

Women were considered as a weaker sex. They were given a subordinate status in the Hindu Society. **'She is protected by the father in her childhood, by the husband in her adulthood and by the son in her old age'.** The male - dominated paternal system allows her to survive as secondary member of the family and lower citizen of society. The condition or the material state in which poor women live is characterized by low wages, poor nutrition, and lack of access to health care, education and training. Emphasis on improving the daily conditions of women's existence curtailed women's awareness of, and readiness to act against, the less visible but powerful underlying structures of subordination and inequality. While receiving material benefits women should not be deprived of their urge to achieve a better role, their will power to reach a higher quality of life and their commitment to an enhanced status in family, community and society.

Poverty is known to have driven countless women to low status, low paying occupations in domestic service or organised prostitution frequently as migrants away from their homes at times across international borders exposing them to considerable risk of economic exploitation and sexual abuse.

Within the family poverty strikes women disproportionaly hard. As women are entrusted with the responsibilities of home management the absence of resources and entitlements to meet base minimum needs for the survival of the family burdens women particularly. In material terms also women and girl-children in ultra-poor families are the worst sufferers as the distribution of family resources under patriarchal system tends to be skewed against them. When total resources are very limited in any case, it is easy to surmise why this tendency may spell disaster in the life situation of these women. If they are unable to emerge from poverty the cycle tends to be perpetuated through their children.

The majority of Indian women reside in rural areas and urban slums and the majority of women workers are engaged in subsistence agriculture and the informal sector with little or no regulation, legislative protection and trade union support.

The structural adjustment process has generally increased the quantity of employment for women , however, this increase has been mainly in non-regular forms of employment including self-employment in the informal sector. Such workers are often not covered by labour legislation and lack job security. The downscaling of the public sector, budgetary restraints and privatization have affected women adversely, particularly through the reduction of subsidized welfare services. Rapid technological advances are likely to affect poor women by devaluing their traditional skills, thus jeopardizing their survival strategies and pushing them into extreme poverty.

There is also increasing evidence of women entering home-based sub-contract work, which almost always denies them protection under labour laws and isolates them from fellow workers thereby reducing opportunities to organize. These workers are often not recognized in national labour statistics as economically productive workers. Structural adjustment programmes that emphasize privatization and the role of the market have sometimes resulted in reduction of the level of labour standards even in formal sector jobs. At times women have suffered a disproportionate reduction in labour market opportunities under economic reforms especially in economies in transition.

Women's access to wage and salaried employment is heavily skewed towards lower paid jobs. When new job opportunities are created specifically for women they tend to be in low wage, low skilled occupations often under highly exploitative conditions. The vast majority of women work in self employment outside agriculture in low paying trade or service activities.

The major difficulties encountered by women in self employment activities relate to access to credit markets and technical skills. Customary law and convention in most countries preclude women from claiming family assets. Women also lack adequate access to institutional credit facilities.

A considerable amount of abuse and harassment of women also takes place within the family. The phenomenon of violence in the home is common and is not confined to poor or illiterate families as is often presumed. In some communities female babies and girl children have been known to be systematically condemned to pervasive neglect. The extreme form of such neglect and abuse is manifested in female foeticide and infanticide. Dowry or the perceived inadequacy of it has been the cause of harassment of young brides in thousands of reported cases at times leading to death.

One of the main reasons for the high incidence of obstetrically difficult births and anemia in women is poor nutrition of women and girls and the excessive workload women and girls are made to bear from early childhood. These factors continue to shape the conditions of women's daily lives in many households. Furthermore facilities for the treatment of infection toxaerma and hemorrhage which are the major cause of maternal morality are generally inadequate in many countries.

The incidence of unwanted pregnancies is still very high suggesting among other factors inadequate access of women to education about reproductive choices and to family planning services or lack of control over their reproductive roles in an unequal sexual partnership. Excessive workload, lack of proper nutrition, repeated pregnancies, poor education and lack of access to health care facilities mark the lives of the majority of women particularly those who are poor. Many countries continue to suffer from inadequate and very skewed distribution of medical services. Distribution is heavily skewed in favour of urban and against rural areas while within each access to services is skewed in favour of men and against women. Poor rural women are the most neglected of all groups. In addition one quarter to one third of all maternal deaths occur when births are too numerous or to mothers who are under 16 or over 33 and when the births are too closely spaced. Early marriages and teenage pregnancies which have continued to flourish despite legislation to the contrary in some countries have contributed to this problem.

According to the 1991 census, the sex ratio for women is 929 per 1000 men; this has fallen from the 1981 figure where it stood at 933 per 1000men. The literacy rate is 39.42 percent for women and 63.86 percent for men. The literacy rate for both men and women has gone up when compared with the 1981 census. Women's work participation rate according to 1991 census showed that it was 13.99 percent and men's work participation rate was 51.62 percent.

Women's participation in labour force has been declining and the status of women has not improved much over the years, and they continue to remain a disadvantaged group.

Women have been playing very important and significant economic roles in both the urban and rural areas. We see that both in the organised and unorganized sectors of the economy, be it agriculture, industry or services, woman has been contributing substantially and yet very often her contribution goes unnoticed by both the family and society. Her work remains mostly **"invisible"**

Women play dual roles, one is as the paid worker and the other, as an unpaid worker, involved as a part of the family labour in the fields, family trade, craft, etc. through her labour, she also contributes in running the family by doing different domestic chores.

The work of hers in the family by virtue of her being the mother, wife, daughter, daughter-in-law and home maker takes up a lot of her time and very often she is the sole contributor in running and keeping the family going. Yet, this contribution of hers is not recognized in the economy.

Even her contribution as a worker on the family lands, in traditional household crafts, etc., is not recognized. Thus, although woman does double the amount of work and contribute doubly to the economy, she is still considered a burden and instances of female infanticide and foeticide (which are not uncommon even today) bear testimony to this.

Only 5-6 percent of the working women have an employer-employee relationship. These are across the three income groups . There are some women who are engaged only in household work for their own families. These women mainly belong to the middle income groups. The women in the low income group con not afford not to earn some returns for fending the family, so they have to combine household work and return earning work. The women in the high income group rarely do their own household work themselves; they engage other people to do it for them. It is the women in the low income group who are fending for themselves, without a regular job, an employer employee relationship which constitutes the majority of the female workforce in our country.

Poor women are engaged in a variety of occupations: small farm agriculture, livestock tending , processing livestock produce, gathering and processing fruit produce, tree- growing, small trading and vending, producing manufactured items such as garments, *bidis*, shoes food stuff, etc. at home or in small worksheds. They also provide manual labour in fields, at construction sites, in factories and worksheds, providing services such as - domestic labour, washing, cleaning, transportation, child care etc.

Woman's biological and social reality has created several distinct roles for her in society: that of wife, mother, daughter, homemaker, worker, citizen, etc. these multiple roles of woman make several diverse demands on her time. The social system in our country recognizes wife, mother and homemaker roles as the paramount roles of women.

As elaborated earlier, poor women living at sub-subsistence level, have no choice but to be primary wage-earners and assume responsibility for the livelihood of their children. Any attempt to change the situation of poverty for the vast majority of the population in our country today, needs to recognize and validate the "worker role" of poor women, and enable them to meet their basic livelihood needs over which they have no control.

It is impossible to even think of affecting the situation of the poor people in today's economy. The forces against the poor are so many and the social system so biased in favour of the rich that it will not respond to the demands of the individual poor woman. In the economy, the various forces that work against the poor are highly organised, It is so-far the poor self employed workers, as well as the poor women workers, who are not organised as workers. To be able to ameliorate the situation of poverty of women workers, some direct interventions have to be made in the economy as it exists today. This is possible only by organising the women workers and enhancing their collective strength. Their strength lies in numbers and these need to be brought together.

Feminist Strategies for Development

The authors of the ***Human Development Report*** (UNDP 1990) argue that to live a long and healthy life, to be educated and to have access to resources needed for a decent standard of living are the most critical of human capabilities and choices. Additional choices include political freedom, guaranteed human rights and personal self-respect. Development enables people to have these choices, by creating a conducive environment for people, individually and collectively, to develop their full potential and to have a reasonable chance of leading productive and creative lives in accord with their needs and interests. **" Development is ultimately ¼ [a matter] of the capacity of a society to tap the root of popular creativity, to free up and empower people¼"** (**Levitt** 1990). Both the imperatives of distributive justice and concerns about societal development call for women's access to productive resources (employment, training, credit, land, extension, legal reform), access to basic goods and services (household needs, education, health), and external resources flows (such as debt reduction). **In turn, these contribute to the long-term goals of gender equity and the empowerment of women.**

The World Conference of the UN Decade for Women held at Copenhagen in July, 1980 defined **Development as the total development, including**

development in the political, economic, social, cultural growth of the human person. "Women's development should not be viewed as an issue in social development but should be seen as an essential component in every dimension of development", according to this definition.

Why Empower Women?

Discrimination of women from womb to tomb is well known. The **National Perspective Plan for Women 1988- 2000 AD (1988)** which has made a free, frank and objective analysis of the impact of developmental plans and programmes of Indian women, with special reference to rural women, gives us the following profile of women in India:

There is continued inequality and vulnerability of women in all sectors - economic, social, political, education, health care, nutrition and legal. As women are oppressed in all spheres of life, they need to be empowered in all walks of life.

Kamala Bhasin (1992) asks the question **why women need to be empowered?** They need to be empowered, she believes, because women have and will lead us in our search for a world free of violence and war. Women have led the peach and ecology movements in many parts of the world. She believes that sustainable development has to be woman centered. She does not say this because she is a women or a feminist. Historically and even today women take care of the basic needs of society like food, fodder, fuel, shelter, nurturing. They are also more in tune with nature. As child-bearers they have had to be more in tune with their own nature. They have also been creating and nurturing. She does not say that. It is because of women's socialization for centuries, and because of their preoccupation with sustenance, nurturing, nursing.

Empowerment of women, means many things to **Bhasin** (1992):

- It means recognizing women's contribution, women's knowledge.
- It means helping women fight their own fears, and feelings of inadequacy and inferiority.
- It means women enhancing their self-respect and self- dignity
- It means women enhancing their self-respect and self- dignity.
- It means women controlling their own bodies.
- It means women becoming economically independent and self-reliant.
- It means women controlling resources like land and property.

- It means reducing women's burden of work, specially within the home.
- It means creating and strengthening women's groups and organizations.
- It means promoting qualities of nurturing, caring gentleness, not just in

Women but also in men.

Women's empowerment includes both a personal strengthening and enhancement of life chances, and collective participation in efforts to achieve, equality of opportunity and equity between different genders, ethnic groups, social classes, and age groups. It enhances human potential at individual and social levels of expressions. Empowerment is an essential starting point and a continuing process for realizing the ideals of human liberation and freedom for all.

Thus when we talk of women's development and women's status, it is important for us to recognize that interventions at all levels namely, social, cultural, political, economic are required and are possible (real changes) only if changes take place in the existing system and social structures, which are not at all, favorable to the women today.

Any intervention that does not contribute substantially towards women's active and critical participation in the overall development process of the society, needs to be re looked at as women's development in the real sense can take place only when the systems or structures of the society are changed in favour of women.

Women's empowerment is not and cannot be separate from empowerment of nature, empowerment of all the marginalized people and countries. Women's struggles are and should be linked to peace movement, ecology movement, working class movement, human rights movement and movement for democratization and decentralization of society.

Women, especially rural women, are also the ones whose survival is most threatened by ecologically disastrous development. Women are the poorest, the most vulnerable. When forests, or lands or rivers, or wells die, these women mourn the most because they are the most affected. Because women know the pains of creation they hate destruction most. This is why in struggles to save forests, struggles against pollution, in movements against militarisation women are in the forefront. For all these reasons women have to be at the centre of sustainable development. Women are more likely to insist that basic needs be satisfied, that killings be stopped. Women are also said to be more emotional, more passionate and movements for sustainable development definitely need heavy doses of passion and emotion. Cold rationality alone is not enough.

Empowerment of women is very much essential to achieve sustainable development. Quoting from a **UNFPA** report, "the state of World Population 1992", the News Letter of Bernard Van Leer Foundation says, that there can be no sustainable development without development for women, because it is women who contribute most for the development for children.

In order to play their various roles in the preservation of ecological balance and in maintaining sustainable development there is the urgent need for strengthening their hands by empowering them. For, based on a United Nations 1991 report, "Challenges to the year 2000", the world ecology report says, that the empowerment of women has multiple benefits not only for the environment but also for humanity as well. Ensuring sustainable development requires women's empowerment and their full, equal and beneficial involvement in decision making process related to sustainable development. it also requires their full participation as planners, managers, scientists and technical advisers in all environment and development fields.

During the **Earth Summit** held in Rio (3-14 June 1992) Women's treaty for NGOs seeking a just and healthy planet, **pledged their commitment to the empowerment of women which is the central and powerful force in the search for a safe environment, economic and social justice, adequate reallocation of resources, the survival of all species and the common goal of a healthy planet in which future generation can flourish**. According to the treaty, for raising the social, economic, political and health status of women, there is the need for policies and actions to assure then to equal access to education information, fair wages, land safe working conditions, inheritance rights, credit and appropriate technology, environmental friendly consumer products and health care. There should not be any depravation of women of their reproductive freedom, the knowledge required to exercise that freedom, the provision of comprehensive reproductive health care and family planning, including the right to parental care, safe and legal voluntary contraceptives and abortion, sex education and information.

Empowerment of women also implies avoidance of crimes and atrocities against women and improvement in education, health etc. Improvement of the status of women and their access to family planning services, make a triple contribution to sustainable development such as they make their own contribution to the quality of life and eradication of absolute poverty, they contribute to economic growth, by raising the quality and skills of the work force and slowing down population growth thus reducing the burden on the environment which will improve sustainability, says a **UNFPA** report.

Empowerment of women would necessarily mean redefining the notions of femininity and masculinity changing man-woman relationship. This is something more and more women are now talking about. Contrary to the rumors which are spread, feminists are not against men. They are against patriarchy as a system; against aggressive masculinity, against macho men. They want men who are gentle, who are caring. The models of good men for us are not muscular, aggressive, supermen but men like Mahatma Gandhi, Jesus Christ, Guru Nanak, Buddha. They want husbands who can not only act as fathers but also as mothers.

Many men tell us (**Bhasin** 1992) **"why do you want to be like men".** We really do not want to be like men if being a man means being aggressive. We would like men to be like us. We feel male and female qualities are not natural; they are cultural and therefore men can also learn to be caring and nurturing.

Empowerment of women is not a one way process - it is not the adult educators and activists can go and empower others. It is a two way process in which we empower and get empowered. This is an ongoing journey for all of us. No one can become empowered for good and then become an expert in empowering others.

As women account for more than half of the world's illiterate population achieving literacy could be one of the first steps to empowering women to participate more equally in society and free themselves from economic exploitation and oppression. The empowerment of women and the improvement of their status, particular in respect of education, health and economic opportunity is a highly important end in itself. In addition, this also enhances their decision making capacity in vital areas, especially in the areas of reproduction. Education is one of the most important means of empowering women and of giving them knowledge, skills and self confidence necessary, to be full partners in the development process (**Lucy**, 1995).

Women need to be empowered for gaining collective strength. Why do women want collective strength? When we are discussing of role of women, we are talking of changing the equilibrium of social forces to treat them as equal partners in the society and to bring recognition to all their roles. When we are concerned with poor women, we are seized of changing both social and economic forces in favour of their worker-role in particular and other roles in general. Such a perception of poor womens' work places, their **empowerment as the central thrust of the desired goal**, which is beyond increase in income levels, and, in financial terms. **Empowerment entails struggle; it entails learning to deal with the forces of oppression; it entails having a vision of a new society; it also entails conscious and deliberate interventions and efforts to enhance the quality of life. Collective strength is necessary for building solidarity and support among workers to achieve empowerment. On the one hand, a struggle against existing forces of oppression has to be undertaken and on the other, support for women workers has to be generated through collective strength. Empowerment through organising helps to sustain both the struggle and the support base.** In order to fight against the socially constructed gender biases, women have to swim against the stream that requires more strength. **Such a strength comes from the process of empowerment**(quoted from the book "Work and Empowerment: Management of women's Economic Activities(A Manual for Activists, New Delhi, 1991).

Empowered Women's Characteristics

According to **Hall** (1992), the **empowered women** share the following characteristics:

- Empowered women define their attitudes, values, and behavior in relation to their own real interests. They have autonomy because they claim their freedom from existing male hierarchies, whether they live in traditional societies or modern, industrial societies.

- Empowered women maintain equal-mindedness, rather than act out roles that merely confront and challenge male dominance. Empowered women do not aim at being superior to men. They respond as equals and cooperate in order to work toward the common good.

- Empowered women use their talents to live fulfilling lives. They has not only survived the harshness of their own subjugation, but they have also transcended their subjugation, thus moving themselves through survival to fulfillment. Empowered women maintain their strength in the presence of pressures of family, religion, and work, and they contribute toward the empowerment of all women.

- Empowered women may continue to meet their family responsibilities and participate in religion. They choose to do so in ways that strengthen rather than debilitate them, however, which is also advantageous for others. Empowered women do not retreat form these traditional responsibilities, but they forge their own ways of doing things.

- Empowered women define their values and formulate their beliefs themselves. They do not derive their sense of being from male authorities, and they do not live vicariously through men. Empowered women strengthen themselves through other women's support and sustain their own moral visions. Their actions flow from their own distinctive ideals.

- Empowered women can be found in all social groups and all societies. However, the optimal conditions for empowered women are both individual and both individual and social, and there are more empowered women in modern societies, because the collective actions of women are more visible and more palpable in those in settings.

What Does Women's Empowerment Achieve?

Women's empowerment helps women to make necessary transitions over their life courses (**Foner & Kertzer**, 1978; **Marks**, 1977). As the patterns of women's interactions have an impact on broader social structures, to the extent that they make changes in these exchanges, they will be in more advantageous positions to make changes at broader levels of social organization (**Sanday**, 1981).

When women find their real selves, they will be more able to recognize that many of the institutional demands on them are alien to their true interests (**Turner**, 1976). Empowering changes in women's attitudes result in new values that motivate them to participate more actively in broader social contexts (**Mason, Czajka, & Arber,** 1976; **Roper & Labeff,** 1977).

Women's empowerment allows women to be appreciated and acknowledged for who they are and what they do (**Kessler-Harris**, 1981; **Levy**, 1989). Women's support of other women (**Oliker**, 1989) heralds a new stage of women's development, where women can unite and act collectively to reduce and remove oppressive social structures (**Fitzpatrick**, 1990).

On both individual and social levels women's empowerment neutralizes and sometimes negates their pervasive devaluation (**Reskin**, 1988). Women's empowerment also modifies women's existing sexual ideologies (**Mason**

& **Bumpass**, 1975) by introducing women's own goals and values into their decision making. Women become more autonomous through their empowerment and, consequently, institutionalized patterns of gender arrangement will continue to be scrutinized and questioned.

Women are empowered when they are in touch with their own traditions, shared achievements, and real interests. Women's expansion of power depends on their abilities to stay centered in their own uniqueness, as well as to be open simultaneously to the range of action possibilities demonstrated through other women's lives (**Gerson**, 1985).

Women's personal exchanges with other people are unavoidable influenced by their historical circumstances. women act most effectively when they can recognize the inevitability of this interdependence of influences and can formulate their goals on the basis of this interdependence (**Hall**, 1990a).

It is not particularly the ideology of feminism that empowers women, but rather their capacities to face bravely the individual and social facts of their actual situations (**Lengermann** & **Wallace**, 1985). Through examining the facts of their lives, women understand themselves and their circumstances more fully and become freer of the extent and internal controls that would otherwise define their lives for them. This process of empowerment also may be thought of as the way in which women observe, interpret, and assess their realities as objectively as possible (**Andersen**, 1988).

Empowerment allows women to move beyond others conventional gender stereotypes and rigid gender role definitions . When women deliberately turn toward the most significant sites of their oppression-families, religion, and work-they begin to see the complexities and nuances of their own exploitation (**Mills**, 1967). Women must know themselves sufficiently to be come freer, and this occurs only when they understand how much society controls them and perpetuates their subordination (**Randour**, 1987).

When women make their own empowerment into a goal close to their hearts-a primary task of each day-they will inevitably become an integral part of grassroots activism (**Diaz-Diocaretz** & **Zavala** 1985; **Iglitzin** & **Ross**, 1986). However, when women choose to ignore or deny their need to be empowered, they become pawns of the social mechanisms that perpetuate their subordination (**Durkheim** 1984).

The first state of women's empowerment is women's awakening to the facts of their existence-throughout the United States, in different ethnic groups, in different social classes, and in the world around them (**Charlton. Everett, & Staudt**, 1989). **Empowerment is the initial phase of women's liberation freedom, and equity as well as a long-range goal of women's political participation. It is the first step in a long journey toward the formulation and realization of human rights and responsibilities that transcend gender role stereotypes and the objectification of women and the men.**

Empowerment of women and their equal status etc., are more easily said, than put in to practice. This is, more especially so, in a society ridden with orthodox and conservative ideals and ideologies for which religious sanction and support are not lacking. In such societies any improvement in the status of women is almost impossible without the cooperation and change of hearts from the part of men (**Lucy,** 1995).

•

CHAPTER - II

CONCEPT OF EMPOWERMENT

Empowerment: Meaning And Concept

Women's empowerment is a global issue, and discussions on women's political rights are at the forefront of many formal and informal campaigns worldwide.

The concept of women's empowerment appears to be the outcome of several important critiques and debates generated by the women's movement throughout the world, and particularly by Third World feminists. Its source can be traced to the interaction between feminism and the concept of "popular education" developed in Latin America in the 1970s (**Walters** 1991).

Lorraine Gutierrez et al (1995) feel that during the past two decades, empowerment practice in the human services has emerged from efforts to develop more effective and responsive services for women, people of color, and other oppressed groups. The goal of this method of practice is to address the role powerlessness plays in creating and perpetuating personal and social problems. it can be distinguished by its focus on developing critical awareness, increasing feelings of collective and self-efficacy, and developing skills for personal, interpersonal, or social change (**Bricker - Jenkins & Hooyman,** 1991, **Freire,**1973, **Gutierrez,** 1990; **Pinderhughes, 1989; Rappaport,** 1981; **Solomon,** 1976; **Staples,** 1991). Within our increasingly diverse society, empowerment has emerged as one perspective on practice that can be inclusive and supportive of diversity.

The most conspicuous feature of the term empowerment is that it contains the word power. To sidestep philosophical debate, it may be broadly defined as control over material assets, intellectual resources and ideology. **The process of challenging existing power relations, and of gaining greater control over the sources of power, may be termed as *empowerment.* This broad definition is defined by feminist scholars and activists within the context of their own regions (Batliwala** 1995).

Empowerment in its simplest form means the manifestation of redistribution of power that challenges patriarchal ideology and the male dominance(**Chandra** 1997). It is both a process and the result of the process. It is transformation of the structures or institutions that reinforces and perpetuates gender discrimination. It is a process that enables women to gain access to and control of material as well as information resources. The concept of women's empowerment, throughout the world, has its roots in women's movement. It is since the mid 1980s that this term became popular in the field of development, especially in reference to women. In India, it is the Sixth Five Year Plan (1980-85) which can be taken as a landmark for the cause of women. It is here that the concept of women and development was introduced for the first time. It was realized that no more piecemeal strategies but an integrated approach would deliver the desired goods. The realistic and regenerative developmental efforts in the direction of progress, in terms of economic independence for women and educational advancement of them is what would answer the basic questions raised for empowering women (**Chandra** 1997).

The literature describing empowerment practice is based primarily on **empowerment theory** and case examples of empowerment practice. The focus of this literature has been on definitions of empowerment practice (**Parsons**, 1991, **Rappaport**, 1981; **Simon**, 1990; **Staples**, 1991; **Swift & Levin**, 1987) and the description of specific methods (**Freire**, 1973) and outcomes (**Butierrez & Ortega**, 1991; **Maton & Rappaport,** 1984; **Zimmerman & Rappaport** 1982). Less attention has been paid to how the structure, culture and management of human services organizations can support the empowerment of workers and consumers.

The mid-1980s saw the term empowerment becoming popular in the field of development especially in reference to women. As **Srilatha Batiwala** observed, "In grassroots programmes and policy debates alike, empowerment has virtually replaced terms such as welfare, upliftment, community participation, and poverty alleviation to describe the goal of development and intervention". Empowerment has become the key solution to many social problems like high population growth rates, environment degradation, low status of women. The concept of women's empowerment appears to be the end result of a number of important critical discussions, dialogues and debates generated by the women's movement throughout the world and particularly by Third World feminists (**Apte**, 1995).

Dodd and Gutierrz (1990) say, "although empowerment has been a social work "buzzword" since the 1960's most members of the profession have not taken serious, systematic look at the major root of the word - **power**. Yet understanding power is essential before one can discuss what empowering practice is".

Power is usually defined in two ways: as (1) the ability to get what one wants and (2) the ability to influence others to think, feel, act and/or believe in ways that further one's interests (**Parenti** 1978). This relational concept is reflected in two kinds of power - personal and social power. A third kind of power political power depends not only on who influences whom. Personal power is based on **Bandura's** (1981) concept of perceived self-efficacy. Personally powerful individuals actively engage in their world and know both how to get what they want and how to influence others in ways that further their own interests. In contrast personally powerless individuals avoid challenging activities and give up readily in the face of difficulty, either because they cannot get what they want or because they cannot influence others in ways that further their own interests.

Social power emanates from the social resources that individuals bring to relationship. **French and Raven** (1959) describe five bases of social power- **reward, coercive, legitimate, referent** and **expell** power. These sources of power derive respectively from (1) One's ability to provide rewards or remove punishments, (2) one's ability to impose punishment, (3) one's normative, role-oriented values, (4) one's degree of conformity in identifying with others, and (5) one's degree of credibility or informational influence.

One currently popular way of viewing these bases of social power is an exchange where each person in a relationship contributes some kind of reward to the other (**Emerson**, 1982). Thus the person who has more reward, power is said to have a power advantage in the relationship. However, the danger in thinking of all relationships in this way arises from the fact that in an extremely asymmetrical power relationship, the weaker person may indeed gain nothing, a situation that can hardly be classified as an exchange (**Parenti**, 1978). This risk may be especially potent for oppressed communities.

Political power is based on the fact that there is a scarcity in society of social desiderata, which are tangibles and intangibles such as financial security, a nutritious diet, good health, meaningful and useful work opportunities for self-development, and self-esteem (**Parenti**, 1978). Another way to define political power is who determines who gets what or influences whom. Understood this way, power then belongs only to those who make policy and set standards. Through collusive consensus, the politically powerful are able to maintain and perpetuate the status quo, which they then hold up as the only acceptable system and one which the powerless have no choice but to accept.

Each of these kinds of power-personal, social and political - is important for community practitioners to understand, for they each play into the cyclical nature of powerlessness which keeps certain individuals and groups oppressed, impairing individual functioning and the functioning of family and community systems.

Clark and Stewart (1992) say that empowerment is a theme which requires clarification. Like any idea 'whose time has come' there is confusion and a lack of clear understanding. it is a theme which underlies the approach of both the government and the opposition to public services as set out in their statements on Citizen's Charters. To some empowerment is about increasing the power of the public over public activities, giving the public greater choice and/or greater and better defined rights over those services. To others it is about increasing the power of the public over both public and private sector activities. Advocates of the first position may argue that the public do not need empowerment in the private sector because the market gives power to the customer. In the latter case, advocates would argue that the market does not operate that way and needs action in the public domain. Thinking empowerment must start therefore with a consideration of the basis of the power of the public both in the public domain and in the private sector. The danger is that a public body can become an enclosed organisation against which the citizen can feel powerless. And there are other forces at work which insulate local authorities from the influence of their citizens: the power and influence of professionals, bureaucratic organisation and an unwillingness to be open. All these things can reinforce one another.

In thinking about empowerment, the crucial issue is to clarify what is meant by the term. Central to this is who is to be empowered. It is not sufficient to speak of empowering the public because a distinction can be drawn between:

- the public as a customer;
- the public as citizen;
- the public as community.

The public as customer focuses attention on the individual user of a service, although it has to be recognized that in many public services there is more than one customer. Empowering the public as customer involves extending the choices available to them or at least by making clear the service to which they are entitled and giving them the means of securing redress, as well as providing equality and ease of access. It does not need to be recognized, though, that this may escalate the demand for services and thus the requirement to ration them.

The public as citizen focuses attention on the individual as part of the process of government itself. Citizens may or may not be users of a service, but irrespective of whether they are users of a service, they are entitled as citizens to a share in decision- making on issues in the public domain. It is not only the users, but also the citizens who can be empowered. Empowering the public as citizens involves being clear about rights (the rights to know, to explanation, to be heard, and to be listened to) and also of considering how the right to vote can be enhanced. These are basic civil rights necessary for discourse and decision in the public domain. Empowering the public as citizens involves treating civil rights as basic conditions whose full potential has economic and social rights, for without these a citizen may lack the basis to play a full part in society.

Karl (1995) feels that, Empowerment is a word widely used, but seldom defined. Long before the world became popular, women were speaking about gaining control over their lives, and participating in the decisions that affect them in the home and community, in government and international development government and international development policies. The word 'empowerment' captures this sense of gaining control, of participating, of decision making. More recently, the word has entered the vocabulary of development agencies, including international organizations and the United Nations.

According to **Pillai** (1995), "Empowerment is an active, multi-dimensional process which enables women to realize their full identity and powers in all spheres of life. Power is not a commodity to be transacted; nor can it be given away as aims. "power has to be acquired and once acquired, it needs to be and once acquired, it needs to be exercised, sustained and preserved".

Empowerment is a process and is not, therefore, something that can be given to people. The process of empowerment is both individual and collective, since it is through involvement in groups that people most often begin to develop their awareness and the ability to organize to take action and bring about change. Women's empowerment can be viewed as a continuum of several interrelated and mutually reinforcing components:

- Awareness building about women's situation, discrimination, and rights and opportunities as a step towards gender equality. Collective awareness building provides a sense of group identify and the power of working as a group.

- Capacity building and skills development, especially the ability to plan, make decisions, organize, manage and carry out activities, to deal with people and institutions in the world around them.

- Participation and greater control and decision-making power in the home, community and society.

- Action to bring about greater equality between men and women.

In short, **empowerment is a process of awareness and capacity building leading to greater participation, to greater decision-making power and control, and to transformative action.**

At a workshop of pacific women entitled 'women, Development and Empowerment', (1987) **Venessa Griffen** spoke about what empowerment means to her: To me, the word simply means: adding to women's power ... To me, power means:

- having control, organizing further control;

- having a say and being listened to;

- being able to define and create from a women's perspective;

- being able to influence social choices and decisions affecting the whole society (not just areas of society accepted as women's place);

- being organised and respected as equal citizens and human beings with a contribution to make.

Power means being able to make a contribution at all levels of society and not just in the home. Power also means having women's contribution recognized and valued.

Gutierrez et al (1995) say that the term "empowerment" is ubiquitous, used by presidents and poets alike, yet its meaning often seems hazy and undeveloped. The concept of empowerment has been unevenly developed and has been unevenly developed and has been unevenly developed and has been used in different ways. Some describe empowerment primarily as a goal, others as a process, others as a form of intervention.

As regards the definition of empowerment, practitioners describe it as a psychological process to change. One critical element of this change is gaining awareness of the power that exists within any individual, family, group, or community. This focus on empowerment as a process is emphasized by practitioners involved in different levels of practice (for example, individual, group, or community work) and with different populations. The applicability of empowerment to varying foci of practice suggests an underlying unity to the concept; although practitioners may work with individuals, groups, or communities that have different goals, empowerment is described as a method for developing personal and interpersonal power through a process of self-awareness.

'Power' is the key word of the term 'Empowerment' which means 'control over material assets, intellectual resources, and ideology. The material assets over which control can be established may be of any type - physical, human, financial, such as land, water, forests, people's bodies and agencies, labour, money and access to money. Knowledge, information, ideas can be included in intellectual resources. Control over ideology, signifies the ability to generate, capacity to propagate, capacity to sustain and institutionalize specific sets of beliefs, principles, values attitudes, actions and behaviours - 'virtually' determining how people perceive. think, and function in a given socio - economic and political environment (**Apte**, 1995).

Staples (1990) argues that the ability to act or to prevent action goes to the heart of any definition of **"power".** The prefix **"em"** is attached to the noun **"power"** to create a verb. According to **Webster's New World Dictionary** (1982), this prefix is used to form verbs meaning "to make, make into or like, cause to be". Thus, "to empower" is to make or cause power. Yet, the actual definitions offered for "empower" are: "(1)to give power or authority to; (2) give ability to; enable; permit", with the example, "Congress is empowered to levy taxes.

Clearly, these definitions all refer to a process whereby power is given granted, or permitted. Yet, power is not likely to be handed to "have-not" groups in out society. Power must be developed or taken by the powerless themselves, as well as being granted (Hess, 1984). It is possible for individuals or groups to empower themselves rather than merely being the recipients of power bestowed by others. Our own definition of "empower" as a transitive verb relates back to the connection of the prefix "em" to the noun "power". Staples defines this term as: (1) to gain power; (2) to develop power; to take or seize power; (3) to facilitate or enable power; (4) to give, grant, or permit power.

The noun **"empowerment"** which is not listed in Webster's New World Dictionary (1982). refers to the process by which power is gained, developed, seized, facilitated, or given. An individual or group moves from a condition of relative powerlessness to relative power through the empowerment process. Yet, to be empowered" also refers to the state of possessing or controlling power, being able to act or prevent action. In this sense, "empowerment" (holding power) is the product of the same process. The empowerment concept includes both process and product dimensions and the relationship between them often is complex. The following discussion examines each in turn and the relationship between process and product.

Effective action on behalf of self (whether individual or collective) is essential to the notion of both the empowerment process and product. The concept refers to the ongoing capacity of individuals or groups to act on their own behalf to achieve a greater measure of control over their lives and destinies. The literature on empowerment offers further insights. It has been characterized as the antithesis of paternalism (**Swift**, 1984) with key themes being the participation of people in their own empowerment (**Rappaport**, 1984) and self-help for social change (**Kahn & Bender**, 1985). A number of writers emphasize the importance of recognizing existing competencies (**Rappaport**, 1984) and building on individual and collective strengths (**Pinderhughes,** 1983; **Biegel**, 1984). Individual qualities associated with empowerment includes self- efficacy (**Barton**, 1984), participatory competencies (**Kieffer**, 1984), critical analysis (**Kiefer**, 1981), rationally motivated action (**Mondros**, 1981), skill (**Biegel**, 1984), self-esteem (**Pinderhughes**, 1983; **Rappaport**, 1984), and a sense of control or actual control (**Rappaport,** 1984).

According to **Zippy** (1995), empowerment represents a means for accomplishing community development tasks and can be conceptualized as involving two key elements giving community members the authority to make decisions and choices and facilitating the development of the knowledge and resources necessary to exercise these choices.

The Social Work Dictionary (**Barker**, 1991) defines empowerment as "the process of helping a group or community to achieve political influence or relevant legal authority" (p. 74). Empowerment is often described as building "community capacity" which involves enhancing the aptitude of community groups to procure and manage social and economic resources (**Mayer**, 1984), implies a focus on developing the resources and skills necessary for individuals and communities to exert authority and power.

Bandura (1986), Empowerment is the process through which individuals gain efficacy, defined as the degree to which an individual perceives that he or she controls his or her environment.

Generalizations About Empowerment

In order to stay empowered, according to **Hall** (1992), women will have to be familiar with at least some of the institutional trends that had previously restricted them. Knowing what to expect from others in the course of their empowerment will enable women to maintain stronger functioning positions.

Some of the generalizations that can be made about women's empowerment as a social change process are listed below. The welfare of one woman, remains inextricably tied to the welfare of all women.

1 Women's empowerment is a social process that neutralizes women's oppressions. If women do not take decisive action on their own behalf, their victimization will continue automatically through their traditional subordination.

2 Grassroots political activism growing from women's empowerment derives from women's decisions to be empowered. The actions that follow women's resolves to develop their potential and to take broader roles in community and societal activities.

3 Women's empowerment is synonymous with the achievement of equity and equal mindedness in society. These are not accomplished at the expense of others, but in a mutually cooperative spirit wherever possible.

4 Women's empowerment will result in traditional female values being more respected in society at large, it is not women's purpose to take

power while respecting men for who they are.

5 Women's empowerment is a base for human liberation and empowerment for all. Although initially women will neutralize patriarchal structure in order to ground their own rights in social realities, women cannot be empowered effectively at the expense of others.

6 Women's empowerment will bring more balance to the male value hierarchies in current traditional and modern societies. Empowerment reestablishes cooperation as a viable social process and makes the development of all people more possible then is the case in fiercely competitive patriarchies.

Empowerment Propositions

Propositions relate directly, if hypothetically, to patterns of predictability in society. The propositions below , given by **Hall** (1992), suggest some strategies for women who want to empower themselves, as individuals or as a group.

1 The more empowered women become, the stronger the resistance this empowerment will initially produce. However, in the long run, women's empowerment will bring balance and not disruption to social relations.

2 Whether individual women or groups of women purpose their empowerment, social resistance is predictable. Empowerment will continue to be feasible only if women continue working in the direction of their own goals. If they capitulate, women will move back into their positions of subordination.

3 Women's empowerment moves women in the direction of living more fully. The more empowered women are, the more fully they live, and the more meaningful their lives become.

4 To the extent that women's empowerment increases in a particular social class or cultural setting, those women are empowered will necessarily depend on other women for their well-being. Not until all women move out of their subordination will all women be truly empowered.

5 Women's work outside the home can be a primary avenue of their empowerment. When women have economic independence, they will be

able to take firmer stands against their oppression in families.

6 If women can integrate their needs for empowerment with their religious beliefs, their motivations for empowerment will intensify. Women's collective mission includes expressing their real selves in order to neutralize existing restrictive patriarchal structures and to build a truly new world.

Individual And Collective Empowerment

Empowerment is a very positive concept with the capacity for self-action and the transformation of self. It is inextricably linked to both the ability and opportunity to make decisions and to act for oneself. Thus, empowerment is egalitarian in nature, stressing the competence and right to people to take charge of their own destinies. For the powerless, this entails a bottom up process whereby they transform from passive or reactive subjects to positive actors in the drama of their individual lives (**Friere**, 1973). They become active participants in the creation and implementation of the policies, decisions, and processes which affect them. They are accorded basic respect and dignity as capable individuals who are willing and able to take ownership and responsibility for their own choices, decisions, and actions. And material resources, information, and knowledge are developed and made accessible so that opportunities can be maximized.

The concept also is dynamic, since change is a constant phenomenon in life. The dialectic process ensures that future problems will arise from current solutions, that some individuals and groups will lose power in the process, and that existing competencies will be insufficient to meet every need. And just as there is no final synthesis, there is no final state of empowerment. Rather, the empowerment process strengthens the ongoing capacity for successful action under changing circumstances.

Individual empowerment occurs through the process of personal development. This entails both the growth of skills and abilities, as well as a more positive self- definition. At the psychological level, people who become more empowered, feel better about themselves, there is an increased sense of personal dignity, self- respect, and self-esteem. A new confidence and sense of self-efficacy emerges as the person redefines him or herself as a more capable and worthy individual. Closely connected to the psychological redefinition of self is the actual increase of individual knowledge, competencies skills, resources, and opportunities which enable more effective action and interpersonal relations. Self-perceptions should be based in reality. There clearly is a positive interactive effect between the development of self-confidence and the strengthening of personal ability.

Such an individual transformation of consciousness and capacity is exciting to behold in others and a profound experience to undergo oneself. While one can foster and facilitate the empowerment of another, it can not be done for another. The ability to redefine oneself and to act effectively for oneself is the essence of individual empowerment. This is a basic human need, rather than merely a nice positive phenomenon. Even before, they can speak, young children exhibit a strong desire and drive to "do it myself". The person who lacks power and control over his or her own life has been stripped of a fundamental element of one's humanity. This transcends even the loss of dignity-it is the loss of self. The individual who has become more empowered has become more human in the fullest sense of the word.

Individual empowerment is not now, and never will be, the salvation of powerless groups. To attain social equality, power relations between "haves", "have-a- littles", and "have-nots" must be transformed. This requires a change in the structural problems, then solutions logically should be collective rather than individual in nature. Groups as well as individuals must be empowered in order to change the social structure. Empowerment must be conceptualized, operationalized, and measured in collective as well as individual terms.

And in this area, the existing literature is deficient. Generally, empowerment is interpreted and examined in an individualistic manner. This undoubtedly results from the fact that much of the relevant literature has been developed within the field of community psychology. Not surprisingly, a number of these studies have focused on psychological indicators to measure whether empowerment has developed among individuals. Even when social action organizations have been recognized as the primary vehicles for empowerment, the concept has typically been measured through the perceptions of individual leaders (**Kieffer**, 1981; **Mondros**, 1981; **Hoffman**, 1978).

Such an approach is inadequate for measuring collective empowerment for at least three reasons. First, and most fundamentally, the above studies characterize empowerment as an individual equality and developmental process. There has been no assessment of collective capacity. Thus, what is examined is the achievement of individual empowerment through collective action rather than any notion of collective empowerment itself.

Secondly, the above studies focus only on the perceptions of the leaders in social action organizations. Yet, **Mondros** (1981) acknowledges that "....while a person or group may feel empowered, others may disagree". However, none of these research projects employed other measures. It is insufficient to consider only subjective impressions. The perceptions of opponents, allies, and observes should be included in any evaluation of empowerment.

Finally, perceptions, whether by insiders or outsiders, are only a piece of the empowerment equation. Certainly, the importance of perceptions should not be underestimated. **W.I.Thomas** (1928) dictum correctly holds that perceptions, whether accurate or false, lead to real consequences. Self-perceptions of their own power by leaders and members of organized groups are critical variables in the efficacy of those groups. Likewise, the perceptions of a group's power by opponents, allies, and other third parties also is an essential factor in the capacity to achieve collective goals.

However, empowerment is more than merely a perception. Actual results also are crucial. The concept must entail the ability of an individual or group to act effectively in their own behalf and the process through which this action takes place. In addition to transformations in consciousness, beliefs, and attitudes, empowerment requires practical knowledge, solid information, real competencies, concrete skills, material resources, genuine opportunities, and tangible results. The capacity for effective action is an essential component of any meaningful conceptualization of empowerment.

The empowerment process is a continuing development involving many changes whereby an individual or group is able to strengthen and exercise the ability to act so as to gain greater control and mastery over life. It is a process of both thought and action, which is dynamic and constantly evolving. Through it, individuals and groups develop an ongoing capacity to act effectively in their own behalf. The empowerment process is positive in the sense that it implies that many strengths and abilities already are present or at least possible. It entails that particular methods, actions, activities, and interactions that are employed (the "what") and the way in which social action is conducted (the "how") to produce empowerment. Yet beyond this, it is the dynamic process whereby consciousness is transformed while individual and collective capacities are developed.

Simply because there is a dynamic empowerment process (as well as no "final state" of empowerment), it does not follow that the concept cannot be assessed at a particular point. For empowerment is a product as well as process. It is analogous to the situation of an athlete who is trying to "get in shape". "Getting in shape" is a dynamic process that necessitates a training regimen with particular requirements for exercise, diet, and sleep. But one can be in varying degrees of "good shape" at a particular point in time. Empowerment works the same way.

The empowerment product moves beyond the realm of the perceived to the domain of concrete reality. It is critical to the empowerment process that there be a sense of control and feelings of the ability to act successfully. But the empowerment product requires an actual capacity for effective action. Obviously, feelings of efficacy and real capacity interact positively in the empowerment process. Successful action requires self-definitions of effective individual and collective capacities. The process is dynamic with no finished empowerment product. Yet, like a snapshot of a mighty river, one can capture and gauge the presence of individual or collective empowerment at a given point in time.

The capacity for successful action refers to the ability to make and carry out decisions in a purposeful way in accord with individual or collective interests. At the individual level, the ability to act in behalf of oneself is a function of factors such as critical consciousness, sense of entitlement, knowledge, resources, opportunities, competencies, skills and self- respect. Collectively, a group's efficacy is a product of such variables as its size, the quality of its leadership, resources, allies, opportunities, and strategies. At both the individual and collective levels, self-perceptions and the impressions of others are important determinants of the capacity to act effectively. Time is another important element; both historical experience and potential prospects for power shape current ability to act. Overall, the development of a number of specific qualities, competencies, relationships, resources, and opportunities constitute the ongoing capacity for successful action.

Thus, the process of empowerment produces a greater capacity to act effectively in order to gain more control over life. And the capacity, the product of being empowered, makes possible the process of achieving individual and collective goals. Some of those goals may be instrumental to increasing control over life by altering relations of power with relevant institutions, groups, and actors. When this type of power yield occurs, it increases both individual and collective capacity. At such times, empowerment generates power, and that power in turn contributes to greater empowerment capacity.

While the actual power generated through social action increases capacity, this does not mean that the achievement of goals is synonymous with empowerment. Accomplishment of ends is an important indicator of the ability to act effectively. Empowerment itself refers to the process of gaining power, the capacity to wield it, and the degree of control that actually exists.

This product dimension of the empowerment process cannot be evaluated accurately through the use of perception scales either at the individual or collective levels. For the most important product is power itself, not simply the perception thereof. A conception of empowerment which is devoid of the elements of real power is hollow and potentially illusory.

Choices Women Can Make For Empowerment

Women must make several choices, according to **Hall** (1992), in order to assess the usefulness and meaningfulness of empowerment. Also, women must make choices that are predictably effective in order to maintain their empowerment. Some of the choices women must consider are listed below.

1 In order to be empowered, women must want to be empowered. Although it may be comfortable to live dependently for a short time, sooner or later women must address the issue of becoming independent and make deliberate choices in one direction or another.

2 Choosing to be one's real self and choosing to develop one's potential are synonymous with the choice to be empowered. Empowered has many phases, and choosing actions that constructively build one's resources is one aspect of an overall empowerment that must be continuous in order to be effective.

3 Choosing to lead a meaningful life will eventually lead to empowerment. Women must be sufficiently courageous to ask basic questions about the quality of their lives in order to live fully and productively.

4 The choice to be empowered needs to be renewed continuously. Empowerment is a process that has to be forged at all stages of the lifecycle.

5 The accomplishment of women's empowerment does not mean that others will necessarily be oppressed. When women choose their own empowerment, they are in stronger positions to support others and to make more solid contributions to society.

6 Empowerment requires women to face the facts of their lives at all levels of social organization. Choosing to be realistic in interpersonal and community matters is essentially the choice to be empowered.

Women's Participation in decision-making

Gender discrimination is a universal phenomenon. Both inside and outside the households women are excluded from positions of power. They are denied opportunities to participate in the decision making process. Even when the decisions are to affect their well-being, they are only passive observers. The primary challenge facing women today, therefore, is to increase their participation so that they get hold of the situation and become actively involved in the process of decision making(**Chandra** 1997).

Participation has two dimensions - quantitative and qualitative. Many a time only the quantitative aspect of participation is taken care of. People's participation in terms of mere numbers has no meaning. Women often make up majority of the rank and file and compromise a minority as far as decision-making process is concerned. Today, there is a need for change - change in the right direction - change from quantitative to qualitative. As long as women would be left behind in the process of decision-making, it would be hard to get the democratic process started. Active participation in social, economic and political spheres would help in enhancing the process of empowerment and it would also give women the desired self-respect and social dignity, and these, of course, are the pre-requisites of empowerment.

Obstacles and opportunities in the direction of empowerment need to be looked into in depth so as to give meaningful interpretation to the term participation. " An idea which is gaining momentum these days is that increased participation of women in decision-making at all levels will help to "adjust" the goals pursued through the development"(**Karl** 1995).

Women's Participation in Development Process

Improving women's opportunities in the area of decision-making requires long-term strategies. They have to be systematic and they must aim at challenging prevailing structures. Society imposes gender roles on women and men that inevitably follow them inside and outside their households. Traditional and contemporary definitions of womanhood are based on women's subservient roles. The behavioral expressions reduce women to a mere nothing, as far as their ability to give services are concerned. Economic independence and awareness both are looked upon as negative attributes. " The lack of economic opportunities for women socialized through a life style of dependence, leads to a condition of emotional insecurity. Indian women's socialized dependence and status have programmed women's psyche t believe in the patriarchal process which control the female gender(**Jethmalani** 1995).

Things all over the world are similar. It is understandable that many factors affect women's ability to participate in the process of development. For a longtime, a certain image has been given to them. The household status the women hold, the educational and training background they have, their health status and the burden of work they have to bear are some of the factors that affect the decision-making ability of women. It has been recognized that empowerment is a process and this process has both individual and collective phase. It is a continuum and consists of several inter-related and mutually reinforcing components, such as awareness building, capacity building and skill development. Concrete measures are needed to remove many obstacles that make the process of participation difficult. New strategies for women to increase their access to decision-making, need to be developed. Building a critical mass of women who could act as a pressure group would enhance the process of empowerment. Gender emphasis on peoples participation by policy makers and growing awareness among people, would create a favorable climate here empowerment could get a fertile land to flourish.

Creating Linkages Between Women in Public Life and Women working in Other Areas

There is a growing interest all over the world to being women in the forefront in the process of decision making. The governmental, inter-governmental and non-governmental agencies all are working in this direction of empowering women. Now that the process has started, there is a need for new strategies and mechanisms for gender equity and here one must be sure that unless these are translated into policy options and policy-action, not much could be achieved.

Male domination and gender discrimination in the form of child marriages dowry, demands, wife-beating and wife burning , bigamy and polygamy and discrimination in food intake, employment, education, health and nutritional facilities are some of the things which need immediate looking into as new understanding towards empowerment makes it clear that discriminatory behavior has to go. By expanding the family resources and by making men partner to the elated better halves, it enhances the male ego to a greater extent. Women get liberated, because they start recognizing the importance of reversal of the values and attitudes which had given rise to oppression and subjugation. As they grew up believing what existed was just and natural, the new look makes them think differently. The power of questioning which was denied to them all these years stealthily gets an entry into their lives and they start believing that rights to equality dignity and justice are as innate to them as to their male counterparts. It is essential that the subjugation and oppression of women perpetuated by family, class, caste and religion must be curbed. Women in both the worlds - developed and the developing - are discovering that they can translate their efforts to protect themselves into effective political, social and economic participants.

Women's Participation in Governance

There can never exist a true democracy unless there is true participation of women, both in governance and developmental programmes. Without equal participation of women and men, it is very difficult to attain what is desired to be attained. Gender and development taken together is emerging as a progressive approach. It is a part of larger basket of creating alternative models for development. For a dynamic approach, which looks beyond the economic analysis, it is essential to include environmental , sustainable and qualitative aspects of development into its models, which are progressive in nature.

Empowerment could be a planning goal in the sense that the governmental support is extended to the voluntary sector as well, both in the field of implementation as well as policy formulation. Empowering women could, thus, be through economic intervention as well as through integrated intervention. The 1990s have new challengers to be faced. With the help of lessons learnt we have to march forward(**Chandra** 1997).

Identity Empowerment Theory

Identity empowerment theory is a recently developed clinical sociological theory that has been built on documented patterns and predictabilities in interpersonal, family, and group behavior (**Hall**, 1990b). It is used as an integrated frame or reference throughout Women and Empowerment, although this practice is not explicitly stated in all analysis, interpretations, generalizations, and propositions.

Identity empowerment theory describes and begins to explain critical clinical and social processes that increases the probabilities and possibilities of women's well-being and optimal functioning. The theory is grounded in the assumption that empowered women make meaningful commitments and undertake effective, goal- oriented activities that they choose for themselves.

Identity empowerment theory suggests that women's understanding of the strengths and weakness of their personal and collective past and present will increase their sense of purpose and direction for the future. Through examination of their values, women become more able to consciously determine life-time goals in their own interests.

Identity empowerment increases women's knowledge about their options in everyday life. In time, they become more able to cope with conflict in their relationships, although initially they may be perceived by other people as being less productive or less cooperative than they were previously. Identity empowerment necessarily entails some disruption of the status quo, because it is established relationships that or problematic for most women.

The increased breadth and clarity of women's views of society and the universe can motivate them to articulate new values and goals. When women's attention shifts from their personal troubles to social issues, they can more consciously connect their biographies with the historical times in which they live (**Mills**, 1967). Moreover, attention to the value components of women's behavior increases their motivation for meaningful individual and social actions (**Weber**, 1964).

Although identity empowerment theory needs much additional substantiation, patterns in women's behavior are discernible, and tentative predictions can be made from the repeated trends in women's interpersonal and collective behavior. Furthermore, the clinical use of identity empowerment theory suggests that, when women choose to make changes in their lives. they can accomplish sometimes dramatic shifts in their life courses.

Legislative changes must remain women's highest priorities in both traditional and modern patriarchal societies. However, other kinds of changes can transform significantly the quality of women's lives. The advantage of working toward changes in values and levels of functioning is that these are not dependent on legislated equality between women and men. Women can claim their equality and then work toward the legislative equality that needs to be attained. As long as women remain in positions of subjugation, they have much work to do to heighten their awareness and to free themselves.

Empowerment And A new understanding of power

Empowerment should also generate new notions of power. Present-day notions of power have evolved in hierarchical, male-dominated societies and are based on divisive, destructive and oppressive values. The point is nor for women to take power and use it in the same exploitative and corrupt way. Rather, women's empowerment process must evolve a new understanding of power, and experiment with ways of democratizing and sharing power - building new mechanisms for collective responsibility, decision-making, and accountability.

Similarly, once women have gained control over resources, they should not use them in the same shortsighted and ecologically destructive manner as male dominated capitalist societies. Women's empowerment will have to lead women - and the "new men" - address global concerns and issues, including the environment; war, violence, and militarism; and population (**Batliwala** 1995).

Summing Up

The most conspicuous feature of the term empowerment is that it contains the word **power**. To sidestep philosophical debate, **it may be broadly defined as control over material assets, intellectual resources and ideology(Batliwala** 1995**).** The material assets over which control can be exercised may be physical, human, or financial, such as land, water, forests, people's bodies and labour, money, and access to money. Intellectual resources include knowledge, information, and ideas. Control over ideology signifies the ability to generate. Propagate, sustain, and institutionalize specific sets of beliefs. Values, attitudes, and behavior virtually determining how people perceive and function within given socio- economic and political environments.

Power thus accrues to those who control or are able to influence the distribution of material resources, knowledge, and the ideology that governs social relations in both public and private life. The extent of power held by particular individuals or groups corresponds to the number of kinds of resources they can control, and the extent to which they can shape prevailing ideologies, whether social, religious, or political. This control , in turn confers the power of decision- making. **The process of challenging existing power relations, and of gaining greater control over the sources of power may be termed empowerment** (**Batliwala** 1994). This broad definition is defined by feminist within the context of their own regions. For instance, the term empowerment refers to a range of activities from individual self-assertion to collective resistance. Protest and mobilization that challenge basic power relations. For individuals and groups where class, caste, ethnicity and gender determine their access to resources and power, their empowerment begins when they not only recognize the systemic forces that oppress them, but act to change existing power relationships. **Empowerment, therefore, is a process aimed at changing the nature and direction of systemic forces which marginalise women and other disadvantaged sections in a given context** (**Sharma** 1991-1992).

Theories that identify any one system or structure as the source of power, for instance the assertion that economic structures are the basis of powerlessness and inequality, imply that improvement In one dimension would result in a redistribution of power. However, activists working in situations where women are economically strong know that equal status does not necessarily result. If anything, ample evidence exists that strengthening women's economic status, though positive in many ways, does not always reduce their other burdens or eradicate other forms of oppression. In fact, it has often led to intensifying pressures (**Brydon** and **Chant** 1989: **Gupte** and **Bokar** 1987: **Sen** and **Grown** 1985). Similarly, it is evident that improvements in physical status and access to basic resources, like water, fuel, fodder, health care, and education, do not automatically lead to fundamental changes in women's positions. If that were so, middle- class women, with higher education, well-paid jobs, and adequate nourishment and health care, would not continue to be victims of wife beating or bride burning.

There is widespread confusion and some degree of anxiety about whether women's empowerment leads to the disempowerment of men. It is obvious that poor men are almost as powerless as poor women in terms of access to and control over resources. This is exactly why most poor men tend to support women's empowerment process that enable women to bring much-needed resources into their families and communities, or that challenge power structures that have oppressed and exploited the poor of both genders.

Resistance, however, occurs when women compete with men for power in the public sphere, or when they question the power, rights, and privileges of men within the family-in other words, when women challenge patriarchal family relations (**Batliwala** 1995). This is, in fact, a test of how far the empowerment process has reached into women's lives; as one activist put it, "the family is the last frontier of change in gender relations.... You know (empowerment) has occurred when it crosses the threshold of the home"

(**Kannabiran** 1993).

The process of women's empowerment must challenge patriarchal relations. Thus it inevitably leads to changes in men's traditional control over women, particularly over the women of their households. Men in communities where such changes have already occurred no longer have control over women's bodies, sexuality, or mobility; they cannot abdicate responsibility for house-work and child care, nor physically abuse or violate women with impunity. They can not (as is the case in South Asia at present) abandon or divorce their wives without providing maintenance, or commit bigamy or polygamy, or make unilateral decisions that affect the whole family. Clearly, the, women's empowerment does mean the loss of the privileged position that patriarchy allotted to men.

A point often missed, however, is that women's empowerment also liberates and empowers men, both in material and in psychological terms. First, women greatly strengthen the impact of political movements dominated by men not just by their numbers, but by providing new energy, insights, leadership, and strategies. Second, as we saw earlier, the struggles of women's groups for access to material resources and knowledge directly benefit the men and children of their families and their communities, by opening the door to new ideas and better quality of life. But most important are the psychological gains for men when women become equal partners. Men are freed from the roles of oppressor and exploiter, and from gender stereotyping, which limits the potential for self-expression and personal development in men as much as in women.

•

CHAPTER - III

FRAMEWORK FOR EMPOWERMENT

The core of the **Women's Empowerment Framework** is its argument that women's development can be viewed in terms of five levels of equality, of which empowerment in an essential element at each level. The levels, according to **Longwe**(1990) are **welfare**, **access**, **conscientisation**, **participation** and **control**.

1. **WELFARE** - the first level, address only the basic needs of women, without recognizing or attempting to solve the underlying structural causes, which necessitate provision of welfare services. At this point, women are merely passive beneficiaries of welfare benefits.

2. **ACCESS** - the second level, is essential for women to make meaningful progress. The involves equality of access to resources, such as education opportunities, land and credit. The path of empowerment is initiated when women recognize their lack of access to resources as a barrier to their growth and overall well-being, and take action to address this.

3. **CONSCIENTIZATION** - is a crucial point in the Empowerment Framework. For women to take appropriate action to dose gender gaps or gender inequalities, there must be recognition that their problems stem form inherent structural and institutional discrimination. They must also recognize the role they can often play in reinforcing the system that restricts their growth.

4. **PARTICIPATION** - is the point where women are taking decisions alongside men equally. To reach this level, however, mobilization is necessary. By organising themselves and working collectively, women will be empowered aim increased representation, which will lead to increased empowerment and ultimately greater control.

5. **CONTROL** - is the ultimate level of equality and empowerment. Here,

the balance of power between men and women is equal, and neither party has dominance over the other. At this stage in the Empowerment Framework, women are able to make decisions over their lives, and the lives of their children, and play an active role in the development process. Further, the contributions of women are fully recognized and rewarded.

Using the Empowerment Framework, development planners can determine whether a project or programme is at the welfare, access, conscientization, participation of control level, and determine the point of intervention, to move women to higher levels of equality and empowerment. An empowerment approach to development can also mean people's participation in the policy making and planning processes.

Tenets Of Empowerment

Since empowerment is a necessary part of any intervention to enhance women's income, it is essential, as given in the book 'Work and Empowerment' - Management of Women's Economic Activities: a Manual for Activists, New Delhi(1991), to understand some of the **critical tenets** of empowerment. These are :

Collectivization

Bringing a group of women together at a base to become an integral part of an economic activity is an important part of the strategy towards their empowerment. The coming together of poor women provides then an identity which is different from their other identities and helps highlight their worker role. It also provides them a sense of belonging in a totally different power equation - that is, of mutuality. Both of these are empowering experiences in themselves. For providing support to each other, the group of women can met periodically and there is a reference available for each group of women can meet periodically and there is reference available for each woman. For bargaining and negotiating activities, like bulk buying and selling, bulk acquisition, credit and other facilities, necessary for economic activities, collectivization can be there. This collectivization also brings in the possibility of pooling and sharing resources, skills, time-frames, space and other facilities. Pooling is an important way of strengthening the capacities of the poor women to work together and to develop a sense of strength.

Capacity Building

Once women start coming together, the next step is to enhance their capacity tot work as a group and play different roles, necessary for development and maintenance of the group. It is important from the point of view of empowerment that women are not only capable of functioning as a group but also are able to effectively participate in the process of economic activity undertaken by the group of women.

Capacity building of women in the areas of planning, executing and monitoring all aspects of the economic activity is equally desired in this context. This will include capacity to use legal framework to their advantage and the capacity to build as well as sustain a culture of the economic activity compatible with the realities of the women involved and to the nature of their activity.

Ownership and Control

Once women start acquiring the capacity to work as a group, planning, executing and monitoring the activities, the issue of taking control over the whole activity becomes critical. A sense of belonging and owing good and bad consequences of their own activity, is the first step in the direction. It implies that women being to consider the group and the group activity as their own activity, is the first step in that direction. It implies that women being to consider the group and the group activity as their own. Taking responsibility of more and more functions in the entire process of economic activity helps them gain control over their ventures. So, managing different components, apart from operational aspects of activity, like record-keeping, accounts-keeping, handling cash, being signatory to bank accounts, etc., are helpful in building this control.

Mediation

Another important aspect of empowerment of women is to strengthen their capacities to mediate with the external world, Mediation entails relating with the outside world, with the markets, with financial institutions, with competitors, with suppliers, with a host of policy-makers and other important segments of external environment, i.e., politicians, bureaucrats, officials, etc. Mediation also requires mediating with experts, with those who can provide some technical assistance in the conduct of the economic activity.

Women's sense of empowerment gets a concrete base and mediation becomes an integral part of women's work in that economic activity.

Working towards the empowerment of a group of poor women is an ongoing and gradual process, which cannot be short-circuited under any circumstance. Therefore it is important that these different aspects are dealt with through a series of carefully planned and deliberately made interventions over a period of time, keeping specific requirements of a particular group and the economic venture it has undertaken, in mind.

Elements Of Empowerment

A quantitative element of empowerment is control over economic resource; but progress in this matter is by itself no indication of enhanced social power of the underprivileged to assert their developmental aspirations and their freedom to take initiatives for their self-development. The essential qualitative elements of empowerment are well suggested in many writings on participatory development, from which the following three are highlighted (**Rahman**, 1990).

1. **Organisation** of the disadvantaged and underprivileged people in structures under their own control, or sufficient strength, derived from direct numerical size and/or linking with other organisations of similarly situated people.

2. **Social awareness** of the disadvantaged, in terms of understanding derived from collective self-enquiry and reflection, of the social environment of their lives and the working of its processes. The knowledge itself, and a feeling of knowing from self-enquiry, are both important in giving the disadvantaged a sense of equality with the formally 'educated' classes of society, rather than a sense of intellectual inferiority which is often a powerful force inhibiting the generation of confidence in the disadvantaged to rely on and assert their own thinking and take their own initiatives for development.

It is possible to acquire social knowledge without literacy, through methods of verbal enquiry and communication. But in many contexts not being literate amounts to surrendering power to literates, who claim knowledge which the disadvantaged cannot verify. Illiterate people depend on the literate for much information, as well as for dealings with public and other agencies which require the use of written instruments. Such dependence produces a sense of helplessness vis-à-vis institutions and structures which use the written language, and is liable to have powerful adverse effects on self-confidence in situations where relations with such institutions and structures are an important element of normal life and development effort of the people .

At the same time, the mode of acquiring literacy can have a significant bearing on the development or otherwise of self-confidence in the disadvantaged. A vertical mode of learning from conventional teachers coming from the more privileged social classes can perpetuate a sense of inferiority vis-à-vis the teachers and their social classes, who are regarded as the repository of knowledge and wisdom. As the teachings of **Paulo Freire** make very clear, literacy, or for that matter education as an element of social development, must be viewed as an organic component of a process of 'awakening' or 'animation' (**Tilakaratna** 1985). This implies not merely learning, knowing and understanding, but also experiencing and grasping one's own intellectual powers in the same process; to experience, in other words, self-discovery including the discovery of oneself as a thinker and creator of knowledge. This is what makes literacy a qualitative rather than a quantitative process.

3. **Self-reliance:** People's power comes ultimately from self-reliance. Self-reliance is not the same thing as self-sufficiency, but a combination of material and mental strength which one can deal with others as an equal and assert one's self-determination. Once again, any degree of control over material resources is by itself no indication of self-reliance, which is an attitudinal quality, inborn in some and acquired by others by social experience, social awareness, and reflection. Self-reliance is strengthened by a collective identity, deriving not only material strength but also mental strength from solidarity, sharing, and caring for each other, and from thinking and acting together to move forward and to resist domination.

Sequences and Stages of Women's Empowerment

Women's empowerment tends to follow certain **sequences and stages**. When women are aware of these patterns in their own behavior and in their exchanges with others, they will be more able to become empowered on a long term basis. Empowerment inevitably meets with resistance. However, when women are prepared to see, handle, and understand this resistance, other people's resistance is more likely to be neutralized (**Hall**, 1992).

Phases and Aspects of women's Empowerment

Propositions that describe and explain some aspects of women's empowerment are listed below. Although there are many complex **phases and aspects of women's empowerment**, these selected views represent a few of the most vital prerequisites for women's achievement of individual and collective empowerment.

1. To the extent that women can become independent in their families, they will be empowered in diverse social settings. Family pressures toward women's subordination are difficult to counteract, but when women can do so they will be able to maintain correspondingly more control or their behavior in nonfamilial settings.

2. To the extent that women can develop their own religious beliefs and practices within established denominational and sectarian orders, they will be motivated to work toward their equality and the well- being of all. Beliefs in a supreme being can empower women in the search for survival and fulfillment.

3. Women who increase their control over their work at home and outside the home are in advantageous positions for achieving equality and empowerment. Mutual support in work settings in and outside the home is vital to women's empowerment through work.

4. Increased knowledge about women's conditions throughout the world increases women's objectivity about their own conditions, and depends their understanding of women's subordination. Having knowledge of their broader world context to women's lives empowers women, in that they become more able to see their own historical and cultural circumstances.

5. To the extent that individual women connect their biographies with history, seeing the influence of broad social structures on their lives, they will be empowered. Social issues impinge on the quality of women's lives in their domestic milieus, and much of the distress that is thought of a interpersonal problems is the result of patriarchal social structures and institutions.

6. Women's mutual support is a necessary, but not a sufficient, condition of their empowerment. Alone, individual women cannot develop their potential or make their fullest possible contributions of society.

Levels of women's Empowerment

Women's empowerment frequently takes place at a personal level through their friendships with other women (**Bell,** 1981). Both extended family and community networks protect women (**Bott**, 1957), sometimes against violence and other life-threatening situations (**Brownmiller**, 1975). The strengthening of women's personal relationships also assists their growth and maturation (**Cancian**, 1987), making them more immune to their own debilitating and self-destructive patterns of behavior (**Chernin**, 1981). By deliberately counteracting social influences that condition them for dependent lives (**Dowling**, 1982), women can work effectively toward gaining access to power on domestic and international fronts (**Epstein & Coser**, 1981). Understanding the intricacies of personal relationships and everyday choices (**Hall**, 1989, 1990b; **Horner**, 1972) is a vital starting point for forging roles of and avenues to power in the wider society (**Lipman-Blumen**, 1984).

The first stage of women's empowerment at individual or social levels involves the process of reaching the decision to be empowered. Making this initial choice is a vital condition to all further action to be taken. Being open to the possibility of change is a necessary prerequisite for this basic change to become possible.

Techniques Of Empowerment

Within this context of a collaborative helping relationship, and a small group work modality, five specific techniques are suggested for empowering clients. Accepting the client's definition of the problem is an important element of empowering interventions. By accepting the clients definition, the worker is communicating that the client is capable of identifying and understanding the situation. This technique also places the client in a position of power and control over the helping relationship. It also does not preclude the worker's bringing up issues for exploration, such as the connection between personal and community problems (**Beck,** 1983; **Fagan**, 1979; **Fox**, 1984; **Shapiro**, 1984).

By identifying and building upon existing strengths the empowering practitioner gets in touch with the client's present level of functioning and present sources of individual or interpersonal power (**Mathis & Richan**, 1986; **Pinderhughes**, 1983; **Shapiro**, 1984; **Sherman & Wenocur**, 1983; **Solomon**, 1976). This is most effective if the worker can recognize that the client has been involved in process of struggle against oppressive structures and that this has required considerable strength. By identifying elements of the struggle, client strengths can be more easily identified, communicated and the client, and then utilized as a basis for future work.

Raising the client's awareness of issues of power imbalance is a critical technique for empowering practice. This requires that the consciousness of social workers be raised first so that they can fully comprehend the connection between the immediate practice situation and the distribution of power in society as a whole (**Garvin** 1985; **Keefe**, 1980; **Mathis & Richan**, 1986; **Pernell**, 1985). Once the consciousness of workers has been raised, they can implement similar techniques to raise the consciousness of clients. One indirect technique is dialogue between the worker and clients which is aimed at exploring and identifying the social structural origins of their current situations (**Keefe**, 1980; **Lerner**, 1980; **Longres & McLeod**, 1980; **Resnick**, 1976; **Solomon**, 1976). Another, more directive technique involves focusing the client on specific situations, either their own or form vignettes developed for the intervention, on which they can carry out their analysis (**Bock**, 1980; **Pinderhughes**, 1983; 1985; **Solomon**, 1976). As important outcome of this analysis is an understanding of the client's potential sources of power and the ways in which they can be mobilized.

Teaching specific skills is one means of helping clients to develop the resources to be more powerful on the personal, social or political levels (**Mathis & Richan**, 1986; **Pernell**, 1985; **Shapiro**, 1984). The skill areas most often identified in empowering practice include problem solving; skills for community or organizational changes "life skills" such as parenting, job-seeking, or self-defense, and interpersonal skills such as assertiveness, social competency, or self advocacy (**Checkoway & Norseman**, 1986; **Fagan,** 1979; **Garvin**, 1985; **Hirayama & Hirayama**, 1985; **Keefe**, 1980; **Sherman & Winocur**, 1983; **Schechter** et. al., 1985; **Simmons & Parsons**, 1983, 1983b; **Solomon**, 1976 **Withorn**, 1980). The role suggested when teaching these skills is that of a consultant or facilitator, rather than instructor, so as not replicate the power relationships which worker and client are attempting to overcome (**Bchechter** et.al., 1985); **Sherman & Wenocur,** 1983; **Solomon**, 1976).

Mobilizing resources or advocating for clients is also suggested if worker and client together lack adequate resources for empowerment. This would involve the worker in gathering concrete resources or information for the client, as well as advocating on their behalf when necessary. Although some have argued that advocacy can be in conflict with the goat of empowerment because, it can reinforce feelings of powerlessness (**Rappaport**, 1981; **Solomon**, 1976), it can be carried out in a collaborative way which includes the client and involves learning new skills. Through advocacy and resource mobilization, the worker and client together ensure that the large social structure provides what is necessary to complete the empowerment process (**Checkoway & Norseman**, 1986; **Mathis & Richan**, 1986; **Pinderhughes**, 1983; **Sherman & Wenocur**, 1983; **Solomon**, 1982).

Taking a power perspective on community practice, then requires that students develop both an understanding of power relationships and an ability to work with others in an collaborative way. The process of practice is in itself empowering in that in involves an exploration of how power relationships have affected individual and group functioning while assisting clients to develop the means for becoming more powerful. When this process is successful, both the "client" and "practitioner" become empowered.

Categories of empowerment

Anita Dighe (1996) based on her study on "women, Literacy and empowerment - an analysis of the Nellore Experience" in Andhra Pradesh State of India has described the following categories of empowerment:

1. Empowerment for **marginalized groups**
2. **Process-oriented** nature of empowerment
3. **Holistic** nature of empowerment
4. Empowerment for dealing with '**strategic**' rather than '**practical** gender interests'
5. **Cognitive, Psychological and Economic** components of empowerment
6. Empowerment for democratization
7. Empowerment for **understanding the native character** of literacy that empowers
8. **Context-specific** nature of empowerment
9. I.Empowerment for **sustainability**

Models Of Empowerment

Based on an understanding of how community conditions of power and control impact both individual and community problems, the model focuses on both individual growth and development and macro-system change, using interventions at the individual, interpersonal, organizational, and community levels. This multiple approach empowers individuals, groups, families communities to become more effective in their attempts to affect their social environments.

This approach to empowerment is accomplished through interventions which target both individuals and the social environment. In this regard, it is based on a combination of the following theories of empowerment, which emphasize different levels of intervention and change.

First are theories of empowerment at the personal level, which focus primarily on ways in which individuals can develop feelings of personal power and self-efficacy. Developing a sense of personal power can be effective in both enhancing mental health and enabling individuals to work toward broader social change (**Simmom & Parsons**, 1983a, 1983b; **Berlin & Kravitz,** 1981).

Second theories of empowerment on the interpersonal level stress the development of specific skills. Skill development can involve such things as training in problem solving or assertiveness (**Hirayama & Hirayama**, 1985; **Sarri & du Rivage**, 1986; **Shapiro**, 1984; **Sherman & Wenocur**, 1983) or learning how to influence the political process (**Beck**, 1983; **Fox**, 1984; **Mathis & Richan**, 1986). The purpose of such skill development should be to increase both interpersonal influence and political power (**Checkoway & Norseman**, 1986; **Barvin**, 1985; **Schechter** et.al., 1985).

And third theories of empowerment on the political level emphasize the goals of both social action and social change. This level of empowerment is based on both the personal and interpersonal levels groups in society. These theories differ from traditional models of community organization practice in that the development of individuals is equally as important as the development of group action in affecting social action and social change (**Fagan**, 1979; **Kahn & Bender**, 1985; **Longres & McLeod**, 1980; **O'Connell**, 1978).

Unifying these three levels of empowerment is a belief that the primary goal of community practice is not to help individuals of communities to accept on adjust to problems, but to help them develop the ability to change negative situations and prevent the recurrence of problems (**Gutierrez**, 1988). Because the effects of powerlessness occur many levels, these efforts toward change are directed toward both individuals and institutions. Therefore, it is not sufficient to focus only on developing a sense of personal power, or on developing skills, or on working toward social change. Instead, the goal of a truly empowering community practice is a combination of these three elements.

This integration calls for new kinds of interventions. Many social work practitioners may be aware of how powerlessness affects clients, but may lack knowledge of how individuals can gain power, especially in the context of interpersonal practice. This can lead to feelings of frustration and be "dis- empowering" for individual workers. Fortunately, the literature on empowerment suggests specific techniques and forms of intervention which can lead to the empowering practice.

Empowerment : Multiple Dimensions

What is the texture of this empowerment and how does it operate in the different areas of women's lives? How do women handle power? Differently from men? If so in what ways? Do women, singly or in small numbers in a man's world, follow given patterns of power-play? And does a critical mass of women behave differently? What has 'empowerment' meant to many empowered women? How does the age-old internalised self-image of the sacrificing, nurturing, do not know anything woman articulate with the newly acquired ability to "make things happen"?

These are not new questions for which there is one clean, easy answer. **Mahila Samakhaya** experience has shown that the women have acted in myriad ways - all along the scale, from continuing to stay oppressed to taking on the attitudes of power they see around them. There however, appears to be a pattern for the majority bunched in the middle. By and large, the women who have felt some power within, have acted in practical ways - give a little, take a little, two steps forward, one step back. They have negotiated rather than confronted; maintained relationships rather than acted in terms of ultimate and abstract 'truths'. And this is visible in their encounter with the community and now, increasingly, in Panchayats. Their immediate political arena, the home, is possibly the last one for demonstrated change.

It is possible to discern a pattern in the **'empowerment'** of women, which cuts across the specificity of their environment? The experience broadly demonstrates **three stages** in the process of shedding off 'powerlessness'. These are demarcated more at a conceptual level rather than seen as a chronological ladder. More often than not, the three layers are intertwined through continuous struggle for change in women's position at home, in the community and in society as a whole.

The **first stage of empowerment** is visible when they can distance themselves from a given situation and recognise the structures of power, decode the symbols and look into them straight without fear. This may not later the situation at all, but it alters the chemistry of the encounter. Women learn to analyse the situation and in the process, the 'fear' gradually turns into an 'understanding'. This can only happen when they discover that their personal suffering is a 'kind' of systematic phenomenon, a chronic situation, which need not cripple their morale.

The next stage in this process is when women can experience the change of not only being able to 'name' the injustice but also by resisting it: What is not 'right', need not be accepted. Hence, the courage to protest is experienced. And this is possible in the 'togetherness' of the collective.

At the third stage a more mature state of realisation emerges: viz. that we need to know more - before making simplistic judgements. Basic confidence in oneself generated by predictable support from a group nurtures the learning spirit and humility in one's own stand.

Moving away from this board pattern, and as a clean contrast, one can discern multiple cases of those women who took family violence as a quiet suffering. What they do with ease in a public forum becomes the most difficult battle at home individually. The important message here is that empowerment processes exhibit their impact, to begin with in the public situation where the collective can visibly by together. Whether it is wage or caste or other struggles. Women have tempered justice with their conditioned reflexes of nurturance. Also, in most community level action, perhaps because women become a critical mass, they are more easily able to act in deviant (from the traditional) ways; unlike at home, where they battle the very roots of power, ultimately, alone.

Empowerment Approaches

Three experimental approaches to empowering women have been undertaken in South Asia; **integrated development, economic empowerment, and consciousness- raising.** While these approaches differ from each other in concept, most organisations working on the ground take a mix of approaches. Common to all three is the importance placed on group formation to build solidarity among women (**Batliwala** 1995). The **integrated development approach** views women's development as key to the advancement of family and community. It therefore provides a package of interventions to alleviate poverty, meet basic survival needs, reduce gender discrimination, and help women gain self-esteem. This approach proceeds either by forming women's collectives that engage in development activities and tackle social problems. Examples are dowry, child marriage, and male alcoholism (**Proshika** in Bangladesh; **RDRS** in Rajasthan India). At times an "entry point" strategy is employed, using a specific activity. These include literal class or health programmes, to mobilize women into groups (Gonoshastya Kendra in Bangladesh and United Mission to Nepal Redd Barna in Nepal).

The **economic empowerment approach** attributes women's subordination to lack of economic power. If focuses on improving women's control over material resources and strengthening women's economic security. Groups are formed using two methods organising women around savings and credit, income generation, or skill training activities (**Grameen Bank** in Bangladesh, Programme of Credit for Rural Women in Nepal); or by occupation or location (**SEWA** in India. Proshika). These groups may work in a range of areas, including savings and credit, training and skills development, new technologies or marketing, as well as provide such ancillary supports as child care, health services, literacy programmes, and legal education and aid.

The **consciousness raising approach** asserts that women's empowerment requires awareness of empowerment requires awareness of the complex factors causing women's subordination. This approach organised women into collectives that tackle the sources of subordination (**ASTHA**, **Deccan Development Society**, **Mahila Samakhya**, **WOP** in India, **Nigera Kori** in Bangladesh).

Education is central and is defined as a process of learning that leads to a new consciousness, self worth, societal and gender analysis, and access to skills and information. In this approach, the groups themselves determine their priorities. Women's knowledge of their own bodies and ability to control reproduction are also considered vital.

The long-term goal is for the women's groups to be independent of the initiating NGO. This approach uses no particular service "entry point" and attempts to be open- ended and non-directive. It gives considerable emphasis to fielding "change agents", who are trained to catalyze women's thinking without determining the directions in which a particular group may go These forums should enable women to evolve from an aggregate of individuals into a cohesive collective, wherein they can look at themselves and their environment in new ways, develop a positive self-image, recognize their strengths, and deplore sexist misconceptions.

The activists also help women collectively to claim access to new information and knowledge They also begin to develop a critical understanding of the ideology of gender, the systems and institutions through which it is perpetuated and reinforced, and the structures of power governing their lives. This is the process that expands women's awareness beyond their "condition" to their "position".

With a growing consciousness and collective strength, women's groups prioritise the problems they would like to tackle. They begin to confront oppressive practices and situations both inside and outside the home. Gradually they alter their own attitudes and behavior. This often includes changing their treatment of their girl children and asserting their reproductive and sexual rights.

In the course of both individual land collective struggles for change, women also build their skills of collective decision-making, action, and accountability. They may forge new strategies and methods, such as forming alliances with other groups of exploited and oppressed people, or involving sympathetic men of their own communities. With the help of training and counsel provided by the NGO or activists working with them, they also acquire real skills - vocational and managerial know-how, literacy and arithmetic competence, basic data collection techniques for conducting their own surveys. This enhances their autonomy and power.

Women's collectives then begin to seek access to resources and public services independently; demanding accountability from service providers; lobbying for changes in laws and programmes that are inaccessible or inappropriate; and negotiating with public institutions such as banks and government departments.

Collectively they may also set up and manage alternative services and programmes, such as their own child care centres, savings banks, or schools. Finally, village or neighborhood-level women's collectives may form associations at the local, regional, national, and global levels. Through these poor women can more effectively challenge higher-level power structures and further empower themselves for the well-being of society as a whole(**Batliwala** 1995).

Three major approaches to women's empowerment were identifiable in a study of selected South Asia NGOs engaged in women's empowerment. These were integrated development programmes, economic development and consciousness-raising and organising among women. The above are not mutually exclusive categories, but they help to distinguish among the differing interpretations of the causes of women's powerlessness and, hence, among the different interventions thought to lead to empowerment.

The integrated development approach ascribes women's powerlessness to their greater poverty and lower access to health care, education, and survival resources. Strategies are focused on providing services and enhancing economic status (some NGOs also emphasize awareness building). This approach improves women's condition mainly by helping them meet their survival and livelihood needs.

The economic development approach places women's economic vulnerability at the centre of their powerlessness. Economic empowerment has a positive impact on other aspects of women's existence.

Its strategies are built around strengthening women's positions as workers and income earners by mobilizing, organising or unionizing, and providing access to support services. This approach undoubtedly improves women's economic position and condition. But it is not clear whether that this change necessarily empowers them in other dimensions of their lives.

The consciousness-raising and organising approach is based on a more complex understanding of gender relations and women's status. This method ascribes powerlessness to the ideology and practice of patriarchy and socio-economic inequality in all the systems and structures of society. Strategies focus more on organising women to recognize and challenge both gender and class-based discrimination in all aspects of their lives, in both the public and private lives.

Women are mobilized to struggle for greater access to resources, rather than passively provided with schemes and services. This approach is successful in enabling women to address their position and strategic needs, but may not be as affective in meeting immediate needs.

These approaches are contrasted with that more generally used by women's organizations and other NGOs: empowerment through awareness building, capacity building and organizing women that leads to transformation of unequal relationships, increased decision-making power in the home and community, and greater participation in politics.

Some c hese ideas are also taking root in development programmes, and agenc ; are beginning to develop gender training frameworks that include the concept of empowerment. For instance, the United Nations Children Fund (**UNICEF**) is using the Women's Empowerment Framework, developed by **Sara Longwe** of Zambia, as a 'total to be used in its efforts to mainstream gender throughout **UNICEF's** programme planning process' and as a 'conceptual basis for gender responsive assessment, evaluation and programming'.

The evolution in policy on women and development reflects and is in turn reflected by what is happening at the grassroots. Many development agencies are gearing their programmes and projects to the empowerment of women through **capacity building** and through **strengthening both women's organizations and women's participation in rural associations**. Gender awareness activities for both and women have also become an important part of some projects at the community level. Women's participation is grassroots organizations is increasingly recognized as crucial to their empowerment and as a way for them to help shape development policies (**Karl**, 1995). According to the secretary-general of the United Nations, Mr.Boutros Boutros-Ghali.

"Given the importance of female leadership in community and grassroots level organizations, non- governmental organizations have been identified as a key actor in empowering women, and in ensuring that an accurate knowledge of their true situation, of their actual and potential roles, and of obstacles to their economic participation, is reflected in the design of economy-wide policies".

Personal efficacy lies at the heart of **female empowerment**. Efficacy is the degree to which an individual perceives that he or she controls his/her environment (**Bandura**, 1986). Many of the influences on an Indian Village Women create a lack of efficacy. Female infants are regarded from birth as less important than males, they are relegated to inferior status, and important decisions are made for and about them, rather than by them. How can Indian Village Women achieve efficacy? By learning through organized group activities from which they gain control over their lives and their environment (**Rogers, Singhal, Wayanagankar, Shetner,** 1993).

The **female empowerment approach** stresses the capacity of women to increase their self-reliance and internal strength. The empowerment approach to women's advancement in developing countries recognizes that the patriarchal structure of subordination must be addressed through women's organizations at the grassroots level. such local groups can facilitate bottom-up change by providing a social mechanism to raise women's consciousness about their subordination, Becoming aware of women's position in society, and transferring skills to enable women to gain access to education, employment, and health care are key components in many women Empowernment programmes today.

The increasing attention in recent years to the self employment of women dates from the 1985 World Conference on Women held in Nairobi, Kenya, Prior to the Nairobi Conference, **DAWN** (Development Alternatives with Women for a New Era), a collection of women's groups met order to envision an alternative future society in which gender, racial, and class inequality would not exist. The elimination of women's subordination would be achieved together through the self Employment of women (**DAWN**, 1985).

Grassroot organizations of urban poor and rural women are vital instruments to provide collective strength, bargaining capacity, and collective articulation of their interests (**Sharma**, 1992). In recent decades many development programs changed from focusing on economic development as an end in itself, to seeing development as a means for the improvement of women's overall status. There has been a shift from doing things for women, the WID approach, to doing things with them so that women are actively involved in directing empowerment (**Sharma**, 1992).

There are several avenues for future research. Next steps in scholarly research of female empowerment might include:

1. Studying female empowerment in urban areas, where women's self-development programmes like **SEWA** (Self- Empowered Women's Association) are conducted.

2. **Developing** an **empowerment scale** to measure female empower in **general**, rather than in the specific context of women dairy farmers in **India**. Such an empowerment **scale** might include items #7, #8, #9, and **#10** (see Table 2) plus items such as women's right to take a job without her husband's permission.

3. Studies to assess the impacts on female empowerment of other rural development programmes (than CD) in India and elsewhere in developing nations.

The Process Of Empowerment

In order to challenge their subordination, women must first recognize the ideology that legitimizes male domination and understand how it perpetuates their oppression. This recognition requires reversal of the values and attitudes and, indeed, the world-view, that most women have internalized since earliest childhood. Women have been led to participate in their own oppression through a complex web of religious sanctions, social and cultural taboos and superstitions, hierarchies among women in the family (see Adams and Castle), behavioural training, seclusion, veiling, curtailment of physical mobility discrimination in food and other family resources, and control of their sexuality (including concepts like the "good" and "bad" woman).

Most poor women have never been allowed to think for themselves or to make their own choices excepts in unusual circumstances, when a male decision-maker has been absent or has abdicated his role. Because questioning is not allowed, the majority of women grow up believing that this is the just and "natural" order.

The demand for change does not usually begin spontaneously from the condition of subjugation. Rather, empowerment must be externally induced, by forces working with an altered consciousness and an awareness that the existing social order is unjust and unnatural (**Batliwala** 1995).

They seek to change other women's consciousness by:

- altering their self-image and their beliefs about their rights and capabilities;
- creating awareness of how gender discrimination, like other socio-economic and political factors, is one of the forces acting on them;
- challenging the sense of inferiority that has been imprinted on them since birth: and recognizing the true value of their labour and contributions to the family, society, and economy.

Women must be convinced of their innate right to equality, dignity and justice. Armed with a new consciousness and growing collective strength, women begin to assert their right to control resources (including their own bodies) and to participate equally in decisions within the family, community, and village. Their priorities may often be surprising, even baffling, to the outsider (**Batliwala** 1995). In the aftermath of the 1991 Bangladesh cyclone, one of the first demands made by women in a badly affected area was the rebuilding of the schoolhouse and providing of schoolbooks to their children. This was in contrast to the demands of the local men, who talked only about houses, seeds, poultry, and loans (**Akhtar** 1992).

PRINCIPLES OF EMPOWERING PRACTICE

The Helping Relationship

. At the basis of empowering practice is a helping relationship based on collaboration, trust, and the sharing of power. It is critical that the worker perceives him/her self as an enabler, organizer, consultant, or compatriot with the client in an effort to avoid replicating the powerlessness which the client experiences with other helpers or professionals. This requires workers to give up their expert power and to recognize that clients are the experts in regard to their problems capacities, and potential resources. It recognizes that both the worker land client bring equally valued and complementary skills to the helping process.

Therefore, the interaction between worker and client should be characterized by genuineness, mutual respect, open communication, and informality. It presumes that the worker does not hold the "answers" to the client's problems, but instead that in the context of collaboration the client will develop the insights, skills and capacity to resolve the situation (**Bock**, 1980; **Fagan**, 1979; **Keefe,** 1980 **Pinderhughes**, 1983l; **Schechter** et.al., 1985; **Solomon** 1976).

Along these lines, workers can also facilitate empowerment by assisting the client to experience a sense of personal power within the helping relationship. This technique is based on the assumption that the experience of power within the intervention can be generalized to feelings of power in the larger social environment. Specific means for accomplishing this include having clients role play and practice powerful behaviours, engaging clients in roles in which they help others, and having clients take control of the helping relationship by setting the agenda, co-leading groups or meetings, and researching resources (Pernell, 1985; Pinderhughes, 1983; **Bchechter** et. al., 1985; **Bhapiro**, 1984; **Simmons & Parsons**, 1983a, 1983b; **Withorn**, 1980).

Actively involving the clients in the change process is another aspect of the helping relationship which encourages empowerment. Over a decade ago **Solomon** (1976) described empowerment as a

> **..... process whereby the social worker engages in a set of activities with the client or client system that aim to reduce the powerlessness that has been created by the negative valuations based on membership in a stigmatized group.**

Subsequent authors have described empowering interventions as those which are focused on a. .vities ranging from the exploration of a problem to the development of alternative structures in community (**Beckm** 1983; **Checkoway & Norseman**, 1986; **Fagan**, 1979, **Barvin**, 1985; **Hirayama & Hirayama,** 1985; **Kahn & Bender**, 1985. **Mathis & Richan**, 1986; **Pinderhughes**, 1983; **Solomon,** 1976). What is common to all these activities is praxis: the wedding of reflection and action. As clients are actively involved in change, they are also reflecting upon and analyzing their experiences. The results are also reflecting upon the analyzing their experiences, the future efforts (**Bock**, 1980; **Burghardt**, 1982; **Friere,** 1973; Keefe, 1980; **Lerner**, 1980; **Longers & McLeod**, 1980; **Resnick,** 1976, **Rose & Black**, 1985).

Suggested Modalities

The literature of empowerment suggests interventions on the individual, group, family, and community levels. Practitioners are advised to develop skills on all these levels of intervention and to feel comfortable in moving from one modality to another, however, small group work is presented as the ideal modality for empowering interventions because it is an effective means for integrating the other techniques and sub-processes. It can be the perfect environment for raising consciousness, engaging in mutual aid, developing skills, problem solving, and experiencing one's own effectiveness in influencing others (**Coppola & Rivas**, 1985; **Garvin**, 1985; **Hirayama & Hirayama**, 1985; **Pernell**, 1985; **Sarri & Rivaga**, 1986). This emphasis on small group work holds true to known all levels of intervention, regardless of whether the goal is empowering individuals or changing institutions.

In the spirit, involvement of clients in mutual aid, self help, or support groups is also recommended. In the context of empowerment, mutual-aid, self-help, land support groups are formed by individuals experiencing similar problems and who focus on providing aid and support to each other

(**Barvin**, 1985; **Kahn & Bender**, 1985; **Bherman & Wenocur**, 1983; **Withorn**, 1980). They facilitate empowerment by providing clients with a basis of emotional and social support through the change process, a format providing concrete assistance, the opportunity to learn new skills through role modeling, and a potential power-base for future action (**Keefe,** 1980; **Hirayama & Hirayama**, 1985; **Pinderhughes**, 1983; **Solomon**, 1976). They can also provide the context for developing critical consciousness by involving group participants in dialogue with others who share their problems.

Lessons For Women's Empowerment Strategy

No one magic formula or fail-safe design exists for empowerment. Nonetheless, experience clearly shows that empowerment strategies must intervene at the level of women's "condition" while also transforming their "position", thus simultaneously addressing both practical and strategic needs.

Several elements appear essential to challenge patriarchal ideology, and to enable poor women to gain greater access to and control over both material and informational resources. Although these elements are set out below in a particular sequence, they may be reversed or interchanged. Or several may be undertaken concurrently, depending on the context.

An organisation concerned with bringing about women's empowerment must begin by locating the geopolitical region (urban or rural) in which it wants to work, and identifying the poorest and most oppressed women in that area. Activists then have to be selected and trained. Intensive preparatory training is critical. It must impart to activists an awareness of the structures and sources of power, especially gender. It must equip them with skills needed to mobilize, while learning from, the women whose consciousness they plan to raise.

In general, female activists are preferable, since they are in a better position to initiate the empowerment process with other women, notwithstanding differences in class. Caste, or educational background. In the field, the activists encourage women to set aside a separate time and space for themselves as disempowered women rather than as passive observers (**Batliwala** 1995).

Gender Empowerment Measure

The **Gender Empowerment Measure** (GEM), according to Human

Development Report 1994, examines whether women and men are able to actively participate in economic and political life and take part in decision-making. The gender empowerment measure (GEM) concentrates on participation - economic, political and professional. It differs from the GDI, which is concerned primarily with basic capabilities and living standards. Like the HDI and the GDI, GEM focuses on a few selected variables even though participation can take many forms. Given data availability, it concentrates on three broad classes of variables :

1. For power over economic resources based on earned income, the variables is per capita income in PPP dollars (unadjusted)

2. For access to professional opportunities and participation in economic decision-making, the variables is the share of jobs classified as professional and technical and administrative and managerial.

3. For access to political opportunities and participation in political decision-making, the variable is the share of parliamentary seats.

The GDI and the GEM treat the income variable differently. In the GEM, income is evaluated not for its contribution to basic human development - such as a longer life, literacy and freedom from poverty. It is evaluated as a source of economic power that frees the income earner to choose from a wider set of possibilities and exercise a broader range of options. That is why income above the average world per capita income is not discounted as it is in both the HDI and the GDI.

For access to professional opportunities and participation in economic decision-making, the variable chosen in women's share of jobs classified as administrative or managerial and professional or technical. Administrative and managerial jobs lie closer to decision-making, but professional and technical represent opportunities for career development. Women often acquire specialized higher education but are prevented by cultural or economic barriers from taking jobs that will use the valuable skills they gain. Their potential is thus underused. It should be borne in mind that the quality of data for professional careers and decision-making positions is uneven, with some variation in how countries categorize these occupations.

The best record is in the Nordic countries, where the share of women in professional and technical careers exceeds 60% for some countries. Among developing countries , Botswana, the Philippines and Uruguay show similar percentages. Generally, the proportion of women in professional and technical jobs is lower with the average ratio 40%.

In administrative and managerial positions, the share of women is even smaller. An exception is Hungary, where women hold 58% of such positions. In Australia, Canada and the United States, women hold about 40% of such positions. Elsewhere, the percentages are quite low. In most developing countries, the proportion of women in administrative and managerial positions is less than 10%. Even in industrially advance France, Japan, Luxembourg and Spain, the share of women in such positions is less than 10% . Thus, many high-paid career opportunities still are not open to women in many societies.

The third variable is access to political opportunities and participation in political decision making. Here, the facts are even more startling than in the economic arena. No gender-specific training is required t be a parliamentarian. Neither public speaking, nor the ability to represent the opinions of the electorate, nor the art of wining public confidence requires exclusively masculine traits. But politics remains an obstacle course for women.

One of the best indicators of political participation would be women's share of representation in local bodies, such as municipal councils, but these data are unavailable for many countries. So, the variable for the GEM is representation in parliament, in both upper and lower houses, in 1994.

Women have obtained the highest representation in parliament in Norway and Finland, with four-fifths of the seats that men have. The next best record is in Sweden and Denmark, where the proportion was about one third. Some countries, such as Sweden, have made dramatic strides more recently.

Beyond the four Nordic countries, the disparity widens dramatically. In Thailand, 94.4% of the seats are had by men, 3.6% by women. In Republic of Korea, the proportions are 99% and 1%. Even this is better than having no women in parliament, which is the case in some countries. The average representation of women in parliaments worldwide is 10%.

The three dimensions are valued equally in constructing the gender empowerment measure. In computing the index, the parameter of inequality aversion (E) chosen is 2, the same as that for the gender-related development index.

The GEM is not meant to be a prescriptive index, with the intent of setting universal cultural norms. What is crucial is not achieving a certain percentage representation in selected political and economic arenas, but providing equality of choices to both women and men. The GEM examines outcomes in economic and political participation., These outcomes could be caused by structural barriers to women's access to these arenas. Or they could be the result of choices by both women and men on their desired roles in society. this is a matter for the people of each country to determine for themselves.

The GEM is estimated for 116 countries with comparable data for the three dimensions. Sweden and Norway rank at the top. The Nordic countries are not only good at strengthening the basic capabilities of women - through liberal investment in education and health - but they have also opened many opportunities for women to participate in economic and political fields. The Nordic countries are the only ones that have crossed the critical 30% threshold for meaningful participation by women.

The ranking also shows that some developing countries out perform much richer industrial countries in gender equality in political, economic and professional activities. This is also case for Barbados, the Bahamas, Trinidad and Tobago, Cuba, Costa Rica, China, Guyana, the Philippines and Colombia . Trinidad and Tobago has a GEM of 0.533, higher than the GEM for Switzerland, Hungary, the United Kingdom, Spain, Japan or France. France's GEM, for example , is 0.433.

Only nine countries have GEM values above 0,06. Twenty-four have values below 0.25. The low values of the GEM make it clear that many countries have much further to travel in extending broad economic and political opportunities to women than the distance they have already traveled in building their basic capabilities.

A number of countries have very low GEM values compared with their GDI values. Although the GEM and the GDI are not strictly comparable because of differences and their construction. Substantial differences in the values of the two indices are illustrative of important problems that policy makers need to address. Among industrial countries, the widest differences in value between the GDI and the GEM are found in France, Japan and Greece - followed by the United Kingdom, Ireland, and Spain. Greece's GDI is 0.825, for example, and its GEM only0.343. women in Greece hold only 6% of the seats in parliament and only 10% of administrative and managerial positions. Moreover, women receive only 22% of earned income. The story is similar in France and Japan.

Among developing countries, the Republic of Korea, Turkey, Kuwait, the United Arab Emirates and Mauritius have very low GEM values compared with their GDI values. Turkey has a low GEM value (0.234) mainly because women hold only 2% of parliamentary seats and only 4% of administrative and managerial positions.

Comparing GEM ranks with income ranks can help to highlight problem areas. Unadjusted income is part of the GEM, so richer countries should rank higher on the GEM on the basis of income alone. If they do not, this indicates the need for more progress in achieving gender equality. Several Mediterranean countries, such as Turkey, Greece and Cyprus, rank much lower in the GEM than they do in real GDP per capita. The same is true of many Arab states. For example, the United Arab Emirates ranks third in real GDP per capita among the 166 countries, but 94 in the GEM. Kuwait ranks 3 in GDP per capita and 93 in the GEM. One reason: neither country has any women in parliament. In the United Arab Emirates, women hold fewer than 2% of administrative and managerial position and receive only 7% of earned income.

Several countries in East and South-East Asia that have followed an East Asian development model have low GEM values. These include Japan, the Republic of Korea and Singapore-which rank much higher in real GDP per capita than in the GEM. The Republic of Korea, for example, ranks 28 in GDP per capita but 90 in the GEM. The common problem among these countries is that economic and political participation by women is still low.

Some developing countries do comparatively better in the GEM than in the GDI. China Costa Rica and Cuba have higher GEM Values than Japan or France. Nicaragua and the Philippines have higher GEM values than Greece. And Zimbabwe and Cape Verde have higher values than Turkey or the Republic of Korea. Invariably, the difference is that the better-performing countries have opened many economic and political opportunities to women, opportunities that remain closed to women in other countries.

Much progress remains to be made in gender equality in almost every country. And in equality of choice in economic and political participation industrial countries are not necessarily taking the lead. The areas showing the least progress are parliamentary representation and percentage share of administrators and managers.

The clear policy message from this simple exercise is this: In most countries, industrial or developing, women are not yet allowed into the corridors of economic and political power. In exercising real power or decision-making authority, women are a distinct minority throughout the world.

Indicators of Women's Empowerment

Perhaps one of the clearest indicators of women's empowerment is an increase in women's capacities and willingness to support other women and to work diligently toward strengthening women in their efforts to survive or to gain equality (**Bernard**, 1971). It is only through acknowledging women's and men's interdependency in constructive ways (**Durkheim**, 1966) that women can enter into more powerful exchanges with men in society at large (**Blau**, 1967). Women's collective actions necessary to deal effectively with such important issues as violence against women (**Hindberg**, 1988), and the persistence of patriarchy in welfare states (**Holter**, 1984).

The probability of realizing women's freedom is increased through their awareness of the plight and possibilities they share with other women (**Shibutani**, 1955; **Randour**, 1987). When women are able to organize their efforts around crucial goals, such as changing particular values (e.g., prejudice against nontraditional feminine values) or specific behavior (e.g., discriminatory practices against women) in wider society (**Smelser**, 1962), women's empowerment will be realized more effectively.

The Draft Country Paper-India for the 4th World Conference on Women, Beijing, 1995 proposed the following qualitative and quantitative indicators for evaluating the women's empowerment.

Qualitative Indicators Of Empowerment

a. Increase in self esteem, individual and collective confidence.

b. Increase in articulation, knowledge and awareness levels on issues affecting the community at large, and women in particular such as women's health, nutrition, reproductive rights, legal rights, literacy etc., depending on the programme.

c. Increase or decrease in personal leisure time and time for child care.

d. Increase or decrease in work loads of women as result of t he new programme.

e. Changes in the roles and responsibilities in the family and in the community.

f. Visible increase or decrease in levels of domestic violence and other forms of violence perpetrated on the women and girl child.

g. Responses to, and changes, in social and other customs that are anti-women e.g. child marriage, dowry, discrimination against widows etc.

h. Visible changes in women's participation levels e.g. are more women attending public meetings, training programmes; are women demanding participation in other events related to their lives?

i. Increase in bargaining/negotiating power of the women as an individual in the home and community as well as in collectives of women.

j. Increased access to and ability to gather information and knowledge not only about the project, but about what affects their lives.

k. Formation of cohesive and articulate women's groups/collectives at the village level, district, block, state levels.

l. Positive changes in social attitudes amongst the community members towards discrimination against women and the girl child.

m. Awareness and recognition of women's economic contribution within and outside the household.

n. Women's decision-making over the kind of work she is doing; is her income and expenditure in her control or is she still subservient to male member's in the family.

Quantitative Indicators Of Empowerment

a) Demographic trends:
- maternal/mortality rates
- fertility rates
- sex ratio
- life expectancy at birth
- average age of marriage

b) Numbers of women participating in different development programmes.

c) Greater access and control over community resources/government schemes/services e.g. crèches, credit-savings groups, cooperatives, NFE centres, schools, wells etc.

d) Visible changes in physical health status/nutritional levels.

e) Changes in male/female literacy levels - primary, secondary and adult literacy including enrollment and retention rates.

f) Participation levels of women in political processes at the local level.

Process of Evaluation of Women's Empowerment

The scope of empowerment being broad, and somewhat intangible, the evaluation process should also address itself to processes of change, as they affect all participants in the planning-implementation chain, and not only the community. It should also necessarily include an assessment of outcomes that are not directly derived of expected from the given objectives. Several outcome are determined by women in the community and not by outsiders.

In order to build a congruence between the programme implementation and the organizational structure and systems, it is paramount that organizational systems adapt to the changing processes of women's empowerment. Organizational systems need to reflect the values and norms inherent in the perspective and programmes if real empowerment is to be achieved. The evaluation process should thus assess the following aspects of organizational functioning:

a) Congruence between the programme perspective and the organizational structure and policies

b) Whether the implementation staff (both men and women) are sensitive and have been sensitized to women's issues.

c) What support is provided to change attitudes, skills and capacities.

d) Whether there have been changes in attitudes, skills and abilities of staff in the process of implementation.

e) Whether women from the community are involved in the organizational functioning and decision making processes at all levels, and if so how.

f) Whether the structure of communication and information flow is accessible at all levels horizontally and vertically and ensures the involvement of the intended 'beneficiaries' and partners in the programmes.

g) What collaborative mechanism exist between the Government implementing Departments, Panchayats, NGOs, Women's groups or people's institutions and whether there area clear terms of reference for these.

h) Whether one programme to promote to promote empowerment interdepartmentally, links with another programme.

i) Whether information and analysis are shared; Whether and how one programme staff learn from the experience of another to Build stronger programmes.

Institutional mechanisms for monitoring and evaluation need to be built by involving community, programme staff as well as external evaluators. Local institutions such as Panchayats Mahila Mandals, Women's Organisations may be involved and their capacities be built for the same.

It is an accepted fact that women at large, and especially poor women have been a disadvantaged group, trapped in a system that is unjust and iniquitous. Socially, economically, politically and culturally. Development interventions constitute asset of very substantive efforts to overcome this deprivation. It, therefore, demands a qualitative shift in the attitudes of the people involved in their operationalisation and alteration in perceptions of the self-image and social image of women themselves. This would create an atmosphere of reflecting, questioning seeking answers and analyzing the given socio-economic, political context which has been disempowering women. Such efforts will correspondingly need to be evaluated within a framework which is also empowering using some conventional but more innovative methodologies.

Summing Up

We must remember that the world conference on women could be taken as the culmination point for the process of empowerment. It has provided a broad-based activity schedule, to the national, regional and global agencies, in which participation of women has been highlighted. By this method, participation of women in the decision making process could be enhanced many fold and the progress attained in a much shorter-time span. The process of empowerment is helping in identifying areas to be targeted, planning strategies for acting and in analysis of action and outcomes. Empowerment is not a process which is horizontal or vertical. It is a process which goes round in a circle . Here the beginning ends in a change and the change leads to another beginning. No one magic formula or fail-safe design can exist for empowerment. It has to be tailor made to suit the clients (**Chandra** 1997).

CHAPTER - IV
ORGANISING WOMEN FOR EMPOWERMENT

Why Organise Poor Women?

It is impossible to even think of affecting the situation of the poor people in today's economy. The forces against the poor are so many and the social system so biased in favour of the rich that it will not respond to the demands of the individual poor woman. In the economy, the various forces that work against the poor are highly organised. It is so for the poor self employed workers, as well as the poor women workers, who are not organised as workers. To overcome the constraints and effectively use the space, that is, to be empowered, it is necessary for women to organise themselves.

The process of empowerment involves not just an improvement in physical and social conditions, but also equal participation in decision-making processes, control over resources and mechanisms for sustaining these gains. In this context, **Longwe's** (1990) classification of the five levels of empowerment, namely, welfare, access, conscientisation, participation and control, and the need to move from the level of welfare to control, is a useful one. As one moves towards higher levels of empowerment, however, there is bound to be resistance and conflict, as exclusive male privileges are threatened (**Stuart** 1990). The enemy, in a sense, is not 'one' capitalist, but many landlords, trades, contractors, the police, law, municipal service and other state structures, that do not recognize the existence of these women as individuals and workers (**Jain** 1980).

DAWN (Sen and Grown 1987) has advocated a strategy of '**empowerment through organisation**', both to push for major structural changes at the policy level, and also raise basic survival needs as the priority development issue. It is difficult for one woman to bring lasting change, but 'if whole groups of women begin to demand change, it is much more difficult for society to reject them altogether' (**Batliwala** 1993: 10). It is forced to acknowledge, respond to, and accommodate them as best as possible.

Shramshakti too recognizes the need to organise women to claim their rights, stating that,

> **the National Commission has observed that the lack of organisation in the informal sector is the root cause of the exploitation of women workers... Individually women are not in a position to fight against low and discriminatory wages and exploitative working conditions as they lack bargaining power. Laws will also not be so flagrantly violated if workers are organised (Government of India 1988: 294).**

To be able to ameliorate the situation of poverty of women workers, some direct interventions have to be made in the economy as it exists today. This is possible only by organising the women workers and enhancing their collective strength. Their strength lies in numbers and these need to be brought together.

Organising is a slow and continuous process of enabling a group of people to perceive common interests and act collectively. The social activists and those working in the voluntary organisations, who are working with poor women, are organising them in some way or the other. When we are trying to affect the income levels, we are organising women around work issues directly. Organising around work has both occupational and locational aspects. Occupational aspects involve dealing with the specific problems of each occupation separately and focussing on specific occupations as the basis of organising people.. Locational aspects involve dealing with the issues of particular geographical locations and focussing on the specific needs of that area as the basis of organising people. We try to take into the variety of activities that poor women do to understand how we can organise them around work.

By understanding the various occupations in which poor women workers are engaged we are able to recognize the multiple occupational base of poor women workers as well . And this helps strengthen their positioning these occupations by organizing them around work. The problems they face in these occupation become issues for bringing them together. The problems of women in the same occupations across different locations become a focus when the numerical strength of women is necessary for collective action.

The forces keeping poor rural women poor, weak, marginalized, vulnerable and in a "second class citizen" position, are very strong and well rooted in culture. In society, there are many commonly held beliefs and images which dominate culture, and keep things going the way they are. Some of these are:

- all have equal opportunity for education
- anyone who is industrious can become rich
- the Constitutional Rights that we are all equal before the law, is implemented
- the implementation of the present system leads to progress, welfare and betterment of the people.
- men are superior to women and by nature, women are subordinate to men

There are forces in society, people in society, groups in society, who want to have some other people in society kept poor deprived, and prevented from equally sharing the freedoms and resources that they themselves enjoy (**Ginny Srivastava**).

Psychologically, those controlling the system demoralise the poor people by contempt. In so many ways, the vested interests in the country show contempt for the poor - in the way they speak to them, in the way they treat them in banks, government offices, on the street, in buses. This results in a demoralisation of the poor; they begin to think that they are below the rest of society, the dominant society; it is their fate in life - there is nothing they can do about it! "You big people ... were little people". This "breaking of spirit" of more than half the Indian population, is the worst thing that the vested interest group does.

Socially and politically, those controlling and system "divide and rule". The vested interests use psychological means, and political and social manoeuvres, to divide the strength of the poor. One of the key divisions they promote, is to keep the women power weak and separated from male strength. And the men at the village level, themselves numbered amongst the rural poor, are influenced by the male dominance norms prevalent in society. They oppress and suppress the women in their communities, perhaps in an attempt to help them to feel "big" at least somewhere in this world! The totally male dominated caste and community councils (**"Jati Panchayats"**) which exist everywhere, make all kinds of rules and norms to keep women down, separated - they must veil their faces in front of so many categories of people; they should not speak in front of men; women should eat last, no matter if it is less; girls should not vote the way their husbands and sons tell them. And women should not waste their time going to meetings, and getting organised. "Women who wander here and there, on their way to and from meetings, are women of loose character". Or "Women who spend time going to meetings neglect their families". And so on.

Poor rural women live with the reality of "double deprivation" - one deprivation is the fact that they are numbered among the poor/deprived class of society, and the other reality is that, within that class, women are the "poorest of the poor".

Women have been shut out historically from the closed triangle of knowledge, power, economic power and political power. The triangle gives access only to a limited and privileged control-group. Poor rural women live in permanent fear and paralysis due to their powerlessness in the face of events daily, monthly or merely as games played by adversaries. They lack initiative to change the given variables of a situation. All these forces keeping poor rural women weak, poor, marginalized, vulnerable are very strong.

Individuals have failed to break through territorial monopolies. To counter powerlessness women need to collectively alter their self-image and therefore social-image. This can happen when women come together as an organic unit, discover strength of commonality and bonds of solidarity, and initiate joint action, thereby discovering and experiencing their inner power.

Individually, Poor Rural Women can not overcome powerlessness - collectively, they can. Their strength is in organisation.

Unity + Self Respect + Organisation = United Action

for a New society

Individual poor rural women gain a feeling of self-confidence by being a member of a women's group that is working on the problems of the poor. So, a group is not collection of demoralised, depressed rural women who sit together from time to time - the women themselves change fundamentally when they are members of a strong women's group.

"Strength" is the key concept here. Collectively, actions taken and problems solved can be more effective if a strong group works on them. Risk is shared, more people sharing ideas leads to better planning, more ideas for solving problems that arise.

Women Change From Feeling Weak to Feeling Strong

Poor rural women meet together feeling small, weak, vulnerable, opressed, deprived, powerless	**Powerless**
Group	They regularly attend meetings of the women's group, and take part in activities
They begin to feel self-confident, they gather strength from the group, understand themselves as persons, citizens, women, workers, wives, mothers, they gain self respect	**Self-respect**
They develop a "we" feeling of unity with the other women in the group, divisions fade, individual weak nesses fade, unity leads to.....	**Unity**
Collective strength	Developing awareness of common or collective strength
These groups may join with other groups, cooperating on common activities, converns, issues, struggles as part of the Women's Movement	**Cooperation**

To give poor rural women visibility, and to enable society to come in contact with poor rural women, they must get organised into groups. Then society will perceive them, will have to listen to them.

What is a Group?

A group is NOT just a collection of people who come together for sometime - passengers on a bus may be together for several hours, but they are not "a group". Why?

It is because these people are not doing any common task, they have not collectively decided to do anything together. They are together only once. No one is exercising any leadership over the bus passengers.

A collection of people will be called a **GROUP** if:

- they come together to **work for a common purpose**.
- there is a conscious **membership** - members know they are members, and others who are not members, know they are not. Membership criteria and responsibilities, as well as rights are known.
- the members **meet regularly.**
- there is **identified leadership,** whether there is one leader or several. The group recognises the leadership, and the leaders "lead".
- the members **take collective** action, and carry out decided-upon plans. A collection of people that doesn't do anything is not a group.
- they have decided on some **rules and procedures** for their being together and working together. These rules may be formally written down, or they may be only commonly understood.
- the people who come together have a **common interest.** No purposeful dialogue can take place until the members have a common interest.
- the members have a **common understanding** of their reason for meeting, of themselves as members.
- the **size** is big enough and small enough to allow members to interact, participate. In terms of what "feels like a group" and what is a minimum size for effective collective work together, it can be said that when five or more persons get together regularly, meet and talk to each other, it is **"a group".**

The "Culture of a Strong Group

The organiser of women's group has a responsibility to set a good example of a co-operating, sensitive, democratic, group participant. The way the worker alerts the group members group leadership to this important aspect of "group culture", will, to a great extent, determine the strength or weakness of the group.

The culture of the group is determined by the attitudes and customs established by practice by the group members. The culture of the women's groups of poor women should be dynamic, alive, marked by:

- a strong feeling of **UNITY**
  - **FREEDOM** of expression of ideas and feelings
  - **RESPECT** for others
  - **DEMOCRATIC** decision-making
  - **EQUALITY** in the commonality of group membership

- each person **TAKEN SERIOUSLY**, each important

In such a group, each woman feels important, valued, powerful and the group provides a base of security. It is from such a base that the woman can feel **"empowered"**, and work together to change their world.

The culture of a group, according to Ginny Srivastava, is built up over time in many ways:

non-verbal and symbolic gestures

- words
- group processes

A smile, a sniff, rolling of the eyes, a shrug of a shoulder, touching, not touching, seating arrangements, all are examples if the kinds of non-verbal and symbolic gestures that influence group culture. Meeting arrangements, in which the women sit in a circle, communicates "equality", "democracy", "unity". When a group member joins the group, a space for her in the main circle - "each person taken seriously", "equality". Closeness and common understanding will be communicated in many ways.

Size of the Group

If a group is too small, the strength of the group will be weak, and the diversity of ideas, talents and skills, problem-solving suggestions, will be less than if the group is larger. If the group is too large, each member will not have a chance to participate as fully as she would if the group were smaller, and therefore, each member's personal growth will be less. Generally, a group of less than 5 people will not "feel" like a group; a group of about 15-20 women is a good size for a DWCRA group; and probably, the group membership should not go beyond 30 - if more women than that want to be part of the group, a second group may be formed. Nearby groups can meet together from time to time, for mutual strength, and to work on common issues(**Ginny Srivastava**).

Frequency of Meeting

Meetings should be held as often as is necessary. If some issue based struggle is underway, the meetings may even be daily! The frequency of the meetings must be decided by the group members.

Poor rural women are over-burdened with drudgery and survival work, and if the meetings are too often, it truly will be an added burden to the women. Conversely, if the meetings are very infrequent - even once a month, then the sense of the group is in danger of being lost. If, on any particular meeting day, a group member cannot attend because of being out of the village, of sick, or for any reason, then it will be a gap of tow months before she gets a chance to be with the group again (**Ginny Srivastava**).

Participatory Planning

"Participatory planning" is the first activity of the women's group, and this planning process helps both, to being the women's group into existence, and to make it strong. It is not a matter of "making" the women "agree" to already formulated programme targeted activities. It is a matter of helping the women to identify what they want to do, and to decide how to go about doing it. The "participants" in the programme, the poor rural women members of the village-level groups, take the major role in the " planning" of the activities of their group(**Ginny Srivastava**).

Forming Federations of Village Level Women's Groups

The basic building block for widespread social change, according to Ginny Srivastava, is the strong women's group at the village level. Collective action transformers poor women from being week to being strong- and once they get going - they can, and will, change the face of this nation !

Fundamental Social Change "By" and 'for' Women's Groups

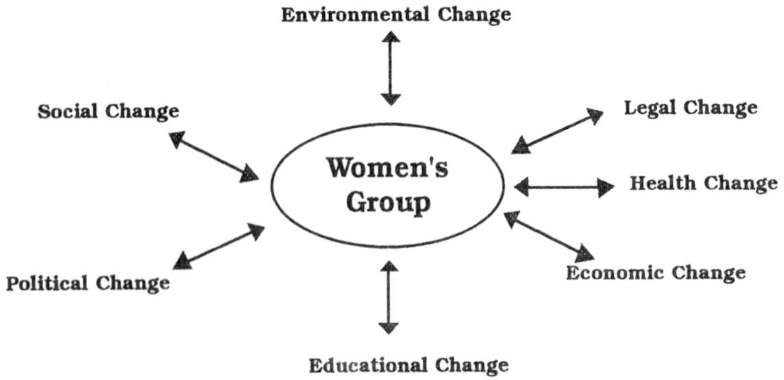

However, fundamental change in the system, to make it more egalitarian, more just, more free, more honest, more democratic, will need the combined strength of strong women's groups united in federations, or broad-based unions and organisations. The single village-level women's group is the "base", but for widespread, fundamental change, women's groups will have to link together, for example"

Environmental Change

- Women's Groups in watershed and catchment areas, planning and working together on soil, conservation and reforestation, will bring change.

Legal Change

- Pressure to amend the laws related to ownership of land in land records, so that married women own land jointly with their husbands, will take legal lobbying of women's federations, may be even form several districts !

Economic Change

- Women's thrift and credit groups, uniting together can create a larger fund for loans and credit than what each could ever do alone

Educational Change

- Efforts to change community attitudes in relation to girls' education and to change the subordinate image of females in the curriculum materials will require a mass movement

Political Change

- Efforts to get women included in the membership of caste and community councils (" Jati" panchayats) will make a collective effort of women in a social region - until it becomes a movement, the men will oppose the idea

Social Change

- Changes in social norms related to windows, marriage costs, veiling, ill require simultaneous pressure on all forces in a fairly large region.

Involvement of men, politicians, administrators will also be needed in the reform of the system. Nevertheless, poor rural women, organised and aware, uniting their organisational strength in federations and networks, can do a lot to bring change in the systems that keep the poor deprived and poor. Indian society, both before Independence and after, has been very slow to work on fundamental changes for half the nation's population - women and girls - that would lead to a more just society.

- Lobbying for changes in policies and laws.
- Planning together for co-ordinated action on common issues.
- Putting collective pressure on exploiters and cheaters of the poor.
- Filling cases in the court for justice – individual cases or public interest cases.

These are all actions that will be more effective , will be stronger efforts, if more than one village-level women's group raises the issues. When groups are mature, and when the issue demands it, women's groups will wise to join their collective strengths, to create larger and more powerful women's organisations (**Ginny Srivastava**).

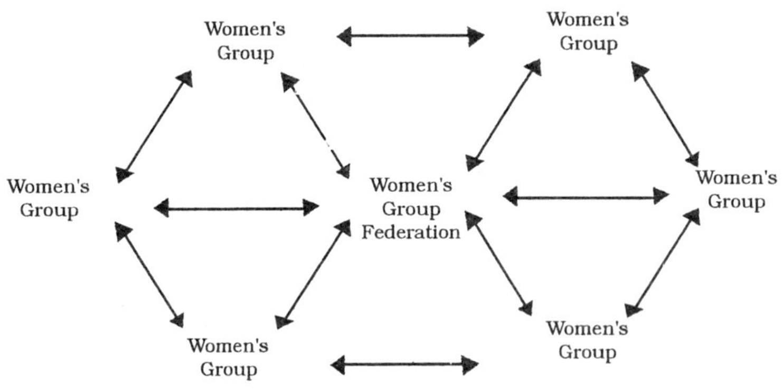

Organising Self Help Groups : the CASA experience

Organising **Self-Help Groups** (SHG's) has been a popular activity with non-governmental organisation since the 1980 . In recent years, several other state and national-level institutions have accepted the SHG concept as well. Many nationalized banks and commercial banks for example, are willing to provide credit to SHGs. The concept of SIGs has spread beyond countries like India and Bangladesh to other parts of the globe.

CASA (Church's Auxiliary for Social Action) views SHGs as a tool for community organisation (**Bose**, 1997), an activity of socio-economic development and a strategy for women's empowerment. CASA organizes SHGs with the objectives of :

(i) inculcating a self-help attitude among the women folk.
(ii) developing collective leadership
(iii) enhancing effective women's participation, control and authority over their development affairs.
(iv) promoting saving habits, developing an indigenous bank system within the village and eliminating exploitation by money lenders
(v) federating these groups under one umbrella or apex body so as to promote women's solidarity and eventually, women's empowerment.

To date, CASA has organised more than one hundred SHGs in Pudu Kkottai and Tiruchi Districts covering seven regions i.e.: Embael, Arimalam, Sembattur, Visalur, Keeranu, Neerapalani, and Manikandam. In Embel region for instance, CASA works in twenty villages. Embel is one of the drought high regions in the Pudukkottai District of Tamil Nadu. This pocket is economically poor, culturally backward, socially nullified and politically denied, The women's problems are innumerable. Our socio-economic survey revealed for example, that women remain as spinsters just because of their impoverished appearance. There were incidents in 1993, when women traveling to purchase rice were attacked due to acute drought and poverty in the area. CASA started working in such areas and carried out Food for Work projects. After having interacted with these villages it was concluded that SHGs would be a means to address their problems.

Ichikottai Self Help Group

In Ichikottai, as SHGs was initiated over an informal meeting between our development workers and the villagers. Mrs.Saroja, one of the villagers, brought a small lamp as an aid for the meeting and that was the day, as the women say that light came into their lives.

To start with 20 women joined together to form a SHG and pooled together Rs.200 each. In six months time, three such groups were organised in the same village. On seeing the first three women SIGs, the men of the village were impressed and the fourth one was formed by the men themselves. Once CASA had organised twenty such groups, these were introduced to the Indian Bank, Thenipatti-Pudupatti. The members now deposit a portion of their savings regularly with the Bank. This has created a linkage between the bank and the womens' groups. The Indian bank patronises these SHGs as its grass-root credit base. In other words, the SHGs becomes a platform between the beneficiaries and the bank.

In April 1997 the village had mobilized nearly Rs.50000. A healthy competition is found among these groups not only in saving, but also in serving themselves. They have engaged in village development activities like road formation, tank deepening, village sanitation, mosquito eradication, availing of government services and linking with nationalized banks.

Porkudi Self Help Group

In Porkudi, a village adjacent to Ichikotai, the pattern was slightly different. An SHG was initiated in June, 1994. Originally fifteen members contributed Rs.10 each per month and started saving. Within a month, however two members dropped out, suspicious that they might not recover their money. Once the SHG started lending money however the members' enthusiasm rose. Within a period of six months, the membership had risen to 24 and numbers continue to increase by the day.

A villager, Mrs.Mangala Mary was given a SHG loan of Rs.2000/- for charcoal making. She invested the money, earned an income of Rs.3400/- and repaid the loan. Encouraged by her experience, the group then decided to avail of a sheep loan for then beneficiaries from Indian bank, Thenipatti-Pudupatti. Mrs.Mangala Mary was also one of the beneficiaries. When the group approached the Indian Bank, officials were impressed with their regular saving and lending systems. Following this, the sheep loans were released to the members. Accordingly, Mrs.Mangala Mary availed of Rs.11000/- for the purchase of one sheep unit i.e. 20 eves and one ram. So far, she has cleared Rs.3500/- out of the sale proceeds from five lambs by September 1997 and clear off the loan. Now she is busy in maintaining the sheep unit which is worth Rs.20000/- and her husband continues managing their charcoal business. She feels secure as the owner of a sheep unit and her life with her husband and three children is much more content.

Few Observations about Self-Help Groups

The growth of SHGs in both cases has followed a similar pattern. It is possible to describe this pattern in stages.

Forming Stage : This is the first stage during which our organisers explain the concept of SHGs. After listening to this, women usually agree to form a group. They give their names albeit cautiously. Some come forward to give their contribution on the same day and some others offer contributions after two or three meetings. It may take from one week to three months time between their first meeting and first lending.

Storming stage : In this stage, a lot of queries arise in the minds of the SHG members. Their hidden anxieties and fears are expressed during meetings Conflict between individual interests and group interests are also evident. The members tend to argue with the organisers that their savings will have to be distributed to them after a fixed period for one year or so. When the members are told that SHG is a continuos process, some of them withdraw their membership claiming back their contributions.

In a meeting at Sembattur village an elderly women queried : " I am more than 50. Suppose I happen to die next year, what will the benefit for me be ?" Questions are also asked about what would happen to the savings made by the unmarried girls after they are married to persons outside the village. Other queries may include :

" Sir/Madam, you are asking us to contribute our money. How much are you contributing for the group ?" or " Can't you give a lumpsum amount say Rs.5000/- or Rs10000/- to start viable in-group lending?" or " Why should we save if you are not contributing anything for this ?"

This is a crucial stage for the organisers, as the members need to be clear that the SHS is not a group which will be wound up after a period of time like a chit fund, The members are appraised that the group's growth is a continuous process which can run not only all throughout their lives but even for generations if they wish; and any problem will have to be solved by the members themselves and not by CASA organisers. At this stage, the group members are ensured that each one of them is the owner of the group and not a nominee by CASA or any outsider. The SHG decides its own bye-laws, whom to make a member, how much to contribute, how long to contribute, how much to lend to each individual and so on. They are reminded that it is a women's owned groups for helping themselves and not a CASA Self Help Group. In fact, CASA plays a facilitating role by not making any financial contribution.

Norming Stage : In this stage, members begin to internalize the concept of "self-help". The experience of meeting, interacting, contributing, saving and lending, builds trust and feeling of co-operation among the members. Once benefit in terms of getting petty loans are enjoyed by group members, the loyalty and attachment towards the group is enhanced. They tend to speak well about the SHG to others. Observing the activities of the SHG, interest among the villagers spreads and more people express a desire to join. Often this option is denied by the SHG. If more than fifteen members are willing, a separate group will be organised.

Performing Stage: Both the task and the maintenance functions of the group are clearly realized by the members of the group at this stage. Their contributions usually double. They approach the bankers for further credit assistance. They began to articulate their social obligations to the village as a whole. The group is perceived as a means for income generation and collective action. At this stage the group matures to function on its own.

Outcome and Impact

The emergence of SHGs has had a great impact on the lives of the lives of the local people, particularly the women in these regions.

Self confidence and security : The women have gained a great deal of self confidence. Previously, when government officials or the bankers interacted with the village women in the absence of their husbands, they generally responded with statements like " I don't know"; " My husband has gone out"; "What can I say ?"; Let him come" or " He only knows"

Now, the same women are approaching the bankers and government officials and demanding their rights and privileges. Many SHGs have placed demands with District Collectors for drinking water, street lights, IRDP (Integrated Rural Development Programme) loans etc. Through these actions their self esteem is being elevated. The women who felt helpless, now realize that they are secure not only in terms of credit support but also in terms of" feeling as members of the group".

Economic Development : Each member of the group is able to improve the economic condition of her family by purchasing assets like goal, sheep, poultry or milch animals. We observed that in almost all the cases, 100% recovery of loans is assured. Hence, the SHG has become model of an honest credit net and this has become an eye-opener for banking institutions to extend support to SHGs .

Group solidarity: The SHGs do not touch common savings for any purposes other than lending. When one of the members is sent to the bank to deposit their savings, each member separately contribute Re. 1 and that money is used to cover travel and other expenses. This implies a financial management discipline among the members.

Attitudinal Change :There have been some amazing examples of attitudinal change induced by the formations and activities of SHGs . In one village, a husband who was involved in the distillation of illicit liquor changed his ways, gave up his obnoxious profession and joined hands with his wife who was running a bakery with money she had loaned from the SHG. Many SHG members are happy to admit that illicit liquor brewing, wife beating and other atrocities have declined since the emergence of SHGs .

Empowerment : The socio-economic activities of the SHGs have generated enormous collective strength among the womenfolk. In most villages, womens' participation in decision making was non-existent. Once, when CASA staff wrote womens' names in the muster roll of the Food For Work Programme, the men objected very strongly. Some even walked out at the time of distribution of wheat under the same programme. In these very areas today, women have been elected to head Panchayats (**Bose** 1997).

THE MAHILA SAMAKHYA EXPERIENCE

The Department of Education (Ministry of Human Resource Development) initiated the **Mahila Samakhya Programme.** Its objectives were delineated by NPE and POA; and initiated under the banner of "***Education for Women's Equality***" (Mahila Samakhya 1988). **Mahila Samakhya** viewed ***Sanghas*** as the means of countering powerlessness. ***Sanghas*** were the instruments that would enable women to plan, implement and direct their own empowerment. The role of the outsider was to facilitate the coming together of women, allowing them 'time and space' to determine direction and pace of social change. 'Delivery' of skills or education was outdated, education could not be thrust upon women (**Sujaya,** 1997). Once the ***Sanghas*** were established, it would come about naturally within the collective reflection of its format.

Unlike most other development plans, the original plan document (October 1988) of **Mahila Samakhya** was kept deliberately amorphous and open-ended. It had to be consonant with the flexibility and philosophy of the programme, which was not centred around predetermined targets and 'timeliness' but as a plan that allowed women to plan. It was hoped that experiential learning would help fill in the gaps left open by the plan.

Since the original plan document, which dubbed **Mahila Samakhya** as women's education for equality, the programme has come full circle viewing the struggle for equality as a necessary condition for women education. The demand for information, knowledge and education is seen as the natural outcome of collective reflection and resistance against gender subordination. This revised theme can be termed as 'Women's Equality for Education'.

Mahila Samakhya was initially operationalised in the following 10 districts from 3 States in India.

- Baroda, Rajkot and Sabarkantha from Gujarat
- Bidar Mysore and Bijapur from Karnataka;
- Varanasi, Banda, Sharanpur and Tehri and Uttar Pradesh.

Each district had its specific socio-economic-political scenario, necessitating a contextually relevant process for initiating the project.

- The first approach consisted of taking an identified group of women created through NGO intervention attempting to weave in the agenda for **empowerment** of women through **Mahila Samakhya**.

- The second approach was to initiate group formation through specially designed processes independently of existing structures. These comprised principally of attempts at establishing emotional rapport and creating a forum for women's issues.

The strategy of initiating the programme through well-established local voluntary organisations, was crucial to the smooth fast and effective launch of **Mahila Samakhya** especially as it was an amorphous and an open-end programme. This method showed quick results; proved that MS is possible, thus increasing visibility of the programme.

Direct Intervention by Mahila Samakhya

The alternative route to **Sangha** formation has been through ***sahayoginis.*** The broad pattern emerging in all **Mahila Samakhya** states is, that **District Implementation Units (DIU's)** select and train a team of ***sahayoginis*** taking help from trainers, either from non-Government, professional groups or from existing human resources within the state. These ***sahayoginis*** are specially trained in building rapport with village women, understanding them and facilitating them to understand themselves. In some states (U.P. and Gujarat) the ***sahayogini*** helps identifying ***sakhis*** who act as women leaders. While the ***sahayoginis*** role is broadly the same in all states of all MS the role of ***sakhis*** and their position in the **Mahila Samakhya** structure shows a wide range of difference. On the whole, the shift has been from grafting the **Mahila Samakhya** programme on existing groups to forming fresh autonomous groups for initiating **Mahila Samakhya** programme. The varied approaches to **sangha** formation include:

- Door to door visits so as to initiate personal contact.
- Getting involved, in and assisting with the daily chores of women.
- Participating in family and community functions like marriages, deaths, births, and festivals, and sharing in the joys and the suffering of women.
- Organising special meets/*melas* and celebrating occasions such as Women's Day, Independence Day, and Environment Day.
- Getting women together to indulge in creative activities like singing songs and *bhajans*, dancing, and putting up plays.
- Organising alternative modes of information dissemination such as puppet shows and street theatre, which foster a sense of fun and collective enjoyment.

Sangha: from an Aggregate to a Group

Collecting women together for a specific purpose, an outsiders objective - is not synonymous with the notion of a group. A group to have an identity must experience and act as a unit with an inner momentum. How does this happen? MS experience clearly demonstrates that in the final analysis, a group emerges only under certain conditions. What are the specific steps that help such an emergence of a group? The response from MS groups is as follows:

- **Training:** At the basic level, women must discover their commonality not merely at a verbal level but as a live experience. To realise that they are a unit in some respect women have to fed a unit. For women who have internalised their role and status as a subordinate member in the society, this experience arises in very authentic way, if and when they can distance themselves from their personal context and look at their shared situation. An in house, residential training situation helps this experience to emerge. And this, initially facilitates a core leadership for a **Sangha.**

- **Support:** Emotional and Institutional. With an altered perception of women's identity, their world view goes through turmoil. What appeared straightforward, God decreed 'destiny' to them, alters into a human cultural situation which needs to be changes. This newly acquired state, which is an inevitable outcome of sensitive training, needs strong support at an emotional level. This is the most critical first step in empowerment which **MS** strictly adhered to. It is this which constituted the major departure from bureaucratically managed interventions (Government or Non-government). Strong sanghas in MS vividly recall their experiences of internalising the supportive gestures by Sahayoginis and DIUs. Also, absence of this can be seen as a crucial factor responsible for the break-up of Sanghas.

- **Strong and Sensitive Sahayogini:** The position and role of the ***Sahyogini*** is crucial to the successful emergence of a **sangha**. She should be a full-time functionary, trained in the MS philosophy and approach, and devoted to not more than ten villages. The three major facets of her position are a **Mahila Samakhya** functionary, a group organiser, and a trainer (Source: Mahila Samakhya, U.P., 1996). The woman in this position should be able to culturally relate to the village women and serve as a role model for them. She should be able to establish emotional rapport, solidarity and a relationship with **sangha** women which requires going beyond the traditional confines of the "government official" (*sarkari*) label that comes with her position. She should avoid potentially conflictual situations and monitor the pace of change closely so as to keep it within 'acceptable' limits. She must always view accountability to the village women as a priority. The ***Sahyogini*** needs constant capacity building through on-going training and educational upgradation. She should have easy access to a contextually relevant information system which will assist her in her role as a facilitator/ motivator of local women.

- **Flexible, Responsive and Supportive MS organisational structure**: The MS structure should motivate and not stifle emergence and operation of **Sanghas**. In addition, timely and appropriate intervention is required by all functionaries to solve problems as and when they arise. The MS structure should creatively facilitate situations that bring women together, encourage them to do things collectively and discover their commonalties as women.

- **Transparency of functioning**: Transparency in the functioning of the MS structure, information sharing, and decentralisation of decision making are crucial elements that contribute to the processes of successful **Sangha** formation.

- **Collective activities**: Besides the role of the ***Sahyoginis*** and a supportive, facilitative MS structure, the **Sanghas** must go through the rites of passage, the necessary steps, and indulge in collective activities before they can build a sense of solidarity. It has been observed that struggle plays a central role in the emergence of **Sanghas**. A **Sangha** that does not go through a history of struggle over issues will remain a loose aggregate (or break apart) and not emerge as a collective in the real sense of the word. This also implies that a **Sangha** needs sufficient time to formulate its priorities and engage in the necessary struggle to achieve success. A sangha formed in a quick manner is generally unstable and unsustainable.

- **Caste and class:** Some interesting common trends have emerged with respect to the caste and class composition of **sanghas** in all the states included in this study. It has been observed that organically strong **sanghas** generally ten to be caste-specific and most **sangha** members hail from lower castes. In addition to one-caste **sanghas** there are many instances of mixed **sanghas** where members come from several lower-caste groups. For example, in Bidar district (Karnataka) there are 44 mixed caste **sanghas** out of a total of 202 **sanghas** in the whole district, and in Bijapur there are 66 mixed **sanghas** out of a total 210 (Refer to Table 1). Mixed **sanghas** have also formed across caste lines as long as there is a commonality of class affiliation. In other words, women belonging to different castes will come together in **one sangha** as long as they belong to the lower class. There are no instances of purely upper class **sanghas** or **sanghas** where there is an intermixing of upper and lower class women. That is to say that while caste boundaries can and are transgressed during the process of **sangha** formation, class boundaries are hard to collapse.

Break-up of Sanghas

Based on the afore-mentioned preconditions for emergence of **sanghas**, the following configurations lead to disintegration of **sanghas:**

- Overpowering leadership at all levels of the MS structure has emerged as one of the leading causes of the weakening and dissociation of **sanghas**.

Leadership that suffocates rather then enables-be it at the **sangha** level, **Sakhi** level, ***Sahyogini*** level. DIU level or the state office level is no conducive to the strengthening of **sanghas**. **Sangha** women, **Sakhis,** and ***Sahyoginis*** need to work collaboratively rather than competitively with each other.

- **Sanghas** also disband when **Sahyoginis** and the DIU/state office functionaries do not respond to **sangha** needs in a timely and appropriate manner. Apathy on the part of programme functionaries kills the **sangha** spirit. This includes lack of regular visits to the villages and systematic reviews of **sangha** activities and progress. Another important factor contributing to the decline and **sanghas** is restriction on smooth information flow both vertically and horizontally through the various levels of the MS structure. This becomes especially problematic where money is involved because it flouts the very basic principle of accountability.

- Situations in which **sangha** activities take on a sense of ritualism leads to the stagnation of **sanghas**. In addition, making personal grudges into **sangha** issues is detrimental to the growth of **sanghas** because it accords precedence to the individual over the collective.

- Intervention from outside agencies - whether governmental or non-governme nt al which follow a philosophy that is antithetical to the basic premises and processes of **Mahila Samakhya** leads to a decline and eventual break up of sanghas. Conflicts with NGOs have been discussed previously in this report. It has been observed that governments schemes for women's economic development (like **DWCRA**) that impose aggregation of women from without rather than building collectivism from within result in the disbanding of **sanghas.** This has been the experience of all four states particularly where governmental (or non-governmental) loan schemes are concerned.

INDICATORS FOR STRONG SANGHAS

Based on discussions on the preconditions for the emergence of sanghas and the factors contributing to their break up, the following indicators for strong sanghas have emerged, the absence of which in turn gives indicators for sangha weakness also. These indictors refer principally to the process of Sangha functioning and not to the initial investments. In other words, the first few steps taken in any Sangha are the choices made by

them out of a whole set of "possible" ways of doing things. What emerges as the outcome from them can be estimated through the following indicators : -

A strong sangha is one which :

- takes initiative in identifying a common cause
- responds with sensitivity to issue of exploitation/ violence on women integrates community concerns in its agenda takes a decision without guidance from ***Sahyogini***
- builds an image of " a power to reckon with " at the community level.
- pressurises the existing system for gather accountability to people.
- attracts and sustains participation from different sets of women and men over varied issues.
- holds regular meetings in which women take active interest and part, and indulge in creative, open-minded problem solving.
- encourages alternative forms of learning
- provides leadership opportunities to gather numbers of women

INDICATORS FOR STRONG SANGHAS

MAHILA SAMAKHYA'S COLLECTIVE ACTION ON COMMON PROBLEMS OF WOMEN

The **empowerment** of poor rural women through knowledge, organisation building and collective action being the main objective of **Mahila Samakhya (MS),** the success of the programme can be gauged from the extent to which the **sanghas** operating in the villages have been able to articulate their demands and to take independent actions. MS has often been faced with the issue of how to capture conceptually the process of development a **sangha** goes through till it can be called a 'successful' unit. Discussions on this have led to the understanding that though empowerment is an ongoing process and has to be defined by the **sanghas** themselves, the programme could be deemed to have played its professed role when the **sanghas** become vibrant and self-reliant in dealing with issues they consider important. In tracing the process till a **sangha** reaches this stage, the Andhra Pradesh team identified four stages of **Sanghas** formation: the rapport building stage when the

Sahayogini meets the women and has casual talks with individuals and groups of women, the formative stage when a structure takes shape with more regular members and perhaps attaching a name to the group; then the consolidation stage when more controversial issues start coming up, days of meetings are fixed, and agendas set and attempts are made to change circumstances through collective action. Leaders emerge, too at this stage. The last stage is that of independent **sanghas** which can mobilise their own support and actively influence the social, cultural, political and economic environment around them. But the path of **Sangha** growth is not linear or vertical, but a series of 'crests and troughs', where they spurt forward in certain directions and slip backwards at other times, only to team up and regroup for more sustained action.

* Groups with social space
* Where women gain strength from the collective
* Where women have developed a perspective on their status concerning them
* Have a common goal and understanding
* A recognised status at social, and legal forums
* They take initiatives
* Have created alternatives
* They have an active social identity

Other than this, the team also collectively defined a strong **sangha** as one which comprises of a group of 20 women or more that meets at regular intervals, has a name and leaders, seeks information and is willing to participate in cluster meetings, takes initiative in decision making, addressing issues that concern it, raised funds for travel expenses for meeting or for visiting officials, and maintains it own accounts. The group concluded that one cannot assume that **sanghas** which were willing participants in the beginning will remain so or that not much achievement could be expected of groups that where initially hostel. The opposite may well be the case.

On the basis of its observations over the years, the Andhra Pradesh **MS** intends to strong' **sanghas** extend the amount earmarked for **Sakhi** honorarium to ' in order to ensure that **sanghas** are adequately prepared for this, it does not break their unity and that the amount is invested on the right direction. The funds are to be used for collective purposes such as literacy, child care, kitchen gardens, **sanghas** huts, to meet travel expenses for group purposes or for emergencies, and not for child marriages, festivals and religious purposes. Other conditions have been added, such as a minimum of ten women should be functionally literate.

Uttar Pradesh, where the sangha process was not too visible three years ago, today boasts of 264 strong **sanghas**. There are 251 **sanghas** which are strong in some respects and weak in others, and 330 (130 in old areas and 200 in the new areas) which are categorised as 'weak'. This opinion was expressed in a workshop in mid-1995 which was organised to analyses the **sangha** process in the State, before any further concrete input is made. Recognising that until two years ago the focus was on indirect strengthening of the **sanghas** through the **Sakhis**, a conscious decision was made to focus on the **sanghas** directly. As a first step there has been clarification of perspectives and concepts at all levels. Sangha women have been encouraged to attend **Sakhi** meetings. This issue of strength or weakness among **sanghas** in Gujarat came up in 1996 when the question of **sanghas** autonomy in terms of continuation of work and financial self-reliance was raised. Strong **sanghas** gather regularly and take collective decisions, share information and experiences, learn from each other, are identified as a collective by outsiders and are sensitive to and prepared to address which gradually brings in financial independence: the amount is split between **Sakhi** honorarium and collective fund; or the **sanghas** decides on retaining the **Sakhi** rotation model.

> Mahila sanghas are entitiles with a definite identity and a purpose I.e. collective action on common problems. It is a forum where women meet and express ideas, concerns and think of solutions and strategies. To this is linked the concept of empowerment involving processes of affirmation, articulation, assertation, emancipation and empowerment at both the collective and individual levels

Karnataka has similarly categorised 713 of its 914 sanghas under 'active sanghas'.

These exercises have been carried forward to the **sangha** level across the country and have thrown up questions and initiated decisions on the part of the Sanghas. Accordingly, in some areas sanghas have decided to take things in their hands beginning with finances. For instance, some sanghas in Gujarat decided to fully or partially bear their travel costs for celebrations, and women from sanghas in Andhra Pradesh attend meetings on their own expenses.

Many of the successful or strong sanghas initiated by Ms are from 'old' areas where the MS process began early. But their strength or weakness does not entirely correspond to the number of years invested in them. Some of the 'old areas' sanghas have fallen into 'troughs' and some new sanghas have risen to relative self-reliance under their own momentum. The strengthening of the sanghas has become an issue of major focus in MS over the past three years, especially after the National Evaluation, 1993 brought this up as a major area requiring focus.

Issues Addressed in MS

Over the past two years, the sanghas, with the assistance of the support units and functionaries have been able to take up several issues that relate to dignified survival in the villages, especially of women and girls. Since life is perceived as one single process in the world view of the villagers and each action taken by the sanghas impinges on this in different ways, it is difficult to articulate the totality of achievements of **MS** in concrete terms. It would be worthwhile to try here to bring out our more tangible achievements in articulating the needs and demands of women, in the form of specific issues that were addressed over the past two years. The fact that the **sangha** women are able to address these issues is indicative of the latent and more qualitative achievements of the programme in empowering women.

Literacy and Learning

MS has recognised right from the beginning that literacy, once a demand for it has been created, becomes an important element in the empowerment of women. This belief has been further reinforced during the last three years, which have witnesses a much greater focus on literacy within MS. This is mainly because of the tremendous demand for literacy that has emerged over the years.

The literacy programme of MS is part and parcel of the **sangha** building and strengthening process mainly because it is seen as a vehicle of **empowerment** and not an end in itself. **'Creating an environment for learning'** has been taken seriously in MS. At this environment emerges and the sanghas becomes stronger on action components, a prominent demand is literacy, either as an action in itself or as part of the struggle for better access to existing government programmes. Since the **sangha** process is also one of gender sensitisation, the demand for girl's education gets crystallised. Very often this demand comes up when the women feel inadequate in dealing with larger forces such as the market, **Panchayats**, Block offices and courts because of their illiteracy. Here adult literacy gets articulated. These processes also bring out issues such as workload and availability of women and girls for literacy, and in the process are evolved a series of activities around creating the conditions and the environment for literacy.

In the **MS** states, various patterns have emerged in children's and adult women's literacy.

Adult Literacy

There are several local structures and processes linked to adult literacy (particularly of women). The most visible one is the Adult Education Programme or Non-Formal Education, which comprises of centres with regular literacy sessions in village. These may be linked or independent of the Total Literacy Campaign. As **MS** emphasises the full participation of sanghas women in the planning and management of these centres, women are involved in the production of literacy materials deciding upon the time and place as well as managing and in some places, even arranging the finances. This further encourages interest in literacy, by the logic of learning by doing. then, MS is fully involved in literacy camps which creates a wider constituency in the literacy missions.

Studies from the States show the various paths that the MS adult literacy programme takes. Gujarat has over the years observed that there are a number of motivating factors in literacy, other than the sheer desire to read and write. For instance, the inability to write applications, the need to maintain child care centre records or write the minutes of the **sangha** meetings, the urge of read newsletters, the necessity to get information through interactions with government offices, or just the urge to reach out to the outside world through the written word compel **sangha** women to venture into literacy. The team encourages this various means. MS has now a regular link with the government Total Literacy Campaign (TLC), to a lesser extent in Sabarkantha and more in Baroda and Rajkot. In Rajkot, **sangha** women decided to prepare lists of illiterate persons in the village and for this there were cultural programme that generated a lot of enthusiasm. Women also prepared literacy manual and other materials. In 1994-95, the campaign ended in Rajkot and Baroda and the Post Literacy Campaign was launched.

In many areas the demand for literacy has led to pressure building for the efficient running of government literacy structures, thus addressing at the same time the vital issue of accountability of the government to its people. The celebration of the Literacy Day, as in the case of the Women's Day has now become an annual affair. These in turn increase the demand for literacy. Today the literacy volunteers, drawn even from among school-going children, hold regular classes in the villages, but the demand for volunteers for exceeds their supply. The demand for literacy is such that when a teacher is difficult to find, women go to other villages to learn. The women are encouraged to write to the **DIUs** and the State Offices. **Apni vat**, a women's newsletter launched by the State office is sent directly to those women who are able to write their names and addresses. The adult literacy programme has thus taken its own momentum in Gujarat.

> *Indicators of rural women's empowerment:*
>
> *Changed self-image*
> *Enhanced access to new information and skills*
> *Larger knowledge base Informed choices*
> *Organisation and collective action*
> *Mobilisation, negotiation and networking*

In Uttar Pradesh, literacy for adult women received a thrust mainly through literacy camps, which in turn created even greater demand for women's literacy. These have region specific curricula. For instance in Sharanpur, where physical violence is a growing concern, literacy was organised around this, while the focus in Varnasai was **panchayat raj** and the wage issue. In Tehri, eco-regeneration found focus and in Banda, the problem of water and wages. A total of 16 literacy camps were organised in 1955-96 itself. U.P. is a case where the need for literacy was first articulated through issue based action where the women felt inadequate without the knowledge of reading and writing. From here there was a progression to regular literacy centres where gender sensitive literacy was imparted through specially trained instructors. Available gender sensitive primers were used, and new ones developed through the participation of the newly literate women. The **mahila dakiya** is now popular and women have even gone in for training in block printing and drawing to make their efforts self-reliant and successful. 'Today there are a total of 133 literacy centres in four Districts. Some sanghas have their own simple library with reading materials, audio records, discussion groups, ecology-club etc. In Banda, adult women, along with young girls, receive literacy also through the newly opened **Mahila Shikshan Kendra (MSK)** which is a residential programme lasting six months each). The curriculum is learner centred, holistic (rather than subject-are oriented), encourages learning and develops a critical understanding. Innovative methods of learning are woven into the method. So far, 80 women and girls have passed through the **MSK**.

In areas of Karnataka where literacy is popular and accepted by women, the sanghas have books and materials for the non-formal education (NFE) and adult education (AE) centres, which are the main village level education centres. Up to mid-1995, there were 119 NFE and 120 AE centres. The sanghas have awarded the title of '**Ghana Gelathiyaru'** (guiding light) to women who have learnt to read and write and are now teaching others. This has added to the status of 'literate'. In general literacy is in great demand, but in some areas such as parts of Mysore where migration is high, progress in literacy is slower despite the demand. Temporary migrants are unable to catch up with learning. An exercise with the village women of this area showed that illiteracy is perpetuated through parental illiteracy, poverty and the consequent preoccupation with livelihood, the lack of opportunities, bad learning environment in schools and the great distances to schools.

> *Making persons literate and aware of prospects in the area cannot be achieved without focusing on their specific situation and thrie local problems and issues. The focus in MS, therefore, should be on local issues--armed with a gender sensitive perspective and literacy--which will ensure mobilization in the right direction for qualitative change.*
>
> *NRG meeting, July 1996*

In Andhra Pradesh the demand for literacy became more persistent since 1993-94. It is now a regular issue at sangha meetings. In may cases, the savings scheme of the sangha had led to the demand for literacy. There have also been attempts to mobilise the literate to teach the illiterate and the sanghas have been able to press upon this. Attempts are also on to train village women to teach the illiterate. The women have demanded states and materials from the TLC. The teaching methods are innovative, as in other States. Literacy kits created by the TLC and the Adult Education scheme too are used, with supplements. The **DIU** teams have held regular workshops as well as training programmes on literacy and its methodology. In 1996, a total of 373 women from 27 villages in Mehbubnagar and 373 from 29 villages in Medak were at various stages of learning to read and write. But analysis of the demand and extension of literacy showed that it remains a problematic issue.

In Medak where the women find it easier to learn to read, the focus has been on strengthening this component, at the same time ensuring that 2 or 3 women from each sangha can write as well. In Mehbubnagar, MS is actively participating in the TLC.

Literacy Among Children and Adolescent Girls

In view of the feeling that literacy among children and adolescent girls has not picked up the momentum it deserves, this was a special focus area for 1994-95 and 1995-96 in U.P. As a result, girl child education has been stepped up and dropout re-enrolment has increased. The '**udankhatolas**' in Varanasi, the '**hindolas**' in Sharanpur and '**buranshs**' in Tehri have gain tremendous popularity over the past three years. In some cases children have attached names even to various grades within the literacy centres. The **anudeshikas** or teachers in these centres, who are selected by the sanghas, are given special training. In places, **Sakhis** too have become **anudeshikas**. Over the past three years in some areas students have been able to organise and run their centres. Saharanpur saw an increase in **bal sabhas** (children's meeting) and **bal melas** (camps with games, nature walk etc.) have increased the potential of children to learn from each other and from their surroundings, as well as display their talents. In Tehri, during 1995-96, '**hilansh**' was launched to increase environmental knowledge. The method of imparting literacy skills in all areas is innovative with painting, singing, dancing, poetry and games are being used. Street plays come in handy, too. **Sanghas** negotiate for resources with MS, which extends such support. The responsibility of discussing the logistics of the support lies with the ***Sahayogini***, who also analyses the needs articulated by the women, the dynamics, and strengths of the group as well as existing problems and their solution.

The year 1995-96 saw a greater demand for units set up exclusively for the education of the adolescent girl child, i.e., **Kishori sanghas** in U.P., as girl child education requires an approach that is different from the education of children of a smaller age group. Health education, law, environmental education and vocational training were decided as the priority areas.

In 1996, a workshop was organised in the State where the scope for the literacy centres to become formalised, the upgradation of **anudeshika** training, better materials and methods, scope of the **bal kendras**, areas requiring DIU support as well as the conceptual issues in literacy, were discussed. On the issue of pedagogy, the workshop concluded that an 'electric' method that combines the alphabet, word and language methods is the best course of action for literacy. It was decided that in the coming year, **anudeshika** and children's training camps will be increased, there will more literacy campaigns for girl children, the curriculum for girl child education will be improved, a magazine will be launched at the State level for articulating of opinion on literacy and that there will be two major workshops on the issue. Decentralisation of literacy efforts will be given further impetus and there will be more linkages and exchanges with other literacy programme. A general decision was taken to broaden the literacy programme. A general discussion was taken to broaden the literacy programme. In 1996 one MSK was introduced in the State.

MS Education empowers women to:

- *Become self confident*
- *Become articulate*
- *Be spontaneous, creative*
- *To face authority*
- *Become aware of themselves, Physical and social environment and to influence this environment*
- *Develop abilities to interact with other people*
- *Function as a team and draw individual strength from this*
- *Increase their self-esteem and respect*

In Andhra Pradesh the literacy programme for girl children so far has not been different from those of adult women. The general experience has been that while literacy among adult women is less problematic, girls child literacy is more difficult. Initially, the camp method was the main venue of addressing this. In 1994, there were specific focus camps with a view to increase enrolment of girls in formal schools. With this also rose the demand for **anganwadis** and girls hostels from the government and in some areas in Medak, the sanghas have managed to get the **anganwadis** shifted to the SC localities. As part of the Mehbubnagar District administration's drive for Universalisation of Elementary Education, surveys were conducted on the situation of children's education which led to the formation of Village Education Committees. Sangha women began taking interest in those Committees, leading to an increase in enrolment of children in schools. The women also expressed the desire to have educational activity for older girls. **NFEs** were envisaged. In 1995-96, it was decided that an approach different from the camp method has to be adopted and hence the **Bal Mitra Kendras (BMKs)** were introduced, although larger issues in this such as child labour have not yet been addressed. The encourage enrolment of girls in the 9-plus age group. These are sangha-initiated and the sanghas select the teachers, too. Every month there is a review meeting-cum-training programme for the teachers. The issue of financial support for the **kendra** teachers was solved with the decision that the **sangha**, the parents of the child and the APMSS will contribute Rs.1, Rs.3 and Rs.6 respectively towards each child. Of the Rs.6 from the MSS side, Rs.3 will be earmarked for ensuring minimum literacy for the child. In June 1995, 18 **BMKs** in Mehbubnagar and 1 in Medak (where the response was lukewarm) were started.

An **MSK** was also started in each of the two Districts in 1995-96, in which the young girls (12 to 18 Years) learn about social, political, legal and current affairs in addition to receiving literacy and vocational training.

As part of the long-term plan, **APMSS** has decided to press for enrolment and retention of children in the 5-7 age category in class 1, to create a model village with 100 per cent access to literacy, to expand the **Bal Mitra Kendras** for girls, to create **MSKs** at cluster levels and to generally strengthen literacy efforts. The sangha-school linkage will also be strengthened through parent-teacher committees.

In Gujarat, there have been spontaneous girl child literacy efforts. An indicator of the interest of the sanghas in girl child education is that in 1995-96, six sanghas in Khedbrahma Taluk in Sabarkantha managed to persuade three girls associated with MS to hold regular classes in their villages for girl children. Young girls in the State have become more enthusiastic towards literacy and many sanghas in the District plan to hold literacy camps to help their illiterate sisters. Literacy camps in general were stepped up during the past three years and camps for young girls were increased. A MSK was started in Sabarkantha District during the past year.

In Karnataka, the Adult Education Centres and the **NFEs** encourage the sangha women to send their girl children to school. There is a conscious effort to establish NFE centres to cater to girl children and in several cases, as in Raichur, the sanghas have been successful in locating literate women and persuading them to teach in the centres. By mid-1996, Bijapur recorded

81 centres with 2250 children, Gulbarga 41 with 534 children, Mysore 21 with 600 children and Raichur 46 with 400 children. There has therefore been considerable expansion over the past three years. Besides, the close link between the sangha and the centres and the ability of the sanghas to run these centres smoothly are becoming apparent. The sanghas in Bijapur are reported to be taking full charge of supervision, motivation of parents, selection of teachers, resolving problematic issues, mediating between MS and the centre and encouraging teachers to participate in sangha activities. Indications are that the sanghas understand their financial responsibilities towards the centres, too. The direct impact on the students is encouraging : there is more interest in further education and the children identify with socially progressive norms between MS and the centre and encouraging teachers to participate in sangha activities. Indications are that the sanghas understand financial responsibilities towards the centres, too. The direct impact on the students is encouraging : there is more interest in further education and the children identify with socially progressive norms.

The **MSK** too is a very popular mode of education of girl children in the State. There are three **MSKs** to date, which contribute to pre-formal education for young girls and towards the education of adolescent girls.

Child Care centres

Child care centres have proven to be a crucial factor in promoting literacy both among children and adult women. Most often as it appeared in Gujarat, basic care of children is itself a problem for women who work the whole day. In such a situation, their education is a possibility that they have not even considered. Hence child care emerged as a problem right from the beginning even when the issue of attending sangha meetings was raised. The support units took this up in earnest, by analysing the problem with the women and making a list of women with these problems. A study in Baroda in collaboration with the Department of Human Development and Family Studies and the Women and Household Development Research and Information Centre analysed the life situation in the villages and the kind of child care support that was desirable under the circumstances. It also evolved participatory, process-oriented training strategies for the functionaries as well as the village women and documented the same. Child care centres emerged as a major requirements, as nine out of ten villages had no child care facilities. The women were too preoccupied with earning a living. When the centres were subsequently introduced, **balsakhis** ('friends of children') were selected by the sanghas. They received special training on child care, pre-school education, child development, health and nutrition, educational opportunities, gender sensitivity, strategies for obtaining support from other MS components, etc.

Over the years, Gujarat **MS** has evolved an organised system of initiating child care centres. The process begins at the sangha level with awareness generation on women's situation, their work and roles, after which collective decisions are taken on the nature and type of child care, choice of time and place, selection of a **balsakhi**, management of the centre, follow-up, and its long-time goals. Committees are formed comprising of senior members, **anganwadi** workers, the ***Sahayogini*** and the **Sakhi**. Internal resources are mobilised as much as possible, e.g., space for the children and payment for the worker. **Mahila kutirs** are used as much as possible and in this process of demanding for a space for the centre, women also learn to exert their right over public places. The pattern is different in different villages: where sanghas are strong food may be paid for by the sangha or by each parent or women may purchase the materials and maintain accounts themselves. In some villages, mothers drop and pick up their children. As the sangha gets stronger, it may be also to bring the ICDS programme into the village. In parts of Sabarkantha, women are now able to keep records of their child care centres as well as maintain regular accounts of the sanghas.

In the selection of **balsakhis** the sangha ensures that she is local, willing and available, has sufficient free time, has the consent of her family, is acceptable and good with children. Sometimes, **Sakhis** volunteer to become **balsakhis.** At present Gujarat has a total of 58 child care centres which cater to the age group of 0-6 years. In Baroda, the sanghas evaluate each other's centres and taken action for improvement of the centres.

> *Training in the political process seems to have helped the women to realise their role and responsibilities in the Panchayat. It is seen that passive practicipation of women in Panchayat activities is found more among those women who do not belong to the sanghas. This may be due to lack of training and orientation and also the fact that where the sanghas are more, passive women have developed self confidence and boldness due to exposure and awareness in various activities, the non sangha women lack this attitudinal adaption. It was decided to encourage such women to take part in training. The decision was taken on the assumption that such a programme will increase women's strength and bargaining power.*
>
> *M S Karnataka*

Analyses have shown that as a result of these efforts, the tensions of women and their families in general have reduced, that the women are able to meet each other and share problems and that even family income has increased because women no longer have to bear the burden of child care through the day. On the part of the children they receive social and moral education, are able to perform better in formal schools and are in general more disciplined. They learn to keep their village clean, plant trees and keep personal hygiene. Girl children particularly are released of work burden.

In U.P., an analysis of the combined effort in child care between **UPMS** and **Nirantar** in Banda showed that the effort has been rather different from the other efforts in the State in that the programme is need based, flexible, managed by the village women, caters to a wide age group using different models and that the child care worker is selected from among the same community, by the sangha.

Karnataka is another State which has progressed substantially where child care centres are concerned. In Bijapur, where more attention has been paid to villages without **anganwadi** centres, there are today 12 crèches. In some villages where there is shortage of funds, the women have begun to provide food for the children. The success of the crèches corresponds to the extent of interest taken by the sangha. Gulbarga had 22 centres by mid-96, an increase of 9 during the year. Raichur has 11 crèches. The children in these child care centres in the State receive medical help in addition to food and personal care. The centres have also contributed significantly to girl child education by relieving young girls of the burden of looking after their younger siblings.

MSKs and child care are also emerging issues in the new MS States, Bihar has 7 **MSKs** as well as informal **jagjagi** centres for children, adolescent girls and women. These are complementary to the DPEP programme. The focus in these is on gender sensitive education, especially for girls. There are awareness campaigns and enrolment drives. Training of **Shiksha karmis** is now on in full swing. Leadership is emerging. The issue of social violence is being addressed as well.

In conclusion, one of the main contributions of **MS** in literacy has been encouraging literacy among girls and adult women and in creating an environment for gender sensitive education as such. Acknowledging the need to strengthen this further, there is greater emphasis today on internalising issues of pedagogy and establishing more effective linkages in literacy.

Women in the Political Process

The 73rd Amendment to the Constitution that ushers in decentralisation of the political process through the Panchayati Raj is eliciting response all over rural India. MS has gone full fledged into this with the view that translating the MS non-negotiable into action needs linkages with the political process as much as with other processes. Political process is an important point of address in order to tackle the issue of women's subordination. But it is recognised that the results will be diluted if women were to merely join the existing structure, without critical understanding of the political process.

A study by Srilata Batiwala in 1995 on the participation of sangha women in the **Panchayati Raj** elections in Karnataka has observed that so far women have either been co-opted or pushed out of the process because of the lack of a critical mass of women in politics, the lack of strategic linkages between the women's movement and the women in politics and because of women not having experienced power in the public domain. So far power has been held over and not on behalf of larger social good. Karnataka has provision for 25 per cent reservation for women in the sill (district) parotid and manual (village) panchayat. As the women became more active in the sangha process, they realised that they were mere fronts in the political arena, and not active women representing women's issues. This led to a demand for training on the political process. Workshops were organised for men and women at the manual level. Soon it was realised that training has to be introduced before elections.

The discussions also threw up several logistical issues such as what would be the relationship of the active parotid members with their sanghas and what will be their accountability to the sanghas. The women in many sanghas came to the consensus that the candidates could stand for election in their own name but have to formally relinquish their sangha roles, so that the sangha does not become another political party. They can make use of the sangha learning process. The successful candidates will not be able to use corrupt means to influence the voting pattern but can use the integrity and respect that the sanghas hold. They will also have the responsibilities of fighting for women's rights and development and giving feedback on panchayat decisions to the sanghas. Sanghas have also evolved systems of pressuring ineffective panchayat members to step down, beginning with a warning, going on to termination from the sangha and as a last resort, organised protests and challenges. The sanghas have therefore emerged as watchdog as well as supporters and guides of the **Panchayats**.

Training issues in the political process:

The nature of the dominant political culture, structures and institutions and strategies for changes.

The nature, powers and functioning of political instututions like the P R Is, the State Assembly and national legislature.

The problems faced by women and SC/ST members and strategies for tracking these.

Functional literacy and numeracy.

The brass tracks of Panchayat functioning including meeting notices, sittings fees, farming resolutions, keeping minutes, procedures, gram sabhas etc.

The State processes have preceded panchayat elections in other States. In U.P. 27 women in Banda and 93 in Varanasi were elected at various levels in 1995. Gujarat has gone into this issue actively in the past years and cases of women's participation in elections are coming up. ***Sahayoginis*** have nominations too in and in one case, a ***Sahayogini*** is reported to have preferred to opt out of politics rather then relinquish her position in MS. In Andhra, 54 women were elected as Ward Members (out of 63 who had contested) and 6 as **Sarpanch.** Attention was focused on the issue on political participation of women during 1995-96 through workshops and discussions. Politically active women and potential political leaders also receive special attention in literacy through camps because very often illiterate women and men are promoted as 'fronts' by the powerful.

Activating the **sanghas** on the political participation issue is now a regular process in MS. In UP the traditional method of story-telling called the **Phad** has been very successful in this, as much as mock elections.

WOMEN FIGHT FOR DIGNITY AND JUSTICE

Physical Violence And The Dignity Of Women

As awareness of gender issues increases, sangha women spontaneously take action against women's oppression and exploitation. Physical violence is a basic issue in this context, to which women are exposed frequently. The MS **empowerment** process has made it evident that what has been assumed to be a 'personal problem of women' is in actuality a social issue. In all the States there have been combined actions against physical violence that targets women. In Sharanpur in U.P. where the crime against women is high, this has become a virtual movement where women gather together to protest and demand legal action. In most places community pressure exerted by women is sufficient and the sangha women actively take up action and negotiation with offenders, as well as bring the problem to public fora. Another issue that has come up prominently in the State is alcoholism among men and its impact on women. In parts of Tehri in U.P., women have managed to take up a two pronged action against this by preventing men from drinking and at the same time breaking the **bhattis** or the local liquor breweries. The women also launched a handout called '**sharab ka dancha**' (structure of alcoholism) showing the larger issues around alcoholism including state incomes through this and vested interests in its maintenance. Similar fights against alcoholism are also reported from Karnataka during the past years. The women now approach courts, police and government offices and when nothing works, they take it upon themselves to demolish the local breweries. The women here have also managed to mobilise women liquor traders against the trade.

The Gujarat group reports that in cases of physical and social violence, where law fails, group pressure succeeds. Some sanghas here have been able to declare a total ban on wife-beating. The **nari adalats** that emerged out of legal committees in the villages are a good example of women establishing their own systems for effecting the provision of justice (**Sujaya**, 1997).

EMPOWERMENT : MULTIPLE DIMENSIONS

In previous sections I tried to explain how 'empowerment' has been operative in the daily lives of women. What is the texture of this empowerment and how does it operate in the different areas of women's lives?

How do women handle power? Differently from men? If so in what ways? Do women, singly or in small numbers in a man's world, follow given patterns of power-play? And does a critical mass of women behave differently? What has 'empowerment' meant to Sangha women? How does the age-old internalised self-image of the sacrificing, nurturing, do not know anything woman articulate with the newly acquired ability to "make things happen"?

These are not new questions for which there is one clean, easy answer. **MS** experience has been that the **sangha** women have acted in myriad ways - all along the scale, from continuing to stay oppressed to taking on the attitudes of power they see around them. There however, appears to be a pattern for the majority bunched in the middle. By and large, the women who have felt some power within, have acted in practical ways - give a little, take a little, two steps forward, one step back. They have negotiated rather than confronted; maintained relationships rather than acted in terms of ultimate and abstract 'truths'. And this is visible in their encounter with the community and now, increasingly, in **panchayats**. Their immediate political arena, the home, is possibly the last one for demonstrated change.

It is possible to discern a pattern in the **'empowerment'** of **sangha** women, which cuts across the specificity of their environment. The experience from all four states broadly demonstrates three stages in the process of shedding off 'powerlessness'. These are demarcated more at a conceptual level rather than seen as a chronological ladder. More often than not, the three layers are intertwined through continuous struggle for change in women's position at home, in the community and in society as a whole.

The first stage of **empowerment** is visible when they can distance themselves from a given situation and recognise the structures of power, decode the symbols and look into them straight without fear. This may not later the situation at all, but it alters the chemistry of the encounter. Women learn to analyse the situation and in the process, the 'fear' gradually turns into an 'understanding'. This can only happen when they discover that their personal suffering is a 'kind' of systematic phenomenon, a chronic situation, which need not cripple their morale.

The next stage in this process is when women can experience the change of not only being able to 'name' the injustice but also by resisting it: What is not 'right', need not be accepted. Hence, the courage to protest is experienced. And this is possible in the 'togetherness' of the collective.

At the third stage a more mature state of realisation emerges: viz. that we need to know more - before making simplistic judgements. Basic confidence in oneself generated by predictable support from a group nurtures the learning spirit and humility in one's own stand.

Moving away from this board pattern, and as a clean contrast, one can discern multiple cases of these very Sangha women who take family violence as a quiet suffering. What they do with ease in a public forum becomes lence as a quiet suffering. What they do with ease in a public forum becomes the most difficult battle at home individually. The important message here is that empowerment processes exhibit their impact, to begin with in the public situation where the collective can visibly by together. Whether it is wage or caste or other struggles. Women have tempered justice with their conditioned reflexes of nurturance. Also, in most community level action, perhaps because women become a critical mass, they are more easily able to act in deviant (from the traditional) ways; unlike at home, where they battle the very roots of power, ultimately, alone(**Sujaya**, 1997).

The Panchayat

A freshly discovered arena for struggle to shake off domination is the panchayat. This being a very recently entered area, patterns are barely discernible. A woman by herself is often squashed or, if sufficiently ambitious, follows (or is urged to follow by those at home supporting her), power patterns that are all around her. However, where there are more than two or three women in the panchayat and receiving support from women outside (in this case the Sangha), there is an attempt to use this newly acquired power for doing good to more than just oneself. This, a more readily recognisable pattern in the longer existing community level action, is only a glimmering in the context of action in **panchayats.**

In the Family

Changes in the power structure within the family are the most difficult to achieve, to reco d or even to observe. In public spheres of the community and panchayat, visible actions reflect changing empowerment. In this private world of the family, this is much more difficult.

> **"We confront men outside but it is a no-win situation with our own family members at times".**

Women who are towers of strength in public, appear willing to put up with beating and being cowed down at home. Women choose their space and it is easier to effect changes outside the home. However, many report to more respect being shown to them in their homes and also of their insistence that their daughters go to school. The change in image outside the home does have its repercussions in the home, but the exact texture of this impact has not been captured.

Apart from the **Sanghas**, there are in many of the MS Districts, forums for hearing cases of violence against women, including violence in the home. Here again, we do not know what effect this discussion of family violence in public, is having on the power relationship in the home. Widows in many of the MS districts now wear **bindi**, jewellery, bright clothes - what effect this has had on their status in the home - we do not know.

How does **empowerment** in the home happen? This needs to be further researched : so that we begin to understand how women are negotiating for more 'space' in decision-making at home and how actions in the family and outside interact in enhancing a women's status. Such that we have a more complete picture of how empowerment works in different arenas.

AREAS OF VULNERABILITY

Future

There is no available experience of large scale programmes for women's empowerment and therefore no precedence to fall back on for weighing alternatives about 'what next?' or will 'x' produce the required 'y'?

Is **empowerment** measurable? Is there such a thing as being 'fully empowered?" and is there a point in the **process of empowerment** when it becomes self-perpetuating? Does the means to empowerment differ according to class, status, circumstance? e.g. The ***sahayogini*** is less dependent on collective action for enhancing her self-image than the sangha woman is. And at the District, State and National Level, MS associates have recourse to choice of several forums (groups) to meet the needs of self-growth.

The above and related questions are of immediate concern in the context of plotting activities for the further. Given that MS is a programme for social change and that empowerment is not a package deal, with a neat beginning and end (like digging a well or building a house), future action is not as clearly visualisable as is habitually expected of planned developmental programmes (**Sujaya**, 1997).

Constraints Facing the Organisation of Women in the Informal Sector in India

Apart from the issue of economic survival, women's double burden, patriarchal controls, and exploitation as cheap labour are major factors influencing not only the participation of women in the informal sector, but also their ability to organise themselves (**Rao**, 1996).

Participation in an organisation is itself an issue for them (**Omvedt** 1986), as it implies challenging the status quo and vested interests in society, and at the same time overcoming their own internal fears and weaknesses. Their limited skills, illiteracy, lack of awareness of the legislation, incompetence informal dealings, lack of access to credit, to markets and other productive resources become further hindrances to organisation.

There are hardly any laws to protect women's interests, and even if these do exist, they are not implemented. A classic case is the bidi industry employing three to five million women workers. Minimum wages exist in law, but are not paid to the workers. The enforcement authority, the labour inspectors, few in number in relation to the largely female and scattered workforce, prefer to turn a blind eye to their exploitation, if not be hand -in-glove with the contractors themselves. In a labour-surplus situation, where alternative opportunities are scarce, women find it difficult to bargain for fear of losing whatever little they get. Most trade unions and their male leadership, unresponsive to women's priorities, fail to take up issues relevant to women.

The invisibility of their multiple occupations and multiple life roles leads to insensitively amongst policy-makers about their needs while their vulnerability is expressed not just in terms of income and employment, but also overwork, poor health, violence and so on, most programmes focus on micro-enterprise development.

A more beneficial approach would be to go beyond this, to look at their livelihood strategies as a whole, and the shift in their goals between survival, stability and growth in response to external conditions and internal constraints. Women's livelihood strategies involve not just an engagement with income-generating activities or with the labour market, but also social networking, changes in consumption patterns, labour and asset pooling, adoption of different technologies, savings, borrowing, investment and so on (**Grown and Sebstad** 1989). **Tripp** (1994), for instance, describes the growth of a range of small business, rotating savings groups, parents' organisations for child care, formation of cooperatives, and informal women's networks, as a response to the economic crisis in Tanzania.

Shramshakti (Government of India 1988:249) emphasizes that 'women's work as home-makers must be recognized as social/economic production'. The neglect of women's reproductive needs by income-generation projects often leads to negative consequences such as the withdrawal of girls from schools, or the withdrawal of the poorest women themselves from such projects.

To attain sustainable gains in improving women's livelihoods, in fact a mix of a broad range of strategies is required, determined by the collective needs and priorities of the women themselves. Productive assistance can benefit women in the informal sector only if accompanied by advocacy, policy reform, asset acquisition, skill training and so on. Stress on both political empowerment and social investment is essential to consolidate economic gains (**Bhatt** 1989).

Mckee (1989) has identified three groups of livelihood-oriented strategies, namely, **area-focused**, **sector-focused** and **function-focused** strategies. **Chen** (1989) sees the sectoral approach as providing a strategic framework for empowerment, by responding to the divergent needs of different groups, and also by helping to coordinate action at the micro and macro levels.

The framework delineated above may be explained on the basis of the experience of **Nitya Rao** (1996) of two women workers' organisations-one in the bidi industry and the other in the stone quarry industry.

The Women Bidi Workers' Organisation

The Jabalpur Women Bidi Workers' Cooperative was initiated in the last quarter of 1985, with support from the Self-employed Womens' Association **(SEWA),** a trade union of women workers in the informal sector. As one of the women workers later vice-president of the cooperative, aptly put it,

> Our wages are far below the minimum. Even government welfare benefits are denied to us, as the contractors and manufacturers are unwilling to certify that we are bona fide workers on the prescribed forms. They are afraid that if they give us an identify, we may demand all our legal rights (**Rao** 1992).

Low wages, lack of benefits, non-payment for long periods, waiting and abuse at the contractor's place, all increased the pressure on women, making them work long hours under poor conditions. Fed up with their exploitation and insecurity of livelihood, some of the women workers decided to organise themselves into an independent production until based on cooperative principles. The cooperative started in a small way, and in the face of warnings from all sources about the impediments likely from vested interests. Apart from intimidation of some women by petty contractors, the major initial bottlenecks came from various government degparments.

The collective consciousness gained through experiences of several struggles enabled the women to respond effectively to make harassment in their personal, individual lives, to improve their bargaining position within the household, and also to face collectively the harassment of contractors, traders and government functionaries. The 'connection between work and home is a key element in the homeworks' predicament... organisation of homeworkers is not simply an economic matter, about low pay, ... it also closely linked to sense of identity and consciousness of self in relation to a social situation' (**Rowbotham** 1993: 15). It was this underlying reality that marked the process of organising women bidi workers in Jabalpur.

The Stone Quarry Workers' Organisation, Tamil Nadu

The second organizational attempt is that of groups of women stone quarry workers in Pudukkottai district in Tamil Nadu, classified as one of the ten most 'industrially and economically' backward districts in the country. The groups here rural-based and organised by the district government under the DWCRA or Development of Women and Children in Rural Areas programme (**Rao** 1996).

Organisation of Women Quarry Workers under DWCRA

DWCRA envisages the formation of groups of 15 to 20 women around a common economic activity. The formation of a group is considered essential to provide women with the opportunity to analyze the issues that affect their lives, form a mutual support structure, gain collective strength to face opposition and create a space for themselves in society. DWCRA was launched in the district in 1989-90.

In 1991, to keep down the auction prices for the quarries, the contractors formed a syndicate and refused to bid over the minimum price. Under the leadership of a women District Collector, the district administration decided to give the unauctioned quarries on lease to groups of women labourers. This set the stage for a constant struggle between the two sets of groups to establish rights over the contested quarries.

Organising women into groups led to considerable economic benefits for women workers. This has motivated them to struggle for survival. However, lack of adequate preparation and support has also aggravated the differences and weakness amongst them, leading some groups to remain subordinate to the dominant classes.

Until women can begin to organise with common goals they will merely continue to fight a holding action that allows them to survive from day to day. Solidarity expressed in an ethic of cooperation and strategizing through manipulating networks may solve individuals problems but only organised solidarity-a group-can bring about significant changes in any system (**Nelson** 1978: 95).

The strategies for organisation adopted in the two situations can be examined in the light of two criteria: (a) **empowerment**, and (b) **scale, replicability and sustainability.**

The essential prerequisites for empowerment through organisation include the following elements: resources in the form of finances, knowledge and technology, skills training, leadership formation, building up of democratic processes, participation in policy and decision-making and techniques of conflict resolution (**Sen and Grown 1987: 89**). These are essential not only for the long-term viability of the organisation, but also to empower women to withstand social and family pressures.

Origins of the Organisation

The first major element one needs to look at is the origin, the very basis for organisation: who initiated the process, were existing networks used, what was the nature of the groups and the form of organisation adopted? The bidi workers' organisation was based on the demands of the women workers themselves. Although initiated by SEWA, the women had a strong stake in the continuance of the organisation. SEWA was responsible only for bringing women from different communities and castes together, many of whom were already working together in common courtyards.

The DWCRA quarry workers groups, on the other hand, were initiated by the District Collector, When faced with a cartel of contractors refusing to bid in the quarry auctions. The groups were largely mixed caste groups, as the issue raised was a common one- property rights for poor women-an issue not specific to any particular caste or community. Moreover, since the women had received the lease for the quarries without a struggle, it took them some time to realize its significance. In many cases the contractors took this opportunity to 'buy off' the leader, or managed to obtain court injunctions to prevent quarrying work, and so on. Experiences reveal that organisations that emerge after overcoming hardships, whether cooperatives or groups, have a greater unity of purpose and a higher morale.

Economic motives provide women with visible 'incentives' to participate in the organizational effort. However, if all economic issues are linked to the questions of access and control over resources, there is potential for conflict, and the organisation may not be sustainable without the capacity for struggle, and a political agenda. And for this the preparedness of the women themselves is essential.

Form of Organisation

The selection of an appropriate form of organisation is critical. Cooperatives have often been suggested by policy-makers as an alternative to the private sector, primarily due to their own inability to enforce protective legislation in the informal sector. The rate of success of cooperatives in India, however, is not very high, due to unequal power relationships in society, lack of workers' access to capital and resources, patriarchal domination, as also complex rules, bureaucratic procedures and controls imposed by the Cooperative Department. Cooperatives are often co-opted by the state through a system of patronage and control. This is one reason why many non-governmental organisations (NGOs) in India prefer to use informal groups or societies for organising women, as these provide the autonomy and flexibility that cooperatives often lack.

Access to and Control of Information, Resources (Financial, Technical) and Services

Mere access to a productive resource is not enough to build a sustainable women's organization, though it could definitely be an entry point. Access to information regarding policy, laws and regulations; access to technology, inputs, markets, credit and training: and access to support services are equally important. Such an approach would, however, require major policy changes (Government of India 1980).

It is necessary here to emphasize the importance of access to financial resources. Poor women are unable to secure even small sums from financial institutions, large amounts beings out of the question (**Berger and Buvinic** 1989). This makes them dependent on informal sources for personal consumption, and donor or government support for group activities. Donors tend to prefer small-scale, income-generating activities for women, instead of striving for structural reform and the elimination of discrimination in all sectors. The government, as a source of finance, is also inflexible in terms of meeting women's needs.

Leadership, Management and Participation in Decision-Making

The issues of leadership, participation and building of democratic processes are topics of heated debate. These especially revolve around the role of external catalysts, their relationship with the local leadership (**Sharma** 1991), issues of their credibility and accountability (**Pearce** 1993), and involvement of members in organizational decisions (**Fredland** 1992). The real challenge is 'to build sustainable social processes from below, to ensure genuine empowerment at the grassroots' (Pearce 1993: 226); this is preferable to NGOs or other organisations in the field developing their own power bases.

Both the cases described above were not spontaneous grassroot movements, but purposive women's organisations. They could not have developed without the support of external facilitators, as interventions were made into complex production and marketing systems. In Jabalpur, the group of women bidi workers were given intensive support by the SEWA organisers, consciously training them in management and organizational issues. These included the nitty-gritty details of running the business, such as maintaining excise, sales tax, raw material and production records, as also general administration. The organisers then withdrew, leaving the cooperative as an independent organisation in the local context, but part of a larger SEWA network at a higher level, that could support them in taking up larger issues.

Rather than be dependent on the facilitator, women must be helped to overcome their inner social conditioning for inequality. A minimum of supports is therefore required for a considerable period of time.

Since most of the women are illiterate, or barely literate, management in a broader sense, not just the maintenance of records and accounts, become a difficult task. SEWA recruited and trained local girls, educated up to high school or graduate level, to take on management tasks. They were responsible to the group leaders, often older women, and were protected by them from wanton gossip. This notion of leadership shared between generations worked well: While the leaders-older women-were able to overcome barriers relating to physical mobility more easily (being relatively free from household and child care responsibilities), the younger and more educated women could provide the necessary communication and managerial support. Simultaneously, the concepts of rotating and shifting leadership, whereby several women could get the opportunity to hold leadership positions (once in every three years), were introduced. To create such an alternative participatory and decentralized structure was, however, a slow and difficult process, involving much effort and experimentation.

Structure for Conflict Resolution and Building Solidarity

The women members of these groups are all economically vulnerable and oppressed. Their organisation has found favour among some groups, but many have directly opposed them (**Klandermans** 1993). The need then arises to recognize points of conflict, to strengthen all supportive networks and build up an alliance system.

Handling Internal Conflicts: Economic

Internally, contradictions arose between individual and group interests. Individual interest in earning more money by increasing the quantity of production led individual women to compromise on quality. The group interest of successful marketing however, required that a high quality be maintained. This implied more careful work, hence a decline in individuals earnings. Followings their disastrous entry into the market, with the product being rejected on grounds of poor quality, the bidi workers cooperative ensured quality through a system of rotating quality control and the use of group pressure.

Handling Internal Conflicts : Social

An effective forum for conflict resolution and organisation support is crucial to the success women's organisations of this kind, particularly as society is stratified, with different sections often having conflicting interests. In Jabalpur, for instance, religion almost became a dividing factor, and in Pudukkottai, caste and class. Attempts were made by fundamentalist groups, contractors and others to aggravate distrust within the groups for their own interests. Overcoming these differences is a slow process that can be facilitated by open, democratic systems of functioning.

Initiatives to Build Solidarity

Apart from structures for resolving conflicts, it is also important to take positive initiatives to build groups solidarity that would help the workers to face external resistance. Group projects, such as group insurance and housing, were undertaken by the bidi workers. An important aspect of the strategy was to recognize and celebrate even small victories, such as access to health care, scholarships for children and insurance cover, when these occurred. Amongst the quarry workers, lack of time and the lack of full-time facilitators led to an emphasis on leadership development, to the neglect of team-building.

Alliance-building

Finally, by raising issues common to all bidi workers, such as those relating to identity cards and health care, by developing structures to help access welfare benefits from the Department of Labour Welfare, and also though personal networks, the bidi workers cooperative was able to build a support base amongst the larger community of workers. They were also formally associated with SEWA's network across the country. Though organised under the aegis of a common programme, the quarry workers groups, however, being widely dispersed across the district, were unable to build a broad-based network. Where groups were concentrated in a particular village, they did support each other, but this related mainly to local issues and problems. In 1993, however, a district women quarry workers federation was formed to provide them support on sectoral issues.

Training

Training has been recognized as an important strategy in building organisations of poor women who are not only faced with economic issues of survival, poverty, assetlessness and indebtedness, but also gender issues resulting from their own internal weaknesses and lack of confidence (**Omvedt** 1986). The importance of the educational and training component cannot be underplayed in any empowerment strategy, as it helps women attain critical knowledge and skills to protect their interests, develop consciousness about the causes of their exploitation and subordination, articulate alternatives and develop the organizational and political skills required to bring about change (**Schuler** 1986).

Economic factors do come first for women on the brink of survival, but social needs such as education, health and child care also exist. These needs often get neglected , leading to a declining participation of women whose reproductive responsibilities are high. Livelihood strategies need not always be income-generating, but could also be income-saving. It is necessary to accommodate the shifting identities of women at the workplace, within the community and the household. Strategies of collective action thus should not dictate to women what their priorities should be, but must allow them to decide for themselves.

Hilighting Women's Positive Contribution

Socialization for inequality, differential treatment of girls and boys from birth, and labeling women as 'supplementary earners' despite their often substantial contribution to household income (**Banerjee** 1989) lead women to have a low self-image and a low sense of self worth. Sen (1987) has argued that the 'perceived contribution' of women, as perceived by both men and women, is often lower than their 'actual contribution', on account of social norms; the form and nature of work and the perception of legitimacy. For instance, household maintenance and child care tasks are considered a labour of love rather than gainful work. However, being unpaid, their work becomes largely invisible. Sen suggests that the visibility of women's participation in 'gainful' economic activities is an attestation of their resistance to an acceptance of deprivation. In organising poor women then, it is not sufficient to only highlight their oppression, but also stress their positive contribution to the work processes.

Role of the State: Government Support

The issue of the state and its relationship to organisation of women, particularly poor women, has been the subject of much debate. More than half the resolutions in the 'Forward Looking Strategies' call for state action. The state is responsible for formulating progressive legislation as well as channeling resources to women, so it cannot be written off. It is up to grassroots groups to identify access points and seize opportunities for development within the state structure.

In addition to organizational and development work then, an essential part of the strategy needs to be sensitization of the state at several levels. First, government personnel and decision-makers need to be informed of the ground realities, the needs and constraints of poor women. As **Longwe** (1990) has commented in the case of Africa, the main problem.... is to shift women's development above the welfare level in the face of resistance from male -dominated government bureaucracies. The second level refers to state institutions and policies, which in a welfare state like India do offer groups of women opportunities to access social and economic resources. The DWCRA programme itself is a case in point. A third level is the state definition of politics, power and gender relations. The Indian Constitution is committed to gender equality (as a Fundamental Right), and this can provide women with a tool in their struggle.

A favourable policy on paper alone is not enough there has to be struggle from the ground to get it implemented. Even then it becomes virtually impossible to make headway without at least some positive government support. The bidi workers cooperative had the potential to grow much faster, if it had not been blocked in its efforts by the cooperative and the forest departments of the government.

Establishing an Alternative Production System

The visibility of an alternative organizational structure, opposed to the exploitative principles of the prevalent structure, provides a source of strength in organising poor women.

Micro-Macro Linkages

The importance of establishing micro-macro linkages has been recognized for bringing about sustainable change. In fact, this has been viewed as the strength of the sector-focused approach, allowing a deeper understanding of a particular sector. Hence the formulation of strategies at all levels form advocacy for accessing resources and changing polices to educating and organising the women to demand their rights.

Action from Above or Below

There is also a difference between collective action and centrally directed action, through the objective of both may be women's empowerment. While the former relates to the profess of organising is bottom-up and longer term in perspective, the latter relates to a process of mobilizing, that can be top-down and linked to immediate, short-term needs (**Prasad and Joseph** 1994).

In conclusion, it would be worthwhile to reiterate some of the issues emerging from the foregoing analysis. It is clear that positive change in the lives of poor women is not possible without organised pressure from the women themselves. Organisation with conscientisation then emerges as the key strategy to strength the hands of weak, vulnerable and isolated women, and prevent their continued subordination in society in the initial stages, however, poor womens organisations need support, or they can collapse. If they do collapse it is doubly difficult to motivate them to overcome all their constraints the second time round, as they also carry the weight of their previous experience with them. It is hence important to consciously develop leadership amongst the local women. Along with this there need to be structures to ensure democratic functioning, participation in decision-making and conflict resolution.

The gains, can, however, be sustained only by adopting a combination of strategies, ranging from policy reform to the elimination of discriminatory legislation in access and control over resources, more responsive state structures and services to provisions for relief and support in reproductive tasks.

A major implication for women workers organisation is the need to bridge the gap between micro insights and macro plans. The benefits of micro-organising are clear, but the issues raised need wider acceptance to bring about sustainable changes in economic and social relations. There is a need to link local struggles with large-scale political and economic processes. Sector- based organisation facilitates this process to an extent, by enabling common issues to be raised. Training, policy protection and building up a supportive social climate are also helpful steps.

In addition, there is a need for constant innovation, for strategies to be dynamic and responsive to changing local, national and international situations. They can range from legal battles to grassroots organisation, from providing alternative organizational forms such as cooperatives to building broad-based alliances, from conflict to cooperation, with a view to combining the practical and strategic interests of these womens groups.

What all this really points towards is that with a gradual shift in perspective from welfare to empowerment, the role of womens organisations is no longer restricted to influencing state policies, but encompasses handling cultural struggles, confronting the power structures in tradition, religion, class and gender as well. To be able to do so, members of the organisation need to have strong stakes and a deep commitment to it.

The disadvantages facing women are many. To confront them, a broad-based, large-scale movement of womens is required. If this broader political dimension is kept in mind, the direction for organizational strategies would necessarily be towards building a strong base at the grassroots, with women involved in the strategic decision-making processes, along with lobbying for recognition and positive policies at the local, national and international levels (**Rao**, 1996).

CHAPTER -V

WOMENS EDUCATION AND EMPOWERMENT

Introduction

Inequality between men and women is one of the most crucial and yet one of the most persistent disparities in most societies. Differences in female and male literacy rates are one aspect of this broader phenomenon of gender-based inequality in India. While about two-thirds of males in the country were literate in 1991, the landmark of 50 percent has still not been achieved for females. The difference between the male and the female literacy rate has hovered consistently around the 25 percent mark for over three decades. For ages, women in India have been subjected to varying degrees of social discrimination and economic exploitation. The most common form of disparity is that the female is confined to the traditionally ascribed roles within the four walls of the house. She is subjected to prejudices in an orthodox milieu and has to be content with a secondary place in society. The exploitation of women is not limited only to the home or to the family, but extends well beyond these frontiers.

Gender inequality in education, depriving women the right to education was in built into the social system very early in the history of our country, in fact as early as later **Vedic** age. The *Brahmanical Smriti* literature reinforced this view categorically, though exception to the prevalent injunctions can be cited. The *purdah* system during the medieval era further distanced women from education, though it did not ban it completely. The coming of the British and the social reform movements started within its rule did lay some emphasis on female education as such, but this was more or less confined to the urban society, largely the intelligentsia or the *bhadralok*, leaving the vast majority of rural women illiterate. *Shudras* along with women were barred from not only learning *Vedic* texts, but even from hearing its recitation according to *dharmashastras*. Given these constraints, the task of making this strata of rural society literate is enormous and a vital task in order to link them to the national mainstream. Women of the lower orders in particular and lower classes and autochthons in general, have suffered from the upper class stranglehold over education and knowledge. Knowledge being power, they have been unable to progress either materially or culturally as access to change social order. Newer technology, marketing and financial schemes remain incomprehensible and distanced from the illiterate masses.

Women constitute an important segment of any community and perform multiple roles as mothers, housewives and wage earners. Women are important productive workers in India's national economy despite the fact that much of their work falls in the invisible or unrecognised category. The female work force participation rate of 51 per cent (which includes women engaged in collection of fuel and fodder, dairy, poultry etc.) is only 13 points lower than the male participation rate of 64 per cent. Added to this is the women's reproductive roles of child bearing and primary responsibility of domestic work.

Women form the pivotal point around whom family life and living revolves. When the economic level of a family goes down women are the worst sufferers. The poorer the family the greater is its dependence on women's economic productivity. Also illiteracy among women often leads to a poor self-image; lack of knowledge and self-worth; makes them susceptible to being deprived of their rights and paying an active role in the society and restricts their economic productivity. Literacy and education are the keys which will allow the conditions of life of women-and men- to be modified and changes made in the social structure. Education of women is essential for them to be able to participate in and benefit from the development process.

ILLITERACY AND POVERTY

Illiteracy and poverty are linked, Illiteracy among women belonging to the lower socio-economic group is higher mainly due to: Inducement into labour force at the school going age to supplement family income; women's heavy work burden which leaves them little time to become literate even when the opportunity is provided; lack of interest in literacy as in some cases it has not helped their economic condition; and negative attitude on the part of the usefulness of education for women.

Most of the World's poor are women. According to the ***Human Development Report 1995***, **"Poverty has a women's face. of 1.3 billion people in poverty, 70 per cent are women".** Illiteracy on a large scale is a major obstacle to development and condemns the battle against equality and empowerment of the women. The **Social Summit** in Copenhagen endorsed that developing countries should move progressively towards earmarking atleast 20 per cent of their budgets to human priority concerns including basic education.

Human development is a process of enlarging choices for all people and not just a segment of the society. Such a process becomes discriminatory if most women are excluded from its benefits. And if women are continually excluded, they fail to play a part in economic, social and political decision making and development, thus hampering the growth of the nation.

Gender equality involves a new way of thinking where in stereotyped roles of women and men give way to a new philosophy that regards all people irrespective of gender, as essential agents of change. According to the **Human Development Report 1995**, gender equality is not a technocratic goal - it is a political process. Further what it requires is a firm political commitment and not enormous financial wealth.

The determination of combat discrimination on the basis of gender and the recognition of equal rights for women have been considered as important as abolition of slavery, elimination of colonialism and establishment of equal rights for racial and ethnic minorities. The international Conference on Population and Development in Cairo in September 1994 underlined the principle, ***"that advancing gender equality and equity and the empowerment of women, and the elimination of all kinds of violence against women, and ensuring women's ability to control their own fertility are cornerstones of population and development-related programmes".***

Equal enjoyment of rights by women and men thus bringing women into the mainstream of economic and social development is what is meant by equality of women. The **World Conference on Human Rights** in June 1993 at Vienna has elaborated the various dimensions of equality.

- **Equal access to basic social services, including education and health.**
- **Equal opportunities for participation in political and economic decision making.**

Literacy And Women's Empowerment

Literacy among women opens the possibility of unlimited exposure to new information and more importantly to new ways of thinking and new perspectives on existing information. Also literate women are able to constructively express their talents and give direction to their aptitudes. This enables them to lead a life which is mote fulfilling and satisfying.

Literacy among women leads to better hygiene improved nutrition practices an greater effectiveness in caring for family health and seeking timely medical intervention. This not only leads to better health status for the woman herself but improved maternal competence lowers infant morality. Better health status of the women makes her a more productive worker both at home and outside, leading the way to her equality and **empowerment.**

Female education also leads to later age of marriage and smaller desired family size by enabling women to take decisions to control their fertility. Further education can enhance their knowledge about contraception thus giving them choice in spacing and number of children and release them from continuous child-rearing and child-bearing. Women thus have more control over how their time is spent and are able to participate more freely in productive work outside the home. Studies have shown that an extra year of schooling for girls reduces fertility rates by about 5-10 per cent. A study on Gender and Poverty in India 1989, has found that the fertility of illiterate women in different age groups is between 30 to 50 per cent higher than that of literate women.

Infant mortality is less among children of educated women and their surviving children are healthier and better educated. The infant mortality rate of Indian children whose mothers are illiterate. Thus education of women emancipates them from wasteful child-bearing thus giving them more time to participate in market activities.

Educated women also make better use of their time. A study in urban south India found that higher education among women led to a reduction in the time they spend in non-market household activities which often go unrecognised. Thus education of women moves them from the non-monetized to the monetized sector, invisible to the visible and unpaid to paid activities thus allowing them to participate directly in household economy. This in turn enhances their status and decision making power within the family which is a major step towards their equality and **empowerment**.

Illiterate women and women with a minimal of education continue to be concentrated in low-paying low-end occupations mostly in the informal sector which not only offers little security but also makes them vulnerable to exploitation by being denied, for e.g., minimum wages; equal pay for equal work; leave benefits etc. Also for most such women there is almost no occupational mobility due to restricted choices in the type of work they can get. A majority of these women are found to be concentrated in domestic or personal service. According to the Census of India, the urban female work participation rate was abysmally low - a mere 7.29 per cent in 1981 which rose marginally and became 8.07 in 1991 census. This clearly indicates that women have not been able to increase their participation rate in formal, 'visible' or monetized sector of work. Conversely women are participating in the work force in the informal, 'invisible' or non-monetized sector and hence are not getting due recognition. Literacy is critical in enhancing women's economic choices by way of improved access to paid employment and higher earnings. Also literacy among women will help in drawing them away from the exploitative informal sector and give them more recognition for their work both at the household and national level.

Literacy levels of high school and above among women supported by vocational training can go a long way in helping women get out of low-skilled jobs which are extensions of domestic work and equip them to take up jobs requiring specific skills which would be better paying and less exploitative. A study of developing countries including India reveals that an additional year of schooling can increase a woman's future earnings by about 15 per cent compared with 11 per cent for a man. Further, low levels of literacy among women leads to their unequal situation in the labour market *vis-à-vis* men by way of reduced earnings and unequal pay for equal work; lack of access to credit which is a barrier to attaining independence and widening choices; and in absence of economic independence lack of status and power in the family. Literacy of women would lead to more and better economic opportunities and hence better income levels which in turn would lead to equality and **empowerment of women**.

If women are in labour force, then even a small amount of education greatly increases their earnings. In India studies have shown that even literacy without completed primary schooling results in higher earnings and that middle school qualifications double women's returns from labour. Education also helps women move out of agricultural labour into non-household manufacturing and service occupations in the modern sector. Just as literacy increases economic opportunities, school attendance familiarises girls with non-family social-settings and increases their skills and confidence to engage in productive work outside the home more competitively. They are better equipped to link into non-traditional work situations and compete with men in the fast paced labour market.

Self employment is a major sector of employment where poor women are concentrated. But in most cases the scale of operation is small and the consequent returns minuscule. If such poor women are educated, they would be in a position to take credit from banks or financial institutions which offer loans to this group of people. Such loans at present are not being fully utilised due to lack of knowledge among the women and insecurity felt by the lending institution(s) due to illiteracy of the borrower. if at all such loans are being taken, they are being awarded to the man inspire of the fact that experience in many countries has demonstrated that poor women invest money more wisely, make sound decisions to maximise returns and are more conscientious in returning the loans. Access to credit is one of the key elements in empowering women and in enabling them to participate in market opportunities.

Education of women will place them on an equal footing with men in decision-making positions in economic and political fields. **Empowerment of women through education** will lead to their greater participation in government and community institutions and better entrepreneurial opportunities. More women in parliament and cabinets, chief executive officers in major corporations, top administrators, managers and civil servants will quicken the pace of progress towards **equality and empowerment**. Having women in top decision making positions will also lead to a better integration of women's concerns into the formulation of national policies and development plans which in turn would result in developing the full potential of women.

Making women literate and educate them are pre-requisites not only for their **equality and empowerment** but for the development of the nation. Women should intimately be linked to the life of a nation because any delay in their education and advancement can only translate education into an impediment for the development of the country. Women are the educators of the next generation. It is through them that innovations that help the communities can be introduced in order to enable women to take part more effectively in modern life.

Literacy and education of women can go a long way in making changes not only in the image women have of themselves but also the roles that they play within the society. It will help change the stereo-typed ideas people held about women's roles and make it clear that the development of a country is linked to women's welfare and productivity as it is to man's. From the psycho-sociological point of view, it is more through the education of women than through the education of men, that changes in attitudes and behaviour necessary for a better adaptation to the modern world are achieved.

Despite strong linkages between women's education and their **equality and empowerment,** female literacy remains very low in India. This is especially the case in rural areas where only about 20-25 per cent of the adult women are literate this is less than half the rural male literacy rate and roughly one third the urban female literacy rate.

Literacy makes the horizon of vision wider and, at a more mundane level, helps to disseminate knowledge of a host of women's issues. The impact of literacy on women's lives has often been dramatic. Experiences of **Pudukottai** in Tamilnadu and of **Nellore** in Andhra Pradesh have shown how women have been **empowered** at individual and collective levels as a result of their participation. In the case of Pudukottai, rural women who participated, felt a new sense of freedom as they learnt how to bicycle and thus acquired physical mobility. They also acquired a new sense of ownership as many women workers in stone quarries acquired ownership rights through newly-constituted women's co-operatives. As part of the post literacy programme in Nellore district, a lesson in the primer about a true incident that had taken place in Doobagunta village sparked off the anti-arrack agitation that later engulfed the entire district and spread to other parts of the state. As recently as a few months ago, the women of Haryana, as a consequence of their deep involvement in the state's four-year-old literacy movement, were instrumental in voting into power a government that was pledged to prohibition.

Its is widely recognised that the literacy classes not only afforded women much-needed respite from their burden of daily chores but also brought about a heightened sense of self-awareness. Today, the one lakh odd neo-literates, mostly women, form a formidable force that serve as a watchdog in ensuring proper implementation of Haryana's new prohibition policy. These experiences show how literacy campaigns have brought about dramatic changes in the lives of women. While evaluation studies have not captured the exact nature of these changes, women have been known to informally communicate because of their participation in literacy, their feeling of greater self-confidence. Women have keenly expressed both privately and publicly how their articulation has improved, how they have become more discerning and how they have learnt to function autonomously as a result of their participation in literacy campaigns.

Also, because of large scale social mobilisation that is elicited by the campaigns, a 'social sanction' is obtained for larger women's participation in social, political and economic life. Women gain substantially because the various patriarchal considerations that hinder their participation become at least temporarily inoperative as women come out of their homes and take part in the campaigns with great enthusiasm. There are other characteristics of literacy campaigns that promote women's participation. The literacy classes in most cases take placc in the immediate neighbourhood of women learners; literacy volunteers largely come from the same milieu as the learners and are in most cases, boys and girls known to them; each literacy class sets its one hours depending upon mutual convenience; the classes have a low learner-volunteer ratio and there is generally a good relationship between the volunteer and the learners. These features promote and enhance women's participation. The use of folk songs and literacy games breaks the monotony and repetitiveness of learning and makes and process more enjoyable and literacy acquisition less daunting. The learning process also encourages experience-sharing among women - women talking about themselves, their problems, their needs - deciding collectively and taking action of ameliorate their present condition.

Experience has taught us the invaluable lesson that a process of critical analysis and reflection, leading to collective action, is crucial if women have to be **empowered** at the individual and collective levels. It is now widely recognised that literacy for poor women has become a means for acquiring knowledge and skills whereby women can begin to understand and analyse unequal gender relations and the structure of poverty and exploitation in society so that they can collectively challenge the existing social reality. Literacy has thus taken on a larger meaning and is regarded as a tool whereby women's access to information, knowledge and thereby to power, becomes possible.

As poor women begin to acquire literacy, they also begin to exercise control over themselves, their bodies, over decisions that affect their lives in the home, the community and society at large. In other words, literacy is clearly perceived as a means for **empowering** women in the wider struggle against inequality and injustice in society.

Literacy is a fundamental component of attaining better living standards for all. The ability to read and write is closely correlated with an individual's capacity for income generation. The proportion of a nation's population that is literate points to the reservoir of human resource potential available for employment and national capacity building. The percentage of women literate gives point to the multiplier effect that can be tapped through the family, young and old, as a strong social and economic unit.

The story of women's liberation in India or searching for an alternative to the existing condition of women in our country is inextricably linked with other social problems like, poverty, poor health and illiteracy. it is hoped that solving one may lead to the solution of the others, as well. In this respect solving the literacy problem seems most important. In the context of women's equality and empowerment, literacy seems to have played a key role.

While talking of equality or empowerment one cannot hope to segregate these terms to use them only in the context of women. For, to strive for the equality of women is to try and integrate them into mainstream social life. The empowerment of women would mean their active participation in the nation's development process and to benefit directly from economic developmental;. It is therefore pertinent to ask if giving loans to poor women benefits the nation? Should women from all sections of society be given the responsibility to solve their problems themselves? Is illiteracy a major block in the development of women and of the nation, as a whole?

Illiteracy does prove to be a major block for developmental work. Illiteracy of the nation as a whole and of women, in general leads to superstitions, economic stagnation and does not help in creating a truly democratic society. All this, in turn, tends to severely lower the status of women. In order to understand how literacy affects he lives of women and thereby of the nation, we may take a look at Kerala and Mizoram. Both these states enjoy a rate of female literacy higher then in other states of the country.

According to a recent article in the Times of India the benefits women derived from literacy efforts, largely by Christian missionaries, resulted in a high percentage of literacy for the state. As a result, family welfare programmes have had more success in Mizoram compared to other states. Mizoram enjoys a low fertility rate(3.3) and a falling infant mortality rate. Kerala, too, shows similar results. Female literacy has played a key role in improving the health situation in the state. Three indicators are used to measure the physical quality of life. These are (i) infant mortality rate (ii) Life expectancy at age one year (iii) Literacy. Significantly it is seen that female literacy seriously affects the other two factors. The infant mortality rate in Kerala is lowest in the country at 32 and highest in Uttar Pradesh at 140. Uttar Pradesh has a very low female literacy rate of 14.04 per cent.

In India, 89 per cent of the women work in the unorganised sector. Lacking literacy they suffer from lack of funds and have to cope with extreme poverty, loss of income and high rates of interest charged by money lenders. Recently, women in Bangladesh have improved their situation significantly through a co-operative banking system. This shows that women are capable of handling their own business and can contribute significantly to the national income. Literacy can help these women to take care of their needs, arrange for loans and to take advantage of welfare schemes.

A discussion on empowerment of women in India must take into account the diversity of problems that exist depending to a great extent, on the religion or social group to which a woman may belong. Illiteracy, gender inequality and female infanticide are common problems, though. It is hoped that literacy will bring in more sensitivity towards women. In turn, female literacy will help women understand their problems and to understand how the legal system can help them. Literacy will certainly help women to cope with superstitions, social systems that exploit them in the name of family ties, religion, social mores etc. The laws that are being formulated to help women can only be effective when women themselves are aware enough to take recourse to them.

Women's development, then, should be looked upon as an exercise in human resource development. In the Indian context, one feels wary of imposing the western model. In the West, women have actively participated in social movements like the, suffragette movement, in order to have a greater say in their nation's politics. Political empowerment, the right to equal wages, divorce laws, abortion are issues that western women fought for. These are still current issues in the west and western feminists regard most of these issues as vital to western civilisation itself.

Although western feminism is blamed squarely for the breakdown of morals and family values, we should not take this kind of criticism seriously. What is important here, is the fact that education helped enlighten the western women so that she learnt to demand a politically and socially more equal position. In comparison, the vote has been granted to Indian women, without her demanding it.

It cannot be disputed that in India, after independence, conscious efforts have been made by the government and enlightened leaders to improve the condition of women. The struggle for India's independence can also be termed as the awakening of the modern Indian consciousness. After 1857, the need to modernise and educate Indian people was deeply felt. Efforts by William Bentick, Raja Rammohan Roy and Ishwar Chandra Vidyasagar spread the message of education of women, widow remarriage and laws prohibiting child marriage, *Sati* were formulated.

These measures were met with strong disapproval. Yet, these were the first steps towards improving women's lot in India. What is significant is the realisation that women constitute a major half of the population and empowerment of women would lead to a better quality of people. Educating women was felt to be the single most important instrument for bringing about social change. This thinking was further developed in the 20th century. Along with the call for freedom the necessity for educating the people was felt. Only a literate people could enjoy the fruits of freedom. Education was also felt to be important for the proper functioning of democracy.

This very elementary requirement for the proper functioning of democracy is being questioned by fashionable salon philosophers who think that the more participatory a democracy is the more efficient it becomes. Although it is desirable that decision making powers cascade down to the panchayat and municipal levels, legislators should not be people devoid of elementary learning skills. This is the unfortunate trend that we observe that both the electorate and their representatives remain ignorant.

While talking about literacy and the empowerment of women this seems to be a valid point of view about the Indian democracy. Not only are women required to be conscious, educated voters but also conscientious legislators. This will make the India a democracy more participatory. However courtesy poor education, the more participatory India's democracy is the lower the quality of the lawmakers.

It is significant, then, to see as to why the quality of education is so poor and inspire of governmental efforts, why the literacy rates are so poor. Literacy since 1971, has been growing at the approximate rate of 9 per cent decade. At this rate, India will have a 38.8 per cent illiterate population in 2001. These 440 million or so illiterate people will comprise about 250 million women. As we have seen, this will pitiable because it will affect family planning programmes, the welfare schemes and the democratic set-up in the country for many decades to come.

Public expenditure on primary education in India has ranged between 1.68 per cent and 1.51 per cent of gross domestic product between 1989-90 and 1993-94. Overall public expenditure on education, including literacy, is now hovering between 3.4 per cent and 3.9 per cent of GDP. But the means of mobilising and allocating resources for primary education is not thought about and the issue of the equality of primary education has taken a back seat. The slow growth of elementary education should cause concern, especially in the context of female illiteracy. A largely ignorant society prevents girls from carrying on with their studies.

Courtesy poor education, we see that the more participatory India's democracy is the lower the quality of law makers. We have also seen how it affects the political process adversely, results in the defeat of family welfare programmes and keeps a major half of the population inferior. Inspire of the best efforts by various governments the lot of Indian women has not changed dramatically. However, certain states have seen the benefits that female literacy brings. Even in these states, female literacy is appreciated for the betterment of society rather than with the idea of empowering women.

This is where the women's movement in the east differs from that of the west. While in the west the rights of the individual have always been important, the East considers and family and society in general to be more important than the individual. This is specially true in the context of women's rights and equality. Both public opinion and governmental efforts consider literacy for women important as long as it helps infant mortality, family welfare and the like. The plight of the girl child continuous to be serious. According to a recent WHO report the survival rate of the female child is far lower than that of the male in India. Women under thirty have less chances of survival and suffer from poor health, under-nourishment besides social inequality. Many agree that the plight of the young girl child and women is mainly due to the attitude which considers women useful only as far as child bearing, looking after the family is concerned.

Both society and the government consider women's literacy and health important only in so far as it is contributory to the success of family welfare programmes. As long as this attitude continues women in the fertile age group will continue to suffer. In this dismal scenario we cannot hope for equality or empowerment for women. Creating a more literate society would mean helping in changing age old biases. Literacy both for women and Indian society as a whole has to mean something more than what mere text books can offer. This again calls for a practical approach towards literacy and the development of alternate methods of education.

However, it will not be fair to the Indian Women if her plight is given up to be lost. Whether in the villages or in urban areas, women shoulder the major part of household duties and responsibilities. They have gone out to work, they manage farmlands and are ready to function as elected representatives. Education will see to it that this trend is not arrested. Besides, it will also ensure that society learns to appreciate the empowerment of women. Only then can women gain most from literacy and enjoy a more fruitful, responsible existence along with the rest of the society.

The **TOTAL LITERACY CAMPAIGNS (TLC's)** have exploded the myth that women are not interested in education and literacy. The large numbers in which women participated in the campaign (constituting 80% of the learners), demonstrates that education comes within the realm of the desirable for women. The experience of the TLC's has moved the debate surroundings women's literacy beyond primarily analyzing the factors that inhibit women from accessing education to sustaining this desire to learn. How can one move from a mere technical acquisition of literacy skills to making education a meaningful, sustainable and continuing activity for women?

One of the most striking features of India's campaign against illiteracy has been its focus upon, and involvement of women. Two out of every three newly-literate people in India are now women. The gender gap is slowly but surely closing. Nonetheless, India's achievements to date cannot mask the daunting obstacles still to be overcome. The **National Literacy Mission** would be the first to acknowledge that its achievements number in the tens of millions, while hundreds of millions yet remain illiterate. For every lakh of people gained for literacy, overall percentages are lost due to pressures of population growth.

This chapter examines how linkages can made to make education a possibility for poor rural women. **Empowerment** plays a vital role in this process. However, we would like to argue that within the process of empowerment, skill acquisition and access to resources are the other crucial elements that influence women's participation in educational interventions.

Women's Education and Empowerment: Evolving a Conceptual Understanding

Education Beyond Literacy

Within the context of sustained educational inputs for women, understanding the relationship between literacy and education becomes crucial. How do we define literacy? When does literacy end and education being? Or, should such a demarcation be made at all?

Over the years, the target of eradicating the 'curse of illiteracy' has been the most important consideration for planners and administrators Knowledge of the three R's is seen as an important stepping some towards reaching out to development process. While radical definitions of literacy - where literacy is seen as a tool or weapon to question existing structures of power - are increasingly invading policy documents, most literacy initiatives continue to be caught in the never- ending spiral of maintaining regular attendance, reducing drop-out rates and assessing the levels of the learners. Acquiring literacy skills becomes their primary focus of basic literacy programmes (NIRANTAR 1995).

Usually, the basic literacy phase is followed by a post-literacy phase which concentrates on arresting replace, strengthening fragile literacy skills and visualizing how literacy may be applied by learners in their specific environments. The shift to development issues is seen as following the initial literacy inputs. The post-literacy phase in thus left to cope with questions of power, information and mainstreaming of marginalized groups.

The underlying assumption in this approach is that learning is a linear process akin to the manner in which learning is structured within the formal school system for children. It is a graded system where progress is recorded in a linear manner - technical acquisition of literacy and numeracy skills are taken care of in the lower classes, and acquiring competencies of self-expression, analytical abilities and independent learning are left for the higher classes.

Women, unlike children, have a rich indigenous information base, highly developed analytical abilities and an understanding of their lived realities. These considerations are ignored in most adult education programmes. Adopting this linear approach for adult women invariably results in their dropping-out from literacy classes in large numbers, after the first flush of enthusiasm. Further, the demands of survival related tasks and labour-intensive coping mechanisms make the sustained and prolonged acquisition of literacy skills a burden and a chore for the women. Since women are central and primarily responsible for these activities, they are most vulnerable to recording irregular attendance and high drop-out rates in literacy programmes. Thus, when the primary focus of adult education programmes limits itself to the acquisition of literacy skills, thereby delinking literacy and education, it decontextualises the meaning of education in their lives. Therefore, it is important to recognize that women's demand for education does not being or limit itself to literacy. Literacy is only one of the elements in the larger process of education, and not necessarily the first.

Literacy and Women's Productive Roles

A strong impetus for promoting women's education comes from the link that has been made between female literacy and quality of life. Numerous empirical studies have brought our the positive correlation between women's literacy and certain indicators of women's status. The Kerala experience is a lucid example of how women's education has lowered child mortality and birth rates, besides improving the sex- ratio in the State. Indeed female literacy is 'so strongly associated with reduced fertility and decreased infant and child morality that it is accepted as a causal factor.' This was the conclusion reached in a recent WHO sponsored study on a comparative analysis of morality, per capita income and educational levels. Female participation in primary education corresponded closely to lowered morality rates.

However, this link between fertility and literacy for women holds within it the danger of women being bound within their reproductive role. It does not make visible the crucial productive work that hinges itself on women's labour. As we have argued in the beginning of this paper, given the centrality of women's role in performing survival tasks, literacy or education for women cannot by-pass this area of their lives.

Moving Towards Education for Women's Empowerment

It is evident, therefore, that strategies and structures that enable children or men to learn cannot be replicated for women. It is to this that review of the New Education Policy draws attention. As we know, education in itself is not necessarily liberating. It has also played a role in maintaining and reinforcing hierarchies. The review criticizes narrow attempts - like changes in training, redesigning curriculum and giving preference to female teachers - within formal and non-formal education efforts to bring about women's participation in education. The review states clearly that only through the process of empowering women can the objective of education be achieved.

However, over the years **empowerment** has now become a development buzzword. It is used by different sets of social actors - women, minority groups, academics, development agencies and even the government - who define it for themselves in a myriad ways. So the issue that must be addressed is - who define it for really mean when we talk about empowering education?

Women's Education and Empowerment

Bringing the concept of empowerment within the realm of education chan... ..e definition and content of education. Empowerment, within a framework of women's education emerges from a live interaction between the Frierien model of people's participation and popular education, and deminist theory and praxis. In working out an alternative politics for daily life, the feminist movement in the 70s rejected the welfarist attitude of the State vis-à-vis education. They critiqued the existing education system as one that was promoting patriarchal systems of knowledge and reinforcing gender stereotypes. The growth of the movement saw women's groups constructing alternative systems of knowledge through an articulation of women's experiences, information systems and skills. Government run literacy programmes were thus suspect and were seen as a means of co-opting the poor and women into the existing hierarchical system. Women's literacy was therefore a non-priority area for the women's movement. Violence against women, dowry and rape related legislation, recognition of women's work and equal wages because the areas of struggle and contestation.

On the other hand, all adult education programmes from the 50s to the late 70s. Whether it was the *Gram Shiksha Mohim* (1956), the Farmer's Functional Literacy programme (1967-68) or the Workers Education programme (1967), adopted a functional approach towards education. Even the New Adult Education Programme, which was launched in 1977, with the progressive agenda of combining literacy with awareness raising and functionality was unable to integrate the three .The crucial factor that made these programmes ineffective was the invisibility of women. None of these programmes focused on the special learning needs of women. Women's education therefore, at this stage, because a case of falling between the two stools.

It was only in the mid-80s that conscientization and literacy found a link within adult education initiatives. Many experiments based on Friere's concept of the liberating potential of literacy were carried out. Within the women's movement the end of the women's decade (1975-85) brought a crystallization of theories, strategies and debates on gender as a category and as a means of protest and change. This process gave birth to the concept of **empowerment**.

Empowerment was defined as a process by which women gain greater control over resources (income, knowledge, information, technology, skill training), challenge the ideology of patriarchy and hence participate in leadership, decision making processes. Within the area of education a creative tension emerged between women's experiential knowledge and formal systems of knowledge. Access to information and literacy became part of women's attempt at redistributing power Simultaneously, education got infused with or broadened its objectives to one that would:

- enhance the self-image of women
- encourage women to become active participants in the process of change.
- build collective and alternative visions of their lived environment.
- question injustice and inequality.
- help women develop the skills to assert themselves.

Empowerment, Skills and Access to Resources

As stated above, **empowerment** involves a process which facilitates women's control over resources, be it technical knowledge, information, income or skill training. An education, that beings to teach women skills that they have been traditionally denied, has tremendous potential vis-à-vis opening up new roles and options for women. Thereby incorporating within it a subversive elements as far as patriarchy is concerned.

Women, even in the most patriarchal of societies, are not devoid of skills. Nor is there a dearth of Government and NGO initiatives that have tried to enhance the skills and income opportunities of women. Teaching women sewing, pickle making and candle making are valid enough initiatives in themselves. After all, it is possible that a women after having acquired these skills will be able to earn some additional income. But the question that needs to be looked at is whether these skills are empowering or merely reinforcing women's reproductive roles? The employment opportunities that these skills provide does not disrupt women's domestic responsibilities or take them away from home thereby keeping the patriarchal ideology intact. Therefore it is very important when looking at skill development programmes for women to think of 'strategic' skills - those skills that will address both women's 'practical' interests (for example lack of water, poor nutrition etc.) and will simultaneously alter the 'strategic' interests (bring about a questioning of the power relations that prevent women from accessing these skills) (**Molyneux** 1981). When women are therefore provided the opportunity of accessing non-traditional skills or technology that they have been denied they can effectively challenge the accepted power structure.

Linking Education with Skill Training

Empowerment is not merely a change of mind set but a visible demonstration of change, which the world around is forced to acknowledge, respond and accommodate. This is clearly demonstrated in the following case studies of Dangarpur and Banda.

A Case Study of Women Veterinary Mid-wives (Dungarpur)

Dungarpur is one of the least developed and most environmentally degraded districts of Ranasthan. The people of the district, sixty per cent of whom are tribal, live in dispersed hamlets, farms a rough terrain for subsistence and migrate annually to supplement their incomes. People's Education and Development Organisation (PEDO), a registered voluntary organisation has been working in nearly 100 villages, in Bichiwada block of Dungarpur for the past 10 years. PEDO has done extensive work in the area of reforestation of common lands and soil conservation. With the women they have started small savings groups and trained them as veterinary mid-wives-locally called 'Dangar Dais' (animal mid-wives).

The **Dangar Dai** programme grew out of the savings societies that were organized by the women in 1991. During village meetings the women did not limit themselves to credit related activities alone. They discussed issues that affected their daily lives, of which, problems pertaining to their cattle was one. Cattle, in large numbers, were lost due to disease or epidemics. The difficult terrain and the prohibitive costs of allopathic medicines made it almost impossible for the locals to access the veterinary hospital. A decision was then taken that some women from each saving society would undergo a **'Dangar Dai'** training.

The programme has been a success as the ***Dais***, through an combination of Ayurvedic and indigenous treatment, have impacted on the problem. They have established their credibility as trained veterinary mid- wives not only within their community but also with the veterinary department. The ***Dais*** became an effective link between the community and the department in organising vaccination and treatment of epidemics. Learning a new skill made the women more articulate, self-confident and effective decision makers. The women are also economically independent now as they support themselves with the nominal amounts that people pay for their services and the medicines used.

Training to be veterinary mid-wives was a new experience for these women. There were many new names of medicines, technical terms and medical procedures to be learnt. While they struggled to pronounce English words, the Dais developed their own ways of identification through different colour packings, varying textures, forms and writing that they saw as different patterns. Gradually many **Dangar Dais** said that they now found it necessary to learn to read and write as they had to maintain a record of their patients, the medicine administered, the money received etc. Besides, their new role had made them leaders within the community. They now had to interact with the local bureaucracy - all this meant that they had to deal with the world of letters.

This demand for literacy however, was the culmination of an educational process that has been initiated by PEDO. The women, through their involvement with the savings groups, reforestation programmes etc., had already been introduced to processes of planning, decision making, acquiring information and upgrading or learning new skills. This they had achieved while still remaining outside the world of literacy and numeracy. As the scope of their activities and interventions in their situation increased, the demand for literacy became part of the women's own agenda a greater control.

Training Women as Hand-pump Mechanics

Another positive experience, where women have made the linkages between literacy, acquisition of new skills and changes in their identify comes from the **Mahila Samakhya Progamme** in Banda district of Uttar Pradesh Banda, one of the most backward districts in Uttar Pradesh, has a chronic water problem. Five years ago, when the programme began its work in Manikapur block, a majority of the handpumps were dysfunctional. Other traditional sources of water are scarce. During the women's meeting at the village level this was a recurrent theme. Not surprisingly, the issue of water has been a major area of work for the MS programme. Over the last five years, women adopted different strategies - demonstrations, petitions, requests for handpump repairs - to come to grips with the problem. When these strategies yielded no results, the MS programme in collaboration with UNICEF and UP Jal Nigam, came together to initiate a project in community based hand pump maintenance and repair.

The project trained rural women as handpump mechanics. Given the fact that handpump repair is a made preserve, this initiative met with stiff resistance both from the community and the Jal Nigam mechanics. Besides, the women were low caste and non-literate women. The initiative thus required intervention not only in terms of technology transfer but also in coping and transforming social and patriarchal values. The training therefore had to provide women the time and space to generate their own confidence in becoming 'mechanics'. A constant effort was made to 'humanize' technicalities and to evolve innovative strategies to make the process less threatening.

The experience of training and getting the women to function as handpump mechanics has had a myriad off- shoots. As with the previous case study, the increasing credibility of the women as technically capable and independent mechanics, has helped dispel stereo-typical images of rural women, both within their community and government departments. The women have developed the necessary skills to deal with the local elite and the government. It has also led to a renegotiation of power dynamics with lower caste women repairing the pumps of upper caste members within the village - as is well known, water is an important symbol of purity and pollution within the caste system.

The process of becoming handpump mechanics has created the confidence among the women about their ability to **learn.** Breaking through their own fears and insecurities has meant an articulation of the need to acquire other skills. Literacy is one of them. Education has become an important symbol of what has been denied to them. This case study validates the inter-linkages between creating a space for women to critically analyze their life situation, providing specific technical skills and literacy - all of which sustain and reinforce each other.

Empowerment, Access to Resources and Education

Women constitute a majority of the poor, under-employed and socially under privileged sections of our society. In addition to this generally not remunerated, is undervalued, and often does not even fall within the definition of 'work'. This is despite the fact that women's role in food production, fuel- wood, fodder, water collection, child-rearing and as farm and wage labour is crucial, if not primary, to sustaining the household economy. Traditional gender- based subordination has denied women access to and control over such productive resources as land, credit and property. Women's vulnerability, is thus reinforced by a system that on the one hand denies or limits their access to means of production and political participation, and on the other imposes a sexual division of labour that allocates to women labour intensive and poorly paid work within and outside the home.

What are the strategies that will break down structures of inequality between gender and class which acts as a barrier to the development process? It is widely agreed that in order to actualize the possibility of women having control over their resources there must be

- **re-orientation of the planning process:**
  The planning process must be oriented to meeting the needs of the poor becomes the principal focus of planning. In this context, recognition of poor women's work must acquire centrality. Planning and implementation, both need to recognize the needs of poor rural women.

- **strong women's organizations**:
  Women's organizations are key to this strategy, because developing political will for major changes requires structures and institutions that have the power the push for such changes.

- **democratic political process:**
  Democratic political processes provides the space and potential for women to struggle for greater access to resources.

The Pudukkottai Case Study: Linking Education to Women's Access to resources

This case study is an example of an attempt that addresses the issues presented above within the framework of a literacy programme. In Pudukkottai women quarry workers were organized into collectives under the Development of Women and Children in Rural Areas (DWCRA) programme and given lease rights over the quarries. Pudukkottai has about 450 stone quarries and 4500 women quarry workers. The workers get low wages and live under miserable conditions. The quarries are auctioned off for three years lease periods. The administration organized hundreds of women quarry workers into groups of 20 women under DWCRA. A total of 150 such groups were formed and were each given quarrying leases for three years. Loans for the purchase of tools, kits, uniforms and initial working capital. This initiative was taken during the Total Literacy Campaign that was initiated in the district in July 1991. The context in which such a radical step was taken in significant. The response and involvement of women in the campaign at all levels - as learners, trainers, project coordinators was tremendous. Further, a major reason for a special focus and sensitivity to women's involvement was the presence of the woman District Collector, who spearheaded the campaign in the district.

This move resulted in a four-fold increase in the women's wages as week as a weekly share of the profits. Economic improvement is a powerful motivator, and the women wanted to preserve these changed circumstances, but they were pitted against powerful vested interests. The contractors, deprived of their quarrying rights and profits, were out of destroy these fledgling groups. Given this strong opposition, providing women lease rights alone, was not enough to sustain this process of change and ensure a sustained livelihood. These new groups were facing tremendous problems ranging from marketing of stones, maintenance of records, and collecting payments to threats by contractors.

At this point the literacy workers decided to respond to the needs of these women, most of whom were non-literate and attending literacy classes. Special trainings, which looked at marketing, legal issues, accounting etc., were arranged for the volunteer teachers teaching the quarry workers. The women gradually learnt to write out bills and receipts and maintain their own production records. They realized the importance of not remaining dependent on contractors and transporters to perform these critical tasks. Their long term survival in a hostile (and literate) environment depended on their independence. As the women acquired new literacy and numeracy skills every day, these skills were put to immediate use, which prevented any relapse.

The Pudukkottai experience demonstrates that 'success' in a literacy programme requires many ingredients - imparting new skills, bringing the people and the skills together in a organised form, providing access to resources, and making credit facilities available - it is the coming together of all these factors that ultimately makes for a successful and sustainable educational process.

The Anti-Arrack Movement: A Case of How Literacy can Impact on Political Processes

The two main thrusts of literacy programmes have been functional and libratory. The functional school of literacy draws its strength from the cross-sectoral impact of literacy, especially with respect to women. The libratory view emphasizes its potential for bringing about structural changes. The anti-arrack movement in Andhra Pradesh emerged from the literacy initiative and validates the liberating aspect of literacy. Women in Andhra were not merely learning the alphabet; the literacy centres provided the space and opportunity for them to come together and critically analyze their life situation as a collective. In addition to learners, the network of literacy activists also became part of the women's struggle. Several organizations and institutions lent support and strength to the movement. Women were able to use spaces within democratic structures to actualize their will and impact upon the political process.

The origins of the anti-arrack movement lie embedded in a history of several such agitations led by left groups. It was these groups that brought this issue on to the state agenda. However, there were some differences between the earlier was a reduction in the retail price of arrack (so that government profits would drop) the recent agitation fought to stop the auction of arrack in villages. Moreover ordinary women were not part of the earlier movement.

The recent anti-arrack movement was ignited by a small incident that took place in Doobaguta village in Nellore district, where two men died after about of drinking. Women; of this area got together and stopped the vending of arrack. Even before this incident took place, men and women were discussing the acute social problems caused by excessive drinking - men drank away their earnings while women bore the economic burden of the family and women were subjected to frequent beatings by their drunken spouses. There was both anger and awareness among the women simmering beneath the surface. The incident in Doobaguta provided the spark.

The Doobaguta episode was described in a lesson in the post-literacy primer. The lesson spoke of the women's suffering at the hands of drunken husbands, how they organized themselves to take collective action, and the success they achieved. The lesson had an electrifying impact on the women learners when read at the post-literacy centres. They started raising questions - would the literacy teachers support a similar agitation? In several villages women's committees were formed. And the agitation against the sale of arrack began. The women started pressuring arrack shop owners to close their shops. Some shop owners consented, others were forced. Women-squads were formed to keep a round the cook vigil to ensure that no arrack entered the village.

By August 1992, the anti arrack agitation had spread like wildfire through out Nellore district. Auctions for arrack licenses are held by the government in August. The government earns significant revenue from these license auctions. The women were determined to stop these auctions. On the scheduled date of the auction there was a major demonstration at the Collector's office. The auction had to be postponed. Each subsequent announcement of the auction, brought on a massive mobilization of women, and further postponement. Gradually all opposition parties, women's groups. NGOs, and civil liberties organizations joined the agitation. By November 1992, the anti-arrack agitation had spread to a large number of districts in Andhra Pradesh.

The government was in a fix. On the one hand District Collectors were active partners in the literacy movement and on their hand they were supposed to carry on with the auction of arrack contracts. The government tried to use strong arm tactics, but did not succeed. Ultimately both the ruling party and the opposition were forced to support the ban on sale of arrack. In the last assembly elections in Andhra Pradesh, banning the sale of arrack was a major election issue. The Telugu Desam party built its entire campaign on banning the sale of arrack NIRANTAR 1995)..

This was a major victory, specifically, for the women of Andhra Pradesh, and generally for the women's movement in India: a women's issue had become major political issue. The anti-arrack agitation thus began by addressing the issue of women's condition in so far as its genesis was the issue of not having enough money to feed the family. But as the agitation gained momentum, it had the potential of addressing 'strategic gender interests' or 'position' of women (**Young** 1988).

Literacy For Empowering Craftswomen

Though women may be deprived traditionally of formal education, they are the repositories of traditional knowledge, especially of art and aesthetics. Folk lore, myth and ritual which are at the very foundation of rural art and craft, are the forte of women of the household. It is women who carry within them the memory and sensibility of culture that they hand down to the next generation of craft persons. With the help of basic educational skills at their disposal, these skilled women will be able not only to assimilate the sheet quantity of memory available to them but also appreciate the roots of their traditions better. From being agents of continuity they will become agents of change in their areas, change that will not erode the basic value system and oral knowledge and skills but rather sensitively combine these with modern know-how for better living standards.

Education has been considered a major agency of socialisation which is intended to ensure continuity rather than discontinuity or radical change. It is in this socialisation that folk-tribal women can and do play a vital role for their reach extends beyond their own kin.

Ganga Devi signed her paintings as Padma Shree Ganga Devi, a visual that was a powerful stimuli for young women to learn both Madhubani painting as well as writing. Similarly Habib Tanveer's troupe of Chhatisgarhi theatre workers and their message of progress within tradition and tribal culture has proved to be a source of inspiration for many. **Teejan Bai, Jamuna Devi, Neelmani Devi, Shiromani Verma, Ambika Devi,** the list of successful folk-tribal artists is long and fascinating and no doubt their fame and effort have prompted women in their areas towards literacy and preservation of folk culture.

Case studies of Andhra Pradesh and Orissa, according to the report of the UNESCO and National Literacy Mission , Directorate of Adult Education, 1996 have revealed certain similar, universal elements seen in the pan-Indian context and certain local specificities borne out of the particular socio-economic and ecological background.

The Deccan province of Andhra Pradesh has as variegated an ecology as craft tradition and yet its literacy level, according to the 1991 Census Report, does not compare well with the national average. Literacy rate for all over India is 52.11 per cent in which only 36.14 per cent with female literacy being 33.71 per cent. Rural literacy rates are even lower being only 20.78 per cent for women.

Pochampally, synonymous with colourful silk fabric in the ***ikat*** style, is a small village sitting, it seems, in the middle of nowhere. Despite it being a centre of silk weaving, most of the women are attired in the ubiquitous nylon *sarees* and most of the village shops do not stock the local produce. Men of the village are involved in the trade side of the business while some are master craftsmen. The village has about 400 women working on the looms at various levels including and up to the actual weaving though like in ***Maheshwar*** in Madhya Pradesh, it is the male master *karigar* who ties the yarn onto the loom and is thus responsible for the design. Interestingly, Narsimhamma, an illiterate woman in her 60s, was the only one who remembered a particular traditional design taught to her by her late husband which she passed onto her son, a master weaver and an invaluable link in the chain of oral traditional design taught to her by her late husband which she passed onto her son, a master weaver and an invaluable link in the chain of oral tradition. It was her determination to see her sons educated that paid dividends as now they are able to negotiate for silk yarn bought from Karnataka and sold at a fair price and not fall prey to middlemen in either acquiring raw material or selling the finished product.

Yashodha earns up to Rs.700-900 from tying and dyeing of yarn. She has been the sole breadwinner after her husband abandoned her nearly seven years age, leaving her to support four children and an aged mother. Not literate herself, she sends her daughters to school "so that no one can cheat them, give them less yarn for more money, or take advantage of their ignorance", she hopes.

Bidi workers, mainly women who earn about Rs.9 a day for rolling bidis out of materials provided by the contractors, have been motivated into joining the local night school by two women, Lata and Lakshmi, who themselves studied up to seventh grade. According to Lakshmi, "if these women study, then we can teach them about hygiene, family planning, post office saving plans, they will improve their living standard but we can't take them away from their livelihood. If they leave their work they will starve and then who will study".

While the economic compulsions remain the same in Warangal, it is different because it is more accessible and urbanised. The seat of Kakatiyas rule in medieval India Warangal is dotted with stone temples carved from the Deccan granite, interspersed with lakes and fields. Here the rural women continue to make the age-old *kolam* (rice flour) design on their doorsteps but the traditional haldi (turmeric) and *kumkum* designs on the doorway has given way to emulsion paint, the aesthetics are there but the utility of turmeric as an antiseptic ant repellent has given way to convenience. Similarly ***Nirmal*** painting on furniture and wooden boxes is being done with emulsion paints for a better finish and long lasting effect. Madhoo Devi, the mother of one of the painters says that "city dwellers buy our products and they use enamel paint so we should give them what they are used to. My son who goes to school tells me and I have seen it with my own eyes in the big city (Hyderabad)".

All over Andhra Pradesh, the big problem is that of school dropout rate which is as high as 52 per cent at the primary school level, of which 60 per cent are girls. The reason is the increasing participation of girls in work situations. Until vocational training becomes a part of literacy in a major way, the situation is unlikely to change.

In Orissa, the land of temples, lakes, rivers ana a variety of art traditions, where tribal art and ritual have not been marginalized. If anything, they have been assimilated into the mainstream of socio-religious life as in the case of the Jagannath cult at Puri or the worship of Sthambeshwari.

Here the tribal and rural women have been educated in the oral tradition over the centuries rather than in any formal sense of the word. They have managed to acquire a vast repertoire of myths, legends and epic poetry that is depicted in their art be it ***patta chitra***, papier mache toys and masks, ***ganjifa*** cards or appliqué embroidery. Yet literacy rates in most districts are not very high. The 1991 Census Report revealed that in Sambalpur district, 24.57 per cent of rural women were literate while in Mayurbhanj, the percentage was 17.44 per cent and in Kalahandi it was an abysmal 10.56 per cent. In the relatively higher literacy rate areas, women have responded to developmental initiatives like milk co-operatives in Samblapur, but in the Mayurbhanj and Kalahandi districts, poverty is palpable and a strong movement is needed in order to bring relief to rural women.

The effects of education on ***patta chitra*** painters is most visible in their village near Bhubaneswar, as now many of the painters put their signature on the works, women in their wattle and *duab* huts sit in the doorways preparing paper for painting by applying local chemicals, clay and the like on paper. Many have even taken to the brush in an effort to translate their oral tradition into visual images, be it the Dasavatara, Mahabharata or erotic paintings. With the eclipse of feudal monarchies, the patronage for arts such as the exquisitely painted ***ganjifa*** cards has waned so that now the craftspersons involved in the craft an forced to paint them with erotic motifs for novelty interests. Giving this, Gayatri Sahoo, a local artist, is determined to educate her younger son and daughter so that, "even if there is no demand for our art, they will be able to survive in the world". She is one of the few women who feels that literacy is a safe harbour in an increasingly urban world where traditional arts are becoming redundant.

On the other hand, taking advantage of modernisation, contact with the outside world and literacy, are the appliqué workers at ***Pipli***, situated in the shadow of the great Dhauli Stupa. instead of hand stitching colourful pieces of cloth onto the base fabric, one can see women with sewing machines sitting in rows churning out table mats, lamp shades and garden umbrellas to satisfy a large urban demand. "It is either this or we would starve be and forced to leave the land and profession of our forefathers," explained Subhadra Devi who has studied up to the fifth standard and now sends her numerous progeny to the school in the day, while they cut patterns in the evening.

The story is similar in the Balasore area which is a coastal stretch with white sand-filled beaches and palm lined dust roads that lead to a small town which makes lacquered toys. Virtually every house has the women painting the toys in intricate patterns sittings in the front of their houses.

Andhra Pradesh and Orissa illustrate some of the complexities that confront not only the educationist involved in the National Literacy Mission, but also the nation as a whole. On the one hand we have to preserve the rich cultural heritage with which we tend to identify and glorify the nation, a heritage that is in the hands of the folk and tribal artists, the sole practitioners of traditional arts and crafts. On the flip side of the coin is progress, development and integration of these 'underdeveloped' elements into the national mainstream.

The question is whether the urban intelligentsia and the planners should deny them education and the attendant benefits so as to "preserve" a national heritage of aesthetics and craft. To leave them "unspoiled" by progress would be making them pay the price for preservation of culture that the urban elite consume and the tourism industry glorifies. What is required and increasingly attempted by the National Literacy Mission is integrating the traditional value system, oral tradition and arts into education being imparted to craftswomen and folk-tribal artists.

An emphasis on vocational training and the basic three Rs is essential for a sustainable literacy workers. This reduces the dropout rate specially amongst young girls as they are able to continue supporting the household income with their work. It also enhances the skills by making them amenable to efficient organisation of craft and increases income through better marketing networks. Only literacy programmes that take local and popular culture and vocation into account are able to sustain continuing education.

To deny education to any section for the fear of cultural corruption would be selfish, unfair and retrogressive but to on the other hand, educate and enlighten the same segment will enable, especially the women, to comprehend the value of their skills, open them to new aesthetic values and transmit the same to the next generation in a more coherent and self-confident manner. No longer will a hill woman make paper envelops of Kangra miniatures and sell the envelopes rather than the paintings. She will be able to value the art and teach it to her children if she is educated and literate.

The linkages between culture, be if folk-tribal or elite, and women's participation in education are integral to the survival of the former and the sooner we recognise it, the faster we will be able to integrate it to our advantage.

One important criticism of the focus on **empowerment** is that it relegates the responsibility of initiating change, raising question and taking initiative on to the poor. What is the role of the State in this process- whether it is the local elite, the administration, the political parties and the social institutions and ideologies that define, bind and control the realities of the poor or women. What all the case studies point to is the role of different agencies in facilitating or in providing the time and space for the women to articulate their own need for learning and to move from a position of passive acceptance to active participation.

All the case studies also make this clear that irrespective of what the take off point is education and literacy becomes integral to sustaining and vitalizing these changes. Literacy at times becomes the by-product of other processes, such as organizing, agitating, skill building etc. These various processes may run parallel to each other, but they become self-sustaining and irreversible when they converge, and thereby alter the balance of power.

Further, the case studies also point to the fact that gender is not merely a 'category'. Gender issues are integral issues of environment, health, livelihood; agriculture, technology, politics, literacy etc. It does not confine itself to status of women or to sexual violence or such stereo-typical women's issues. Therefore, women's education cannot merely be an 'ADD ON' to the existing education strategies. As is evident, most pointedly from the Banda case study in that the off-shoot of giving women new roles also requires a structure or a support that helps them deal with their new role in society. Otherwise, their education will not relate to their own context and life situation.

Summing Up

The story of women's liberation in India or searching for an alternative to the existing condition of women in our country is inextricably linked with other social problems like poverty, poor health and illiteracy. It is hoped that solving one may lead to the solution of the others as well. In this respect solving the literacy problem seems most important. In the context of women's equality and empowerment, literacy seems to have played a key role.

While talking equality or empowerment one cannot hope to segregate these terms to use them only in the context of women. For, to strive for the equality of women is to try and integrate them into mainstream social life. The empowerment of women would mean their active participation in the nation's development process and to benefit directly from economic development. It is therefore pertinent to ask whether illiteracy is a major block in the development of women and of the nation, as a whole.

Illiteracy does prove to be a major block for development work. Illiteracy of the nation as a whole and of women, in general, leads to superstitions, economic stagnation and does not help in creating a truly democratic society. All this, in turn, tends to lower the status of women. Female literacy will help women understand their problems and to understand how the legal systems can help them. Literacy will certainly help women to cope with superstitions, social systems that exploit them in the name of family ties, religion, social mores etc. The laws that are being formulated to help women can only be effective when women themselves are aware enough to take recourse to them (**Shankar** 1996).

•

CHAPTER - VI

ECONOMIC EMPOWERMENT OF WOMEN

Introduction

When we discuss the role of women, we emphasise on changing the equilibrium of social forces to treat them as equal partners in the society and to bring recognition to all their roles. When our concern is with the poor women, we are seized of changing both social and economic forces in favour of their worker-role in particular and other roles in general. Such a perception of poor women's work places their empowerment as the central thrust of the desired goal, which is beyond increase in income levels, and , in financial terms. Empowerment entails struggle; it entails learning to deal with the forces of oppression; it entails having a vision of a new society; it also entails conscious and deliberate interventions and efforts to enhance the quality of life. Empowerment in this context entails gradually increasing control of poor women over the entire economic process and not merely as producers of some products and services which are otherwise controlled through other intermediaries. Transplanting alien activities which do not have the long-term regenerative and self-sustaining potential do not make the kind of activities that lead to empowerment. Thus, economic intervention is posited not only for enhanced income but also for increased empowerment of the poor women.

Situational Analysis for Women's Economic Empowerment: Issues And Concerns

The Asia Pacific Inputs to the Fourth UN World Conference on Women, Beijing, September 1995 presented the following facts in its paper entitled " **Action for Equality, Development and Peace"** with regard to the economic empowerment of women(ASR Publications, Lahore 1995).

1. Effects of Structural Adjustment Programmes

1.1 Drastic reduction in social benefits-health, education, etc. Without safety nets or production of vulnerable people/women.

1.2 Maximum burden of SAP being borne by the lowest income groups who mainly face :

- retrenchment
- cutback in social services

1.3 Majority of women in South Asian and Pacific are agricultural workers- a sector affected by SAP such as

- seed patent
- power tariffs
- mechanization
- markets

1.4 Number of women in the home-based sector (and unorganized sector) are increasing tremendously.

1.5 Sex industry is rising prolifically especially in development zones, posts and military bases

1.6 Poverty alleviation programmes are becoming the main focus. This is against making the poor productive

1.7 Global relations especially between north and south are exploiting resources in developing Asia and pacific countries which is leading to reduce control over their local resources.

2. Unorganized Sector

2.1 Lack of data - either sector-wise or gender-wise, or women's contribution to the economy - is a major problem

2.2 Women's work is not recognized as "work". This has affected the self-image and self-worth of the women

2.3 Main components of unorganized production-credit-training-raw material-market, constitute the main problem.

2.4 Women are pushed into competitive production without adequate access to either of these components.

2.5 This sector needs to be institutionalized.

2.6 Existing institutions such as international and national banks are not gender sensitive

2.7 Informal credit is exploiting the poor and creating debt.

2.8 total income of nations earned from unorganized production is more substantive than income from organized production-but investment in the latter far exceeds the former

3. Organized Sector

3.1 Work conditions are poor.

3.2 Lower wages for women compared to men for the same or more work

3.3 Lack of child care

3.4 Inadequate / gender blind labour legislation and plans

3.5 economic growth can put women in a vulnerable position. If there is an economic slump the women are the first to be sacrificed.

3.6 Trickle donor does not reach poor women.

3.7 National economic policies are based on inadequate and misleading data concerning women

3.8 Powerful based women workers are exploited for foreign exchange earnings while families at home suffer.

4. Credit And Women's Access To Production Factors.

4.1 Financial institutions are gender-blind, and insensitive to poor women's credit needs.

4.2 Informal credit used by poor women can be detrimental and often aggravate their poverty.

4.3 When women have had access to credit, they have met with remarkable success.

4.4 International debt siphons off large amounts of national income at the expense of social services and other sectors which are especially important to women.

4.5 Credit for poor women need to be accompanied by parallel financial services

4.6 Women farmers not accorded rights as farmers (of their own) and such services continue to be directed at males.

4.7 Lack of legislative/policy framework for informal production and marketing.

B. Strategies For Economic Empowerment

1. Women are beginning to obtain training skills and be in professions which are non-traditional and thus they penetrate the so-called "male" domain

2. Organizing of women on the basis of work is crucial.

3. Strategies must address needs and concerns into development-structures must be created for both.

4. Organizations which are not based on charity or male dominated membership are most likely to become economically empowered.

5. Women's empowerment in the region must be ecologically sensitive. This must be integrated into all strategies.

6. Women's empowerment must not restrict itself to income-generating processes but include other components such as capacity building, control over production, tools and process, conservation of natural resources, strengthening people's organizations and social security.

7. Training processes should be processes of collective learning and empowerment.

8. Training centres have and should establish a link for recruitment of trainees with the relevant job markets.

9. The market should be studied and surveyed adequately before production is undertaken on a large scale.

10. Marketing strategies devised and undertaken suggest that :

10.1 Advertising should be done by the NGO staff themselves;

10.2 Diversify products-leaving a diverse product and price range;

10.3 Develop a theme for the consumers as part of the marketing strategy for example, it could be something that can develop the pride in weaving hand woven clothes.

10.4 Extensive participation in trade fairs;

10.5 Develop an outside market, but first tap the local market completely.

10.6 NGOs exporting the products should interface with NGOs in the importing countries both for market information and lobbying with consumers.

10.7 Women's groups and NGOs should themselves be self-sufficient, and generate their own funds - rather than basing their economic empowerment work on grants and subsidies.

10.8 Devising organizational structures which allow for government bodies to be accountable to poor women, and for women to have a dialogue with governments, can and have become a strategy for economic empowerment.

What Can Be Done

1. Recognizing and valuing women's contribution to the economy.

This requires action to be taken in the following areas:

1.1 Compiling and collecting accurate data on women's work (including national censuses) paid and unpaid with the help of women's organizations and NGOs.

1.2 Redefine concepts of women's "work" and develop methods to quantify this work;

1.3 Introduce national level legislation to recognize home-based workers and ask the ILO to pass a convention for protection of these workers;

1.4 Establish a databse on immigrant and refugee women.

2. Women's access to, and control over resources.

This requires action to be taken in the following areas:

2.1 Credit and working capital needs to be made accessible to women along with financial and technical support services;

2.2 Existing financial institutions should be accessible and sensitive to women;

2.3 Access to raw materials should be given priority;

2.4 Recognize, protect and ensure all women's land tenure rights and other property rights.

2.5 Recognize, protect and ensure all women's land tenure rights and other property rights;

2.6 Women's access to common property resources should be restored and maintained.

3. Strengthening and safeguarding women's existing employment and developing new areas of employment.

This requires action to be taken in the following areas:

3.1 Identify existing areas of employment and those areas which are being eroded by the new economic policies;

3.2 Identify areas of intensive employment for women and reserve these for women (sectors like forestry, dairy, agriculture craft etc.)

3.3 Develop social support systems for women's employment including child care, health care, maternity benefits, productive insurance, shelter and work space;

3.4 Subsistence and food security related activities should be given priority over cash crops and goods;

3.5 Ensure equal pay for equal work and fair working conditions

3.6 Expand employment opportunities for women including the non-traditional sectors.

3.7 Promote technologies that preserve and promote women's employment and discourage those which adversely affect their employment;

3.8 Involve women and women's organizations in planning and implementation of employment programmes and economic development scheme

3.9 Migrant women should be able to practice their professions in the host countries and their professional qualifications should be recognized

3.10 Promote and encourage grass roots level women workers; organizations and groups.

3.11 Promote and encourage grass roots level economic leadership of women

3.12 Extend marketing support including marketing outlets, design support, support and assistance in maintaining quality control of product and process.

4. Develop an appropriate policy framework for promoting, preserving ad strengthening women's economic empowerment.

This requires action to be taken in the following areas

4.1 Recognize women's right to sustainable livelihood and employment

4.2 Gender sensitive analysis and audit of all policies and programmes should be regularly undertaken

4.3 encourage policies which promote and support women's efforts, for self-reliance

4.4 Encourage holistic economic empowerment of women

4.5 Address the situation and needs of migrant workers in order to protect their dignity (both by the sending and receiving countries)

4.6 Create opportunities for women's education and organization

4.7 Develop mechanism to promote dialogue on policies and programmes between GOs and NGOs

4.8 Lobby for the implementation of international protocols and conventions concerning women (e.g. CEDAW,FLLS,ILO Conventions)

4.9 Lobby for the ratification of the UN Convention on protection of rights of all migrant workers and their families.

Planning for Economic Empowerment of women in India

Indian development planning has always aimed at removing inequities in the process of development to ensure that the fruits of development are an equal privilege of all. In recent years it has become increasingly evident that women are lagging behind a great deal both in availing of the benefits of development and as participants in the process of development due to several socio-economic-cultural-political impediments. This has become a cause for concern since women number several millions and constitute nearly half of our population.

In the early years of planning the concern for gender took a welfarism perspective which manifested itself in the form of grants, waivers, subsidies and freeships for girls and women in a few relevant programmes. But these concessions did not elicit the required level of participation. In the later half of the 1970's the focus shifted from merely welfare to development and greater emphasis on integration of women into the mainstream of social and economic development. In due course many social and economic programmes like **Non Formal Education for Girls, Integrated Rural Development Programme**...were evolved exclusively for women or with a percentage set aside solely for them. The benefits derived from these programme had to be sustained and this was posing a challenge. Studies have shown that 'practical gender gains' in improved livelihood, education, nutrition and sanitation are not sustained and easily reversed if the 'strategic need' to give 'women a voice' in the decisions that so directly affect their lives, is not adequately taken care of. The strategy in the 1990's has shifted to **empowerment of women** and 'giving them a voice'.

It is in this context of empowerment and given the vulnerability and powerlessness of the individual woman in the existing socio-economic set up that 'Group' strategies acquire great relevance. The formation of small informal functional groups of women would give them **'visibility'** and create micro level power pockets. Further, grouping would initiate a learning process through sharing of ideas, skills and interactive capacity and in course of time women would learn to articulate their needs resulting in more appropriate participatory and grassroots level plans for them. Some social barriers would also be broken in the process'. Many groups in recent years have started cutting across barriers of religion and caste and working together harmoniously for economic betterment.

Poverty hits women the hardest, as they balance means and ends at the household level and many a time skip a meal to let the rest of the household avail of the little that is available. These women are subject to economic and social discrimination, and credit is not easily available to them. Millions of our women live in poverty and their social empowerment would have little relevance without first empowering them on the economic front. The World Bank studies have shown that enhancement of women's earnings would have a more profound effect on the welfare of the family as a whole since 'increases in women's income result more directly into better health and nutrition for children. Thus grouping women for economic empowerment is of great importance.

The programme for **Development of Women and Children in Rural Areas (DWCRA),** launched in 1982-83, inaugurated an era for systematically organising women in groups for enhancing their earnings on a self-sustaining basis and increasing their access to and utilisation of services like health, child care and adult education, among others. The programme called for formation groups of 10-15 women who would collectively engage in an activity. A revolving fund of Rs.15000 (presently enhanced to Rs.25000) was made available to each group for credit and administrative needs. Supplementing of staff by inclusion of an additional *gram sevika* and appointment of a lady officer to the post of Assistant Project Officer to oversee implementation to the programme were called for. Subsequently with a view to fortifying the programme further and increasing awareness a **Community Based Convergent Services (CBCS)** component and Information, Education and

Communication (IEC) component were included. Upto early 1996, over 1.3 lakh groups covering 2.2 million women were formed. Almost all the districts in the country (except a handful of exclusively urban ones) are presently covered under this programme.

Formation of **Thrift and Credit Groups** of women for self help and economic self reliance has also been encouraged by the government. A **Rashtriya Mahila Kosh (RMK)** was set in 1993 for extending credit with low transaction costs to poor and needy women and women's groups through Non Governmental Organisations. At present (as in July, 1996), the scheme is being implemented in the fifteen states of Andhra Pradesh, Bihar, Haryana, Himachal Pradesh, Gujarat, Karnataka, Kerala, Maharashtra, Madhya Pradesh, Manipur, Orissa, Rajasthan, Tamil Nadu, Uttar Pradesh and West Bengal through a network of one hundred and four Non Governmental Organisations.

The **Indira Mahila Yojana (IMY)** launched in 1995 in 1995 aims at co-ordinating and integrating sectoral programmes relevant to women like health, education, water, sanitation, housing and others at local, block and district levels and increasing their awareness and income through group activities and participation with the aim of **empowering** women. **Indira Mahila Kendras** would be established at village level and **Indira Mahila Block Kendras** at Block level for this purpose. The programme would be a Centrally sponsored scheme. Non Governmental Organisations would also be involved in this process. The Programme has been sanctioned for a period of seven years commencing from 1995-96. During the inception year it was to cover two hundred blocks on a pilot basis and a thousand blocks each year in the subsequent years. The Central Government would provide a one time grant of Rs.5000 to each **Indira Mahila Kendra**. Further funds provided at block level would be used for payments of honoraria to individuals who involve themselves in awareness camps, mobilisation of groups, training group members and functionaries and helping survival of groups through creation of outlets for marketing.

Increased Awareness

Grouping of women has increased their awareness and eliminated exploitation by the middleman, in the case of 'active' groups. In many trades like weaving, processing food items...giving women access to finance through revolving funds and cheap credit has resulted in women directly procuring raw materials and producing and marketing goods without having to depend on the middleman for raw materials to process on measly daily wages, that too at disadvantageously lower levels for women. Incomes have also increased in the process. Studies by the **Self Employed Women's Association (SEWA)**, Ahmedabad on the DWCRA groups helped by them in respect of crafts women and gum collectors clearly show that these groups have strengthened women's economic position, increased their bargaining powers, self sufficiency and thereby social status. Women are held in esteem now and men have become more co-operative on the domestic front and even help women in fuel and fodder collection. Women in turn feel more confident and have a sense of belonging. These self help groups are a new source of social security with the crumbling of the joint family system. Other field level experiences and studies have clearly shown that despite all its limitations, the group strategy has empowered women to approach functionaries and banks to their advantage.

Given the potential power of groups it serves us well to increase their cover. The government has sincerely tried to generate formation of informal groups. But this is a time consuming process requiring a high degree of social awareness of the local area. Finally, the regions which have highly successful groups are those with highly committed *Gram Sevikas* and Project Officers. Such functionaries who are invaluable assets are however not too large in numbers. The government's efforts therefore need to be supplemented to a far larger extent than at present. In the current context, this could best be handled through involvement of local and Non Government Organisations in a big way. Intervention by Non Governmental Organisations with a feel for the people and their problems, in some areas, has brought about very successful and functional groups.

This brings us to the next related issue-Committed Non Governmental and Voluntary Organisations are not in abundance and involvement of greater numbers of committed people is essential.

Starting Point

The process of group formation could thus take the following form: The starting point should be the setting up of local 'Skill Exchanges'. Women possessing various skills like craftwork, tailoring, too making etc., could register themselves for employment. Their motivation to work would be spontaneous as registration is a voluntary act. Also many of the skilled labourers would belong to the poorer sections, though not necessarily below the poverty line. There is a strong justification for this, because as gender experts have pointed out, when we talk of the poverty line we talk in aggregates i.e., of a family as a whole being below or above it. While this is absolutely logical in the aggregate sense, it overlooks the inequities in intra-household distribution of income and consumption, since women may not have access to a large part of the spouse's income but they may be responsible in seeing that all the children and family member are well fed. So technically though the family may be slightly above poverty line, most of the its members may be living in below poverty line conditions. Merely picking up women without skills or motivation from the lost of 'Below Poverty Line' families has resulted in many cases in total waste of effort.

From these skill exchanges, Non Governmental local organisations could group women by homogeneity of skills and location for functional success. Such groups of motivated and similarly skilled women may perform better and result in faster spread of groups through 'Demonstration Effect'. Further, in due course some of the more successful of these groups could themselves become local voluntary organisations and help in formation of groups in their neighbourhoods.

The government would have to play the role of overseer and facilitator in this entire process—a role that it is most competent to play. The government should first group its activities for a co-ordinated delivery systems of services at all the local level. District level teams could be formed with personnel drawn from various departments like health, education etc.,— not the higher planning oriented personnel but middle and lower level implementing functionaries. These teams could cater to various blocks for referral services and problem solving through nodal local organisations or group leaders. The **Indira Mahila Yojana** is a step forward in this direction.

The above system could be tried out along with the existing system which boils down to government *gram sevikas* exploring possibilities of setting up groups, then motivating the women, selecting an activity for them, arranging for training in some cases and so on without ultimate guarantee of the sustainability of the group.

Once **economic empowerment** is achieved it would have major implications on the overall empowerment of women. Intra-family relationships and domestic work culture would change resulting in **social empowerment** and a more equitable participation of women in decisions concerning the family. Leadership and active participation in group culture would improve political acumen and eventually help successful **political empowerment**. Political empowerment in turn would result in more representative planning for women and a strengthening and sustaining of the process of overall empowerment of women (**Sujatha** 1997).

Podupulakshmi : A Case Study on Thrift and Credit Programme for Women's Empowerment

A report on Thrift and Credit Programme, called ***PODUPULAKSHMI,*** brought out by the Nellore District administration in Andhra Pradesh State has clearly demonstrated that how women groups promoted for developmental initiatives in the village by integrating income generating activities of groups with delivery of other services like literacy, health, family welfare, nutrition etc. may lead to women's empowerment.

The rural women in Nellore District of Andhra Pradesh State in India are organised into small groups of 30 to 40 members into Thrift and credit Groups called ***PODUPULAKSHMI*** GROUPS. This programme is being implemented by D.R.D.A., with the participation of all other related Departments.

The Total literacy programme was taken up in the year 1991-92 in Nellore District and a large number of women have participated in this campaign. During 1992 the women in the District agitated against sale of country arrack and Government have declared ban on Arrack in April, 1993. During the implementation of the Ban on sale of Arrack. It was noticed that the women groups which were functioning under DWCRA Programme have shown more interest in the savings. In the year 1992, the Members of DWCRA groups in a village, viz., Lenguntapadu in Kovur Mandal have started thrift and credit groups with the guidance of DRDA. Most of the members of these thrift and credit groups with the guidance of DRDA. Most of the members of these thrift and credit groups have stated that they are now in a position to save small amounts due to the ban on arrack. The youth in this village, who have earlier participated in the total literacy programme, have taken more interest in this savings campaign. The success of these thrift groups in Lenguntapadu village has led to formation of similar groups in the rest of the District.

The women in the other parts of the District have understood the benefit of this programme and started forming themselves into thrift and credit groups with the help of local teachers. Village Administrative Officers, Village Development Officers. Voluntary Agencies and Anganwadi workers. They have started sharing their experience apart from exchanging their achievements among themselves about the benefits that will accrue from the savings. The amounts thus saved under this activity or for meeting the immediate needs of their family.

This scheme is initially aimed at covering rural women only. Two lakh women living in Rural Areas have enrolled themselves in the Thrift and credit Groups by now.

Objectives:

1. To inculcate the habit of saving among rural women and to provide working capital base for rural development activities;

2. To ensure that the savings consequent to the ban on sale of arrack are properly channelised;

3. To build moral trust and confidence between the bankers and rural poor and to encourage banking activity in a segment of population who generally find it difficult to secure loans;

4. To develop group Dynamics so that various welfare and developmental programmes can be implemented in a better way with the participation of these women groups; and

5. To achieve women and child welfare programme goals by actively involving these women groups in Universal Immunisation Programme, Universal Elementary Education, small family norms etc.

Structure Of The Groups:

About 6106 groups have been formed in the 46 Revenue Mandals of the district. The total membership is two lakhs. These women are from low-income group families or rural areas. The optimum number of members for each group is 30 with a maximum of 50. Most of the groups are homogeneous. Each group has selected one among the members as their group leader. Group leader has adequate knowledge to maintain simple accounts and also has the acceptability among the group. Group leaders are drawn from Literacy volunteers. Anganwadi workers, DWCRA group members.

Each group has on guardian who is normally a Government employee working at the village level like the Teacher. Village Administrative Officer, Village Development Officer, Anganwadi Workers. These guardians have played a crucial role in motivating the women, in formation of groups and in initiating the group action.

Initially, the guardian is also the joint account holder of the accounts opened in the banks or post offices along with the group leader. The groups which are stabilised with 6 months to one year experience will select another member as a joint account holder. Then the guardian will remain as a guide but not as joint account holder.

Functions Of The Groups:

The scheme is basically meant for saving Rs. 1/- per member per day for a period of 3 years to begin with. Each member is expected to keep a Rupee aside every day from our of the family earnings. The group leader will collect the amount from each member once in a week or fortnight as per the group's convenience. Group leaders shall ensure that Rs.30/- is deposited by the end of the month in the name of each member in bank account/post office.

Each member is given a pass-book for posting the particulars of savings every month. Each group leader expected to maintain a register (ledger) recording the savings deposited by every member through out the period of the scheme. The group leader will also be in possession of a pass book issued by bank or post office. In the initial period, the guardian is expected to make all entries in the member pass book ad register Over a period of time, the group leaders or any members of group, or one of the family members of the group members will take over the function of maintenance of accounts. The amount in all the three records i.e., the member pass-book, group register and bank pass book should tally every month.

The group leader is also in-charge of promissory note. The loans given to the members will be recorded in the register after obtaining the promissory note from each member. The recovery particulars will also be posted in the ledger. The group has the flexibility for fixing the rate of interest of loan given to the members. Normally groups start giving loans after one year of savings. Each member is normally entitled for a maximum loan of Rs. 1,000.- at a time. In specific cases, the group may decide to give more amounts as loan.

Each group is expected to meet once in a month during the first week and discuss about various topics including thrift, implementation of various welfare and developmental activities for themselves. The important issues raised in the group discussion will be recorded in the minutes book with the help of guardian. The guardians are also expected to attend these monthly meetings.

The group leader is also expected to send a post card once in a month (Bank post cards were supplied by DRDA for each group) highlighting the details of savings, loans, other activities and any problems faced, to DRDA.

The existing Gram Panchayat Level and Mandal Level Institutions of Panchayat Raj Department are also involved actively for implementation, for motivation, for social mobilisation and for monitoring the programme.

Organisational Structure To Implement The Scheme:

A district level committee has been constituted for implementing this programme with District Collector as Chairman, Project Director, DRDA as Convenor-Member, the other District Officials namely Joint Collector, Chief Executive Director, SC, ST Society, Chief Executive Officer, Dist, Central Farming Society and Divisional Level Officers as members. At the Mandal level the family welfare committee which has been constituted for undertaking various family welfare programmes is responsible for the implementation of this programme also. Similarly at the village level, the village level family welfare committee under the Chairmanship of sarpanch of Gram Panchayat is responsible for the implementation of this programme. A special Cell called "***PODUPULAKSHMI*** CELL" in the DRDA with APO (Women) as incharge officer is effectively monitoring the programme at the District level. This cell is mainly responsible for motivation of the women groups, for arranging training programmes for the group leaders, for supply of stationery, books, registers maintenance of accounts and for monitoring the scheme.

Training Requirements:

As large number of women are involved in this programme, it is felt necessary to conduct training programme for all the people involved in this programme for orienting them and for equipping them with required skills. Therefore, the members of the Mandal level committees were trained for a day at District level. A one-day workshop for all the group leaders at Mandal level is now being conducted with the financial assistance of UNICEF. Besides the group leaders, another member from each group will also be trained so that she will assist the group leader in maintaining the group. The Teachers, Village Administrative Officers, Village Development Officers and Anganwadi Teachers/workers who are working as guardians of these groups are also participating in the workshop along with group leaders. The workshops for women will be completed by the end of August, 1994.

This training programme is aimed at preparing group leaders for organising groups and for ensuring continuous savings habit among the members. The group leaders are also being trained in maintenance of accounts and in handling the transactions with the banks and post-offices.

The officers at Mandal level and panchayat level are also being sensitised during the orientation programmes. The field workers of Medial & Health Department, primary School teachers and Anganwadi workers are interacting with the women involved in this programme. Both the official functionaries and women group leaders are given the responsibility of implementing various schemes like enrolment of children in the schools, immunisation programme, small family norm, supply of nutritious food etc. The women group leaders have willingly accepted to share this responsibility. This is acting as a motivation factor for the field functionaries of various departments for giving their best.

Thrift And Credit Programme As Lead Programme Under C.B.C.S.

The Government of India introduced CBCS approach in Nellore District from the current year. The integration of literacy, health, nutrition, primary education, savings ad income generating activities of DRDA other related beneficiary oriented programmes is possible with thrift and credit programme as the lead programme. Therefore, the women participating in the thrift-cum-credit programme are being trained for achieving this task.

About 110 women activists were trained for a period of one week under CBCS. The women who are trained under CBCS are now visiting the thrift-and-credit groups in the villages and trying to integrate all the services in the village. Training of another batch of women will be taken up soon. The women groups are actively participating in adult education. Non-formal education, primary education, nutrition programmes, immunisation programmes. The field functionaries working in the Village viz., Village Development Officers. Village Administrative Officers, Anganwadi Workers, School Teachers, Village Health Workers, Village Extension Officers of Agriculture etc., are also being sensitised.

The stabilised groups under thrift and credit programme are being absorbed into DWCRA programme. The Commissioner, Ruler Development, Andhra Pradesh indicated an allotment of 1000 groups for Nellore district for the current financial year which enables promotion of 1000 thrift groups into DWCRA groups. The beneficiaries under IRDP are also being selected from the members of thrift groups and DWCRA groups.

The willing voluntary organisations in the district namely Bharata Gnana Vignana Samithi, Jagruthi Jana Vignana Vedika are also associated in the training and awareness building programme under CBCS.

Projected Savings:

These thrift and credit groups will be able to save about Rs.2.00 lakhs per day from now onwards as the membership had reached 2 lakhs by the end of June, 1994. At this rate an amount of Rs.700.00 lakhs per year can easily be mobilised. This amount saved throughout the year will be utilised for disbursing to the members as loan for creating working capital base. This scheme is aimed at saving of at least Rs.20.00 crores in 3 years.

An amount of Rs.200 lakhs was saved by the end of June 1994 in the district. From hen onwards, the monthly savings was expected to be about Rs.60 lakhs. The groups had started loans to the members from the amount. 205 thrift and credit groups have already been given assistance under DWCRA. Another 1000 groups will be selected this year. All 6106 groups can be assisted under DWCRA by 2000 AD It is contemplated to form these women groups into a Rural Bank for women Development in the district after three years for providing financial assistance to women members.

Participation Of Women In Other Programmes:

These groups have already shown interest and participated in the implementation of new excise policy viz., Ban on sale of arrack. Several groups have taken interest in collection of information about the availability of arrack, and in communicating the same to the government officials which has helped the administration in the implementation of New Excise Policy. It is also being noticed that the participation of women has increased in the implementation of various welfare and developmental programmes.

The response from the women groups in controlling Gastro-enteritis and in popularising ORS is impressive. In the past few months, an attempt was made to create demand for individual sanitary latrines by propagating the problems being faced in absence of individual latrines. Under Central Rural sanitation programme, an amount of Rs.1600 is available for construction of each latrine. The women have expressed willingness to pay Rs.400/- each and to take up construction of individual latrines. So far 2600 members have expressed their willingness and they contributed their share. These women groups may take more interest in the coming months by observing the construction of latrines in their localities.

While participating in several welfare and developmental programmes, women have started associating themselves with the problems of individual members. The group is coming to the rescue of the individual members whenever a member is facing certain problems from the family or the community-social and financial. These groups are also representing about these problems to the administration at various levels. The status of individual woman member in the family, with the self-confidence and financial independence gained, has improved significantly.

Monitoring:

This programme is being monitored closely by the village level functionaries viz., Teachers, Village Development Officer, Village Administrative Officers. The village level functionaries are nominated as guardians of these groups. The role of guardian is very important in sustaining the interest among the members in this programme. The guardian is supposed to provide required guidance and help in bank transactions. The village functionary will send a monthly report to Mandal Parishad Development Officer indicating the savings. The Mandal Parishad Development Officer will be able to understand the performance of each group and take remedial steps to improve the programme wherever necessary.

The Mandal Level Officers will ensure the participation of the group members in Universal Immunisation programme, Universal Elementary Education, Sterilisation programme, etc., by motivating them during their visit as part of the monitoring of the Thrift and Credit programme. All the Mandal Parishad Development Officers who are the nodal officers at Mandal level are expected to send a monthly report by 15th of every month indicating the savings from each village in the proforma enclosed . This report indicates the optimum savings expected from a Mandal based on the number of women and the actual savings per month. This report helps the DRDA to depute senior officers for improving the performance in case of necessity in a particular Mandal where the programme is weak.

It is proposed to computerise the particulars of 6106 groups and to monitor the groups performance by categorising the groups as A, B, C. 'A' indicates stable groups. 'B' indicates unstable groups where the savings amount is fluctuating and the 'C' indicates, deteriorating groups where the savings amount is gradually coming down.

Each Thrift and credit group is expected to conduct group meetings atleast once in a month. For the sake of uniformity, it is decided to conduct group meetings on 5th or 6th of every month. The group leaders are expected to despatch a post card (12 post cards have been supplied to all the groups for using during this year) indicating the important decisions taken by the group, important achievements of the group under various programmes and any important matters which they would like to report.

The **Podupulakshmi** Cell in DRDA is expected to analyse these letters and take appropriate action in co-ordination with District Officers. Replies are also given wherever necessary. The D.R.D.A., is also bringing out a fortnightly news-letter called PODUPULAKSHMI and circulating it to all group leaders with the help of Zilla Saksharatha Samithi, Nellore. This news letter is being used to communicate with the groups about the developmental and welfare programmes, experiences, success stories etc., The feed back received from the groups is also published. It is being used as an instrument for building awareness among the group members about the programme content and programme strategy.

This programme is being continued without any assurance of matching grant from the Government. This is projected as a self help programme for the women. All the departments in the district were advised to involve these women groups in the for the development of their programmes as they are better motivated for the development of their village. These groups will be given preferential treatment in the sanction of assistance under DWCRA, IRDP, and other related programmes hereafter. The financial institutions are also keen to involve these women as they are disciplined in financial matters and are credit worthy.

Conclusion from *Podupulakshmi* Experiment

The ***Podupulakshmi*** groups are promoting developmental initiatives in the village by integrating income generating activities of groups with delivery of other services like literacy, health, family welfare, nutrition etc. The emphasis is on people's participation through community work. The ***Podupulakshmi*** groups are thus endeavouring to promote a community of women workers with a vision & approach of Small Initiatives in Development Action (SIDA). This would certainly lead to women's empowerment in the near future.

IFAD's Women's Development Programme for Economic Empowerment

Dr. Hemlatha Prasad of the National Institute of Rural Development, Hyderabad carried two case studies, one Salem district of Tamil Nadu and another in ITDP areas of Andhra Pradesh to understand the process of economic empowerment of women. In what follows, I have made an attempt to present briefly the main findings of the study dealing with the economic empowerment of women.

Tamil Nadu is the eleventh largest, seventh most populous and fourth highest state having female headed households in our country with 67 per cent of population living in rural areas. Agriculture is the principal economic activity for the people employing over 60 per cent of the population but contributing only 25 per cent of the state's domestic product. The agricultural sector has stagnated and its contribution to domestic product declined from 40 per cent in 1970-71 to 25 per cent in 1985-86. As a result income in rural areas has declined and incidence of poverty has increased. The various socio-economic indices such as representation in work force, type of economic indices such as representation in work force, type of work in which they are engaged, literacy, health, mortality, dependency upon agriculture for employment revealed that women is the most disadvantaged category of population in terms of income and family circumstances requiring support and gui lance.

In this background, Government of India negotiated with the **International Fund for Agricultural Development (IFAD)** for financing a development project focusing the needs of the women in selected district of Tamil Nadu State. The project is mandated to assist 62,500 rural women over a period of seven years from 1989-90 with a project outlay and Bank loan components of Rs.94.86 crores and Race.35.13 crores respectively.

The principal **objective** of the project is **empowerment of rural women** which is sought to be achieved by socially mobilizing the rural poor women to improve their economic and social status in the family and the community. The social enhancement could be achieved by organising them into **Self Help Groups (SHGs)** which would provide them a power base for self development through group dynamics and improvement in their economic position would be achieved through increasing their income-earning potential by integrating them into regular delivery system for credit and support services.

The Tamil Nadu Women's Development Programme with financial assistance from IFAD has been taken up for implementation in five districts viz., Dharmapuri, Salem, South Arcot, Madurai and Ramanathapuram. The project is being implemented in Dharmapuri district from November, 1989 and it has been extended to Salem and South Arcot districts during 1991-92 and to Madurai and Ramanathauram districts from 1993-94.

In Salem district, the project was started in 1991-92 in three blocks, i.e., Sendamangalam, Erumaipatty and Paramathy. Subsequently, it was extended to eight more blocks covering Panamarathupatty, Namagiripet, Mohanur and Ayodhiapattnam (1992-93) Omalur, Mecheri, Taramangalam and Kadayampatti (1993-94). Overall 11 blocks were covered under this programme.

The women development project has developed during the past four years a successful approach for grassroots development among rural women. It broadly envisages to empower rural women by:

- Expanding their resource base through improvement of socio-economic status of women in the family and the community;
- Improving access to credit, technical advise and training;
- Raising the level of awareness and confidence to strive for a change in status through:
  - a) Formation of strong cohesive, self-help women groups as a source of mutual support; and
  - b) Motivation and guidance by animators;
- Better access to health, nutrition and other services.
- Establish a viable model for women's development which could be replicated.

Organizational Structure

At the state level,, there is a Project management unit headed by a Project

Coordinator who reports to the Managing Director. At the district level, there is a Project Implementation Unit (PIU) headed by a Project Officer is assisted by 6-7 Assistant Project Officers of different sectors like Agriculture, Animal husbandry, Credit, Sericulture, Small scale industries, etc. There are six supervisors to monitor 12 women groups each.

At the Block level, an Independent NGO is actively associated in the selection of women members and formation of self-help groups Three Project Assistants were appointed by the NGO to supervise 20 groups each.

At the village level, one village level worker (animator) is engaged for each village to look after the affairs of the group. She was paid an honorarium of Rs.180 per month through the group from the project.

As all the line departments of Government, NGOs and Banks are involved in the programme, it requires close coordination. At the district level, there is a District Project Coordinating Committee headed by the District Collector, which meets every month to review the progress. At the state level, there is a Central Coordinating Committee to review the work with the Chief Secretary, as Chairman.

Group Dynamics

Two inter-related process are vital for the success of the strategy; group formation and needs assessment. NGO field workers identified the most needy women based on the survey conducted by DRDA and NGO. After identifying the target group the field workers began their work by building rapport with member and brought them together to discuss their problems in smaller groups and identified the animators who could assist in the process of group formation playing the role of facilitator rather than leader or boss. The process of group formation was spontaneous and voluntary.

Right from the initial phase, the field workers managed to develop new awareness, new attitudes and new skills in the community. New awareness may include more precise information on the problem needs and resources of the community or of available resources outside the community. New attitudes promoted at this stage entailed a better identification with other member of the group, more solidarity towards the needs of others and more willingness to speak out, discuss their real concerns. New skills generated included new abilities for articulating concerns in the presence of others These new perspectives and abilities are inculcated through organising regular meetings and awareness camps.

After the first phase of work at the area, the most successful start-up activity was group savings and provision of consumption loans to the members. Therefore, before the bank could commence the lending operations 'self help' groups were promoted and group activities were initiated.

The groups were formed as saving cum loan groups with a membership not exceeding 30 women. The groups have chosen their animators for guiding the activities. They reported that the groups were democratically managed with greater participation of all the members in decision-making. The groups also formed their own bye-laws governing the operations of the savings and loans with the guidance of animator/NGO and supervisors. The members were decided to make regular contributions @ Rs..31 per month per member as savings based on their capabilities. This amount was used to provide loans to members to meet their consumption and emergency needs. The group authorized two of their members and the animator to operate the account on behalf of the group. The loan amount should be repaid in ten equal installments with the interest rate of 24 per cent per annum. The medium size of loans was between Rs.100-500. As a result of prompt repayment, the money circulated was 3-4 times more than the amount saved. The entire lending process helped the members to acquire funds management skills before they were assisted by the bank.

Training is a very important input in this project. As the project is different in many ways from other government schemes. It calls for high degree of coordination and cooperation among participating agencies in implementation. The project has recognized the importance of training at various levels and evolved different training modules for women members and staff involved in the implementation of the project.

All the women members were trained for a period of 7 days. The main thrust was on group dynamics, savings, bank procedures and accounts. Women were paid @ 15 per day during training period. Apart from this, some of the women members attended skill training programmes of 6 days duration for specific trades like sericulture, agro-forestry, oil seeds, khadi and village industries.

An intensive training programme was conducted for animators and supervisors with two modules for a duration of 32 days. The course content included various aspects such as group facilitation and communication skills,, personality development, participatory Rural Appraisal, Potential linked plans and maintenance of Accounts etc. They also organized refresher courses for animators and supervisors to provide additional input on health and nutrition, literacy and other developmental programmes.

The groups unanimously decided that there should be fixed day and time for monthly meetings. An attendance register was maintained and attendance of all members is compulsory. All loan applications were submitted to the group and were scrutinized and approved, modified or rejected in a group meeting. All decisions regarding funds management and fund utilization were recorded and be verifiable through the minutes of the group. The funds management played an important role in the process of group growth in terms of skills, values, self-confidence and sustainability. In addition, numeracy and literacy classes helped the members to acquire the skills necessary to read their pass books and the records of meetings.

The group meetings were also utilized to discuss and to make efforts to solve some problems of the community especially drinking water, latrines and street lights etc. The group members took up these matters with the Block Development Officers and got street lights and hand pumps repaired with accepting the responsibility of maintenance. Some of the members constructed a lavatory at their homes with a probable subsidy from the Block Office. The regular meetings and a higher social visibility also fostered a progressive sense of pride in their efforts to improve as well as growing sense of belonging.

Along with the group saving activities, the programme staff began to identify the opportunities for the income generating activities. They also discussed about the available opportunities for obtaining credit for land based activities like agricultural engineering, agriculture, sericulture and horticulture for women having sole or joint title to the land or land taken on lease and for landless under animal husbandry and cottage and village industries. They also rightly explained to the women that loans would also be given to individuals who had no tangible collateral by providing a group guarantee. This encouraged the members of the group in applying for credit.

After scrutiny of applications and other credentials received the bank branch accorded a formal sanction. Bank claimed subsidy from the project implementation unit (PIU) after giving the details of applications sanctioned. On receipt of subsidy from PIU, the bank branch communicated to the group the sanction details. Animator/supervisor helped the women members in execution of loan documents .

The nature of loan was a medium term loan of composite nature combining loans for fixed asset and working capital wherever applicable. As the subsidy amount was kept as deposit as per policy guidelines of the project, the full cost of investment was released as loan.

Though the subsidy was treated as margin, the same was not allowed to utilize for grounding asset as in the case of IRDP. On the contrary, the subsidy was kept in RIP (Re-Investment Plan) account in the name of women, for a period of three years. It will be adjusted to the loan account either after completion of three years or when 75% of the loan is repaid which ever is later.

The interest was charged at half yearly basis for farm sector and quarterly for non-farm sector advances. The limit for not obtaining mortgage was uniformly fixed at Rs.25,000 for all activities under the project. For limits over Rs.25,000 mortgage of landed properties was obtained.

The full amount of loan was credited to the group's savings account under due authorization. Savings cum loan pass books in regional language were issued to all the women members. The loan amount from the group's saving account was released for purchase of asset thereafter. The assets were purchased in the presence of representatives from NGO/Line Department/Bank along with group animator. Generally, assets were purchased on particular day for one group so as to avoid leakage and ensure the quality of items.

The group was made responsible for grounding of the unit and effective utilization of the asset by the women members. The entire process of sanction, disbursement and asset creation has to be completed within 45 days. However, in exceptional cases, delay was due to seasonality, and non-availability of required items. Since the Bank has accepted the procedure of crediting loan amount directly to the group's savings account, the group accepted the responsibility of furnishing loan disbursement/end use statement to the effect that the amount was properly utilized within a fortnight from the date of receipt of loan.

The animator was made responsible to supervise the members and monitor the progress of their activities in order to ensure the asset created was maintained properly. For this, she maintained a loan ledger for bank credit with individual repayment details. She was also sent reports about recovery and overdue on quarterly basis to the PIU and Bank. The women members said that frequent verification of assets was also done by the joint visits of the project officials and Bankers.

Review meetings were conducted monthly by the Block coordination committee chaired by District Collector. Apart from other issues, recovery performance seems to be one of the important item in the agenda for discussions.

The repayment schedule normally be fixed between three to five years but in any case not less than 36 months. Holiday for repayment was provided during gestation period of the investment. The loan installments were paid in monthly/quarterly/half yearly basis depending on the income generation pattern of the programme. Insurance was provided for all livestock units.

The organization assumed moral responsibility wit a view to ensure group binding on the loans sanction, disbursement and also recovery. In the event of default by any women member they said that group will extend pressure and the recovery of dues were discussed as an agenda in the regular monthly group meetings. In cases where the default was due to reasons beyond their control, the same was brought to the notice of the bank for consideration of replacement in repayment schedule depending on the merits of each case. They reported that repayment rate in these groups was 98 per cent. In this process the role played by the animator was very crucial.

Lessons for Economic Empowerment of women

- One of the factors which helped in the promotion of Women Development Programme was the philosophy and approach which drew heavily on other successful programmes for extending credit to poor women such as Grameena Bank in Bangladesh, Productive Credit for Rural Women (PCRW) programme in Nepal and Self Employed Women's Association (SEWA), Ahmedabad in India.

- The involvement of NGOs in the implementation of the programme helped in doing pre-project work and preparing the people in general and women in particular to accept the programme.

- The coordinated effort in selection of clusters/blocks in concurrence with bank officials helped in net working with other branches to ensure easy access to credit for women.

- The basic strength in the project is the social mobilization through the formation of strong, cohesive women's groups facilitating the group process in terms of exchange of ideas and establishing self-confidence and mutual support.

- Most of the women identified were small and marginal farmers rather than landless poor women due to the project emphasis on proportion (60 : 40) of land based and non-land based activities.

- The resource and market survey undertaken for the district has also helped the implementing officials in guiding and convincing the women in selection of economically viable schemes with possible diversification.

- Generally, the awareness among the women members was very high not only about the programme objectives and their entitlement but also about the repayment procedures and consequences of non-repayment.

- Broadly IRDP type of process was adopted in credit administration and selection of economic activities. However, in practice, more scrupulous procedures were put in place such as joint identification and selection of members by GOs, NGOs and bankers; adequate staff to back-up and monitor the programme at all stages.

- The adequate flexibility in selection of economic activities and easy access to credit through group savings and loans has demonstrated that poor rural women can make productive use of credit in a wide range of farm and non-farm micro enterprises.

- Identification and involvement of single National bank helped in dispensing credit effectively to the rural women.

- One of the innovations in project planning is the dovetailing of long term enterprises like horticulture with short-gestation activities such as livestock production. Such an arrangement will ensure regular employment and quick returns from the initial investment.

- Administration of credit was done on group basis in IFAD programme i.e., the sanction, disbursement and recovery involved group process and was done exclusively on group consensus. This ensured not only timely recovery but removed any scope for misuse of credit.

- The strength of the programme lies in bringing group dynamics bear on the entire process and in this respect it was a departure from the group approach of DWCRA programme where in loans were given on individual basis without much group commitment.

- The income derived from the economic activity ranged from Rs.200 to 400 per month after deducting the monthly loan installment. Majority of them felt that the amount derived from the activity was adequate.

- The creditworthiness of clients increased as group responsibility in repayment was ensured and instituted. The high repayment (89.5%) in the programme corroborates the previous experience with women borrowers in other development programmes.

- They also felt hat prompt repayment was their moral responsibility and would help others to get a loan and qualify themselves for a second loan. The element of social prestige also worked favorably in this direction.

- While the present organizational structure is clearly an improvement, since it provides with a separate Programme Implementation Unit and places it under experienced Project Officer assisted by different line department officers including bank, still there is need for improved coordination and communication between PIU staff and NGOs.

- Apart from their participation in the selected enterprises, group members actively involved in mobilizing community resources and in putting pressure on Government for welfare services like education, health, drinking water and sanitation.

The intermediate objective of social enhancement through group dynamics and bringing rural women into the mainstream of credit delivery seems to have been achieved with reasonable success. This hopefully will lead to capacity build up and economic empowerment which programmes of this type logically endeavor to achieve (Prasad, Hemlatha 1997).

Thrift Society & Grain Bank For Economic Empowerment Tribal Women : A Case Study

In Andhra Pradesh a Tribal Development Project has been designed to assist various tribal communities primarily engaged in shifting cultivation, who are at subsistence level of economy. Historically, this type of farming system is represented as a natural agricultural practice, in response to the Physio-geographic character of tribal habitat with insignificant negative environmental impact. But due to the pressure of immigrant population, changes in the policies, shifting cultivation ***(Podu)*** has increasingly become an untenable way of life, resulting in progressive impoverishment of the tribals, their economy and degradation of the environment. In order to upgrade the situation the Andhra Pradesh Tribal Development Programme (APTDP) was formulated with the aim of improving the living standards of tribals, increase in the productivity of the land, conserve the tribal environment and cultural practices and finally resurrect the ecological equilibrium.

Project Objectives

The main objective of the project are :

1. To improve the household food security by promoting activities which :
   a) generate sustainable increase in production and productivity from rainfed and irrigated lands. Leading to increase in farm incomes;
   b) reduce and reverse the degradation of the environment.

2. To promote sustainable self reliance amongst the participant groups by adopting activities which :-
   a) encourage increased village self-reliance for food production and use of local resources in a sustainable way;
   b) focus on generating awareness on education, health and nutrition, and participation by women in particular in productive sector encompassing activities of Thrift, Village Lending, Grain Banks and Income Generation;
   c) enlist active participatory involvement in planning execution and building up of community assets and common property resources ;
   d) foster community management systems for better maintenance and utilisation of local resources and community assets like drinking water sources, irrigation sources, schools, Anganwadi centers etc.

Approach

Watershed based participatory micro level planning, execution and management is the approach adopted for establishing equilibrium between the ecological security (Macro level) and household food security (Micro level) and human resources development (Macro-Micro levels) facets of the programme.

- Natural Resource Development
- Community And Women's Development
- Health & Education
- Marketing And Credit Support
- Project Management Support

The project area consists of 63,370 families living in 16 identified watersheds in the four I.T.D.A areas viz., Seethampet (Srikakulam District) , Parvathipuram (Vizianagaram District), Paderu (Visakhapatnam District) and Ramachaodavaram (East Godavari District). Seethampet consists of 9050 families covering 86 villages under 4 watersheds. The literacy amongst the tribals is only 7.8 per cent compared with 29.9 per cent for the population of the state as a whole; among tribal women, the contrast is even greater with only 3.5 per cent of tribal women being literate compared with state average of 20 per cent. Almost all the population living in the project villages are tribals and 70 per cent of them engaged in *Podu* cultivation and collection and sale of Minor forest Produce.

The primary focus of the model is on generating awareness among the tribal communities about various techniques to improve and utilize the local resources by initiating new organizational techniques within the existing informal tribal community organizations. The project identified three interacting types of structures viz. Village development committees, women societies with option to involve reputed and locally acceptable NGOs and community coordination teams as an experimental basis to cover certain focused Micro watersheds.

Community development unit was set up to facilitate initiation of participatory development and management process in the area and Community Development Coordinator was appointed. She conducted initial sensitization programmes to project officers and staff at the supervisory levels. The awareness raising workshop, exchange sessions and monitoring workshops were also conducted to the members thrift societies.

Women Thrift Society or Mahila Sangam

This study was conducted by Dr. Hemlatha Prasad of the National Institute of Rural Development, Hyderabad, in Vampaliguda located in Seethampet Mandal of Srikakulam District. Vampaliguda is a hamlet of Pulipalli Village, 60 km away from the Project Headquarters. The total population of the village is 990, of which 481 are male and 509 are female. The proposition of SC and ST are 811 and 135 respectively. The female literacy rate is only 6.5

percent.

Women Thrift Society is a kind of voluntary organization mainly intended to cause necessary initiation towards forming the habit of thrift which is conspicuously absent in the value of cultural system of tribals and is also expected to induce self help and group help mechanism. Because of the fact that women occupies and important role in tribal economy as well as value system, the women societies were formed as levers formed as levers for bringing in necessary attitudinal change in the tribal society. In other words women societies are conceived to act as catalysts in community decision to ensure self-sustenance, household food security and family welfare designed in its larger perspective.

Women thrift Societies are formed in all most all the villages. There are 13 members in this group. Majority of the women are in the younger age group of 20-25 years, remaining are between 30-35 years. They have nuclear families with family size of 4-5 members. Most of them are engaged in agriculture as cultivators and as agriculture labour. Women members reported that they do not get regular employment and hence no income. About 10 households have small landholding ranging from 0.5 ac to 1 ac. Of wet land and 1-4 hects. Of dry land. Majority of them have *Podu* land on the top of hills, where they do practice terrace cultivation. Most of the land holding are Patta lands provided by the Government, and of them have livestock such as cows, goats and poultry. The monthly family income ranges from Rs.400 - 600. The major crop in this area is paddy. Women reported that they also collect the forest products like tamarind, ginger and turmeric and sell in the weekly markets. Generally the women members seem to have adequate information about the programme objectives and the benefits that accrue from the programme. The information about the other development programmes in the area was very marginal.

Group Formation

The group has been in existence for 3 years. The group membership is open to all the women in the village, since there are only 15 households in the hamlet, the membership restricted to 13. They have selected a group leader to organize meetings and also keeping the accounts of the group transactions. The group leader seems to be coordinating well with the group members and project officials. She also conduct group meetings, but most of these meetings were found to be more informal and nothing very significant issues to be discussed.

Group Activities

The women members started the savings activity through contributions towards the group fund. There was no fixed pattern in the contributions and periods of contributions. The group leader along with one member opened the joint saving account in the nearby post office. Every month, the saving amount was deposited in the joint group saving account. The group leader maintaining ledger book with details of individual member savings account. Although the societies are free to formulate their own rules of lending, recovery, interest rate etc. it is said that minimum monthly interest rate of Rs.2 per Rs.100 and repayment schedule of minimum 6 months or within a month after principal crop harvest is fixed as a uniform pattern to all the women thrift societies.

During the year 1991-92, an amount or Rs.1560 was generated by the group as savings and ITDA Project provided matching contribution of Rs.3120 @ 1:2 ratio in the first year. The individual passbooks indicated that most of their savings were not regular but largely seasonal during the harvest season. However , the thrust was to encourage "thrift" to make it a habit. It is commonly accepted that a habit of thrift which contributing to savings and later to investment if opportunities exist, is major factor in generating and sustaining an individual's desire to progress.

The women members used this amount to provide loans to the members to meet the immediate cash requirements for purchase of agricultural inputs mainly fertilizers. In few cases, the loans were also utilized for performing festivals, marriages, to meet medical expenses and other household consumption.

The group saving activity was continued in the second year (!993-94) generated an amount of Rs.1560, and received equal amount (1:1 ratio) as matching contribution from the Project Office.

The group leader maintained the accounts and records with the help of voluntary worker from the local NGO About details of the money transactions, the group leader could not explain properly since most of the transactions were done by their husbands. On verification of group savings pass book and the ledger book, it was noticed that there was no savings after the received the matching contribution in the second year (July 1994)

The officials seem to have not bothered once they released the second installment of matching grant. In view of this fact, it was clear that members were more interested in availing matching grant facility than to continue in a sustainable thrift activity. Such activities promote paternalism and counter very purpose for which they were intended.

Grain Bank

The activity of establishment of Grain Banks were proposed to start during the third year of the project after achieving at least minimum crop productivity improvement. However, during 1994-95, the members of the thrift societies were encouraged to save grain along with their thrift activities. The major crop in this area is paddy. Depends upon the crop production during the season, the women were encouraged to save some grain in order to meet their food requirements during lean season. The members contributed grain ranging form 10 kunchas to 2 putties (1 putti = 20 kunchas, 1 kunchas = 2 kg.) to the grain bank as per their convenience. The members who don't posses landholding, saved grain from their earnings as a part of their wages during the harvest season. In order to provide grain storage facilities to the groups, the project provided an amount of Rs.500 towards the material cost and group members contributed in the form of labour and constructed storage structure in the village.

The group was suppose to provide grain as loans to the members to meet the food requirements of the group members particularly in lean seasons. The loan quantity of grain should be repaid in the next harvesting season in the form of grain with the interest rate of 5 kunchas per putti.

The group leader reported that the grain received from the project as matching contribution i.e. 13.6 putties was sold in the local market and the amount was distributed to all the members on prorate basis of their savings. This means that grain bank activity was no way different from the thrift in that it was managed as a short-term activity to avail the matching grant and nothing beyond. A Serious rethinking is required to correct this malady.

Other Services

Women also started undertaking community nurseries, vegetable cultivation and construction of buildings, soil conservation structures and irrigation structures, as part of income generating activities.

Under complementary health care, tribal local woman was selected by the community as a community health worker (CHW) and trained to meet the specific health and nutritional needs/ problems and diseases / deficiencies of the village.

Tribals generally view educating children as non productive as it reduces the labour availability for agriculture and non agriculture activities. Educating girls is still perceived as a liability. Therefore, attempts were made to motivate the villages to establish community schools within the village with some assistance from Govt. under Community School Programme. The programme has made some provisions under education components like matching grants for construction of community school buildings, community school teacher's honorarium, furniture, black boards, stationary etc.

Besides income generating activities one rice mill and one flour mill was established by the village community members at an unit cost of Rs.22000/- of which the community contributed 50 percent of the cost.

The strength of IFAD programme can be traced in its focus on community involvement at all stages of the programme. By making women societies responsible for construction of school buildings, check dams and satellite nurseries resulted in the capacity build up of the women concern. The long term objective of inculcating saving habit and building up food security have however, not been achieved(Prasad, Hemlatha 1997).

Women's Economic Empowerment Through Thrift Groups:

Evolution of women's thrift groups:

Thrift and Credit Cooperatives have been in existence in India almost for the last 100 years, especially in the urban areas and in the organised sector Most of them are registered under the Cooperative Societies Act, though informal and unregistered thrift cooperatives are also in existence. The thrift cooperatives largely are financially self-reliant and successful. However, for various reasons, they did not have their own system with associations or federations, till **Cooperative Development Foundation [CDF]**, a public society for promotion of cooperatives, based in Hyderabad, helped the local thrift cooperatives in forming their Regional Associations in 1984, and subsequently, Federation of Thrift and Credit Associations - India in 1989. Such groups became popular especially with the reported success of Grameena Banks in Bangladesh. Most of the Credit and Thrift groups in our country are more or less patterned on the Grameena bank Groups in Bangladesh (**Parthasarathy** 1995).

Womens' Thrift Groups' Establishment

The **Federation of Thrift and Credit Associations India (FTCA - India)** and its associations have worked together in helping women set up their own thrift and credit groups and in assisting voluntary agencies in others areas, set up similar groups. The membership in a group normally varies from ten to thirty. The establishment of a group is preceded by:

- at least 2 - 3 meetings of women where the concept of savings, mutual loaning, self-reliance, democratic decision-making, equitable sharing of the surplus etc., are discussed.
- Poor women are encouraged to save what they can on a regular basis.

The group after establishment:

- decides whether there should be uniform amount of thrift;
- decides whether savings should be daily/weekly/monthly;
- decides frequency of meetings for review of loan application to me bers.
- Considers the feasibility of production schemes for which loans are applied.
- Works out repayment capacity, repayment installment, loan duration etc.
- decides interest rates to be paid on savings and borrowings.
- and sets rules for action on defaulters.

At each meetings, new savings and old loan installments with interest come in and new loans go out. The group amends from time to time purposes for which loans are given, maximum borrowing limit for members, maximum payback period, interest rates and so on. Every year, based on the returns, the women pay themselves, an interest on their savings and pay a remuneration to the person in the group who has helped maintain records and accounts. A reserve fund is also created. The interest on savings and loans should be such that a woman should not find the rate exploitative in her role, either as borrower or as a saver.

The entire process of mutual savings and credit is backed by management counseling, financial counseling, literacy and numeric skill upgradation, search for new employment opportunities and search for enhancement of earnings from existing employment. While voluntary of the women groups is never undermined and all decision-making tends to be left in the hands of the members of the group.

The business meetings of the groups are conducted usually late in the evenings, when women have finished their work at home and their 'jobs' for the day. These women are particularly cynical about extension workers, who work during 'office hour', since most rural women are not available during these hours.

As the groups become stable and comfortable with the process of savings, borrowings and feasibility analysis, they become ready for networking with other similar groups in and around their area and for formalizing some of these activities. They are also ready to start new activities such as collectively organising mutual insurance, diversifying lending and saving facilities and so on. For each of these, fresh information, training, credit, manpower inputs become necessary.

The tendency in many groups in fact, has been to issue consumption, education and health related loans initially, giving way to mainly employment related and house improvement loans as the funds become larger.

The employment related loans too make as shift from just working capital loans to investment capital loans as well. The need for external credit beings to be felt when more and more women start to seek loans for production assets and for working capital for expanding business.

Stage of Growth of a Women's Group

A thrift cooperative must be sensitive to changing needs and be ready to meet them. Initially, a group tends to draw members largely from a homogenous occupational group or even neighborhood (perhaps caste) group. This is because of the need for mutual trust and for ability to discipline one another. As the groups gain in confidence, they include others whom they trust. If the number is significant enough, they actually help them to form their own group.

When groups start to relate with one another in order to form a registered society, then the mutual distrust of caste, occupation, village etc., begins to show. The process of coming together to form a larger family is slower than one would hope. Initially, for easier accounting, the women may permit new members to join only once every six months or so. This may change, to allow new members to join any time, once they feel more confident.

Changes in Thrift Pattern

At first, thrift is collected weekly or monthly, because most of the women are not quite literate. Also, they cannot afford a full-time worker. As the members do not have accounting skills, they prefer the thrift to be equal amounts so that interest calculation is simpler. Over a period of time, the amount of thrift and frequency of remittance may change, especially, when networking with other groups starts and there is an outlet for temporary surplus funds.

Changes in Loan Pattern

Initially, women are very cautious and want to see their loans coming back quickly. They also know that there is very little money to go round and every one wants to get at the earliest. Further, their native wisdom informs them that over-financing of an individual vis-à-vis her savings in the group and her repaying capacity may be suicidal for the group. Low interest rates may make group members irreverent towards loan repayment. With these and possibly many other considerations in view, women tend to give out small loans of upto Rs.100 at around 18% per annum, repayable in one to three monthly installments. The loans are largely for consumption, such as buying rations and meeting educational or health-related expenses.

As the group savings continue to grow and with a successful record of default management, the group finds itself left with surplus funds. They give a wider variety of loans such as for working capital and investment capital. One or two group members may be required to stand as guarantors and an item or two or the borrowers may be pledge to the group (in case of default) at the time of loaning. The need for some external capital for production purposes may also be felt. Sudden changes may be harmful and the group must be helped to make the transition gradually. To ensure against risk, a scheme called Death Relief Insurance Scheme (DRAS), was introduced under which every borrower insures his loans amount against the contingency of death of loanee. This protects the group against overdue caused by death of an earning member.

Changes in Management

Initially, all the group members may meet regularly to review all loan applications, thrift collection and loan recovery performance, with just a chairperson to preside over meetings and a paid Secretary to work one to two days a month to maintain books and records. However, with increasing membership, this arrangement may give way to the formation of small representative managing committees to take over loan review and sanction of loans. The entire group may then choose to meet once in six months to review the committee's management performance. This is likely to happen once networking begins. Since by then the loan amounts are likely to be higher and there is need for delegation of power of transactions with other groups. Because, of the financial strength, which successful networking brings, it is possible to meet the local costs of daily collection of savings and loan installments. Where necessary, networking may also result in groups wanting/needing to confirm with one another especially, in areas such as interest rates and other rules and regulations.

Changes in Services Rendered

In the early stages, a group's primary interest may be in the provision of thrift collection and small loan disbursement services. As the group funds grow larger, women begin to appreciate use of loans for productive purposes. They do need to ensure that production loans are actually repaid from increased production.

Financial counseling services, initially provided by the group to members, need to become increasingly sophisticated as the loans become larger and aspirations increase. The value of taking larger consumption loans, as for one time heavy expenditure on a marriage or a death, too, needs to be discussed and counseled on. Individuals need to be helped by the group to express their ambitions and aspirations in the form of family growth plans, so that the group is not taken unawares by the growing, changing needs so that artificial "surplus" in savings is not created at group level. Insurance services, can also be introduced with the strength of numbers when the thrift and credit groups form their own mutual aid society.

Facilitators/Promoting Agency's Role in beginning phase of Group Activity

The facilitators play an important role in the early stages of the group.

- They attend monthly business meetings where savings are collected, loans are sanctioned and rules amended;

- They help groups form first set of bye-laws and duplicate them;
- They design pass-books, obtain cash box, account forms and minutes books;
- They train and help chief executive and President in maintaining books and records.

Role of Facilitators/Promoting Agency towards latter phase of Group Activity:

The facilitator will have to play an important role in the later phase.

- To train functionaries in preparing reports and help them in duplicating them for circulation;
- To analyze accounts;
- to formulate proposals for discussions and decisions by half-yearly formal general body meetings;
- To give financial counseling and helping them select appropriate production schemes;

To help groups organize workshops for preparing growth plans;

- Finding new avenues for use of increasing group savings
- Helping group seek legal redress against unjust attacks against their autonomy and mobilize public opinion

Basic Principles and Practices

The following are the basic principles of Thrift groups:

- Voluntary membership
- Optimum size, small and homogenous groups
- Election of group leaders, where necessary
- Democratic management
- Accountability of managers

- Regular conduct of election of functionaries through secret ballot
- Periodic review and amendment of rules and bye- laws
- External promoting agencies' role limited to facilitating meaningful decisions after under- standing likely consequences
- Enabling members to exercise rights of voting and decision-making
- Educating women on rights, cooperatives principles, finance management, income generating activities
- Training in democratic management, book- keeping, accounting to report preparation
- Making available copies of bye-laws, annual reports and passbooks to members

External capital, may, however, be introduced later, if the group has a track record of sound finance management and democratic accountability practices. The external capital may be introduced initially to the tune of 50% of the group's own collective savings, but, by the end of the third year, the external capital may equal the group's cumulative savings, if financial and democratic performance has been satisfactory.

Certain minimum records must be maintained, whether, members are literate or not. Each member must receive a copy of the constantly changing bye-laws, the annual progress report, the group's financial statements and pass books.

The groups must be helped to conduct their elections regularly, through simple secret ballot, without fear of repercussion. "Unanimous" elections must be viewed with some suspicion till proven otherwise. All staff paid for by the primary groups/secondary society, must be local women known to all and not likely to run away with the funds.

Progress of Women's Thrift Groups in Cuddappah District Structure

The Thrift and Credit system in southern India is a three-tier structure comprising one Federation of Thrift and Credit Associations - India (FTCA-India) and 19 Regional Associations of Thrift Cooperatives (RATC) and almost about 400 affiliated Thrift and Credit Cooperatives in the states of Andhra Pradesh, Tamilnadu, Pondicherry, Goa and Karnataka. The system's objective is to maximize them as decentralized, democratic, self-help and mutual aid financial institutions, effectively harnessing and fostering local resources, in consonance with the principles of cooperation.

Unequal Coverage of Societies

As on 31-12-1992, the Samakhya Women's Thrift and Credit Societies were organised in 15 out of 50 Mandals in Cuddappah district. There is a high concentration of groups as well as membership in Cuddapah, Prodduture, Jammalamadugu, CK Dinne, Kamalapuram, Ontimetta, Attluru and Rajampet. These eight societies together accounted for 80% of the total number of thrift groups and more or less, an equal percentage of members.

Economic Impact: Improved Access to Credit

Among economic impacts of the Thrift and Credit Societies the most perceptible is improved access to institutional credit for the poor.

Increase in Outstanding Loans

Around one-fourth of total households, urban and rural together reported loans outstanding for the period before joining thrift society, whereas, little more than two-third of the households reported loans outstanding as on date of investigation. Most thrift groups under investigation were established around 1989. Within a three year interval, the number reporting loans outstanding rose remarkably.

Decline in Loans Outstanding from Non-Institutional Sources

There was a marked decline in borrowers from non-institutional sources i.e., 70% to 6% and a marked rise in borrowers from institutional and both sources for all societies together, 25% to 61% since thrift societies were established.

Out of institutional sources, currently, thrift societies are prominent. Forty-four per cent of rise in current loanees is attributed to thrift society. Their role is much more prominent in urban areas as compared to rural areas.

The total loans outstanding for households in all societies increased by more than 6 times after the thrift societies were established.

Comparing the situation source-wise on the date of investigation with the past position, amount of loans from institutional sources rose at a faster rate than non-institutional loans. Loans outstanding to institutions increased at a faster rate in rural areas as compared to urban areas. It is also seen the institutional sources do not completely substitute non-institutional sources. But they provide a supplementary sources of loans.

The Importance of Thrift Groups in Institutional Sources

The shift from non-institutional to institutional sources and high rate of growth could be mainly attributed to the functioning of thrift societies. They have undoubtedly contributed to improved access to credit. In the urban areas, the share of thrift society in institutional credit is around 62%. In rural areas, it was around 49%. The role of credit societies in improving access to credit is significant even in outstanding loans in the past three years. Thrift societies account for one-third of the additional credit in urban areas and around 28% in rural areas.

The loan outstanding showed a remarkable increase within the two periods, not only in terms of the total amount, but also in terms of percentage of those reporting loans outstanding. The improvement in the access to credit is observed not only in terms of spread, but also in terms of per capita amount of loans outstanding. Per capita loan outstanding for all societies as a whole, rose from 2219/- to 4283/-. This rise with respect to loans outstanding after establishment of thrift society is observable both in urban and rural areas.

Share of Thrift Groups - Variations Across the Societies

In every society, there is only a small percent of people who do not take loans. In both urban and rural areas, the borrowings from thrift groups is universal in all societies. Those who borrow from thrift societies are found to borrow from others also in all the societies. The role of non-institutional sources in addition to thrift societies is found to be more significant in Cuddappah urban area and Rajampet rural area.

Per capita loan from thrift society alone is small both in urban and rural areas. Thrift socicty lends smaller amounts than banks and also non- institutional sources. There is also a maximum ceiling of 5000/- on loans given by thrift societies. The average loan of thrift society in Cuddappah is generally higher in urban areas as compared to rural except for Rajampeta.

Loans Outstanding by Agency and Share of Thrift Groups

Loans outstanding by different agencies are studied. The agencies covered include non-institutional sources like professional moneylender, village merchant, commission agent, agriculturist and friends and others and institutional agencies like banks and thrift societies. We look at aggregates for the five selected societies. In urban areas, institutional sources account for three-fourth of the total loans outstanding. Among the non-institutional sources, Friends and others are prominent. What needs to be noted is a low dependence on non-institutional sources. In rural areas, a similar picture could be seen. Three-fourths of the loans outstanding are against institutional sources. Among non-institutional sources, village merchant tops the list. Within institutional sources, both in urban and rural areas, a little more than 50% of the number of loans are from thrift societies. Thrift society accounts for the single largest group both in urban and rural areas.

Amount outstanding and Role of Thrift Society

The amount outstanding however, shows a different picture. While for number of loans, thrift society accounts for around 50% for the amount, they account only for 25% both in urban and rural. This is because of relatively small size of loans given by the thrift societies. In the urban areas, Friends and other account for a little more than 40% of total, while in 60% in urban areas and a little more than 50% in rural areas are drawn from non-institutional sources.

Per loan amount given by thrift society is the least both in urban and rural areas. In urban areas, loans outstanding against friends and others shows maximum amount per loan followed by professional moneylender. In rural areas, per loan outstanding against Professional money lender is maximum followed closely by agriculturist and village merchant. On an average, per loan outstanding is higher in urban as compared to rural areas.

Loans outstanding by occupational groups

In urban areas, 66% of loans outstanding are against the artisan group. The rest are accounted for by petty traders, salaried employees and others. Of the total loans outstanding in respect of artisans, more than 50% are to thrift society and 25% to banks. Among non-institutional sources, professional money lender and friends and others are important sources of finance. Thrift society is the single largest credit agency against which loans are outstanding for every occupational group.

In the rural areas, landed agricultural labour and landless agricultural labour are almost in equal numbers. Artisans form the next important group. As in case of urban areas, thrift society is the single major agency for all occupational groups. Its importance is much more in case of landless agricultural labour for whom 64% of the total loans are found to be outstanding against thrift society. In fact, it is the only institution against which loans are outstanding in case of landles agricultural labour. Banks are found to cater to a small number of landed agricultural labour and a significant number of artisans. Among the non- institutional source of credit, village merchant followed by Friends and others are important agencies. Professional money lenders are less significant in rural areas as compared to urban areas. Commission agents are found only against landed agricultural labour.

As regards the amount in urban areas, 69% of the total loans outstanding are against artisans group. Next important category is petty traders, whose loans outstanding account for 20%. Between these two groups, 90% of loans outstanding are accounted for. In the loans outstanding against artisans and petty traders, thrift societies account only for a minor share. Both artisans and petty traders could obtain a significant share from the banks and friends and others. their dependence on professional money lenders is considerably less. The loans outstanding against salaried employees under thrift society form a higher proportion as compared to corresponding proportion to total.

Current Borrowings: Thrift Society as Major source of loans

The preceding account on loans outstanding reflect the current position of indebtedness whatsoever be the year in which loan was taken. Borrowings reflect the loans taken during July 1992-June 1993, and give a better picture of the share of each agency. In urban areas, out of 60 respondents, 48 or 80% are borrowers. Of the 48 borrowers, more than 75% borrowed from thrift society. Reliance on thrift society only is much more in urban arca than in rural area. Banks played a minor role in urban areas. The urban poor are found to have less access to banks than rural poor. This is because of operation of DRDA and DWACRA in rural areas which help the rural poor to obtain loans from banks. In the rural areas, more than 40% of the members were borrowers. Of these, 64% borrowed from thrift society. Thus, both in urban and rural areas, thrift society has emerged as the major source of loaning. The society wise picture of borrowings shows the dominance of thrift society as a loaning agency. In the amounts also, the dominance of thrift society is seen in the overall as well as society level, both in urban and rural areas. As is to be expected, amount per loan borrowed from thrift society is smaller as compared to loans from other sources.

Current Borrowings: The share of Thrift Society in Total amount

But, when amounts are considered, we see a different picture. Thrift society accounts for a minor share both in urban and rural areas. Nationalized banks have the prominence. The role of institutional sources is however, minor, in both urban and rural areas. This is because of the fact that amount of loan per borrower from thrift society is smaller.

Current Borrowings by Occupational Groups

Considering borrowings by occupational groups, landless agricultural labour do not have any access to banks. Their only source is thrift society. Even landed agricultural labour have limited access to banks. Artisans are found to have better access to banks, thanks to support by DRDA and DWACRA. What is to be noted is thrift society stands out as the only institutional agency catering to the poorest of rural society. Even so, for landed agricultural labour, 10 out of 22 loans are obtained from non-institutional sources. The major non-institutional sources for landless agricultural labour is Village merchant. For landless agricultural labour, even access to non-institutional sources is found to be limited. Village merchants do not lend as much to landles agricultural labour. Agriculturists lend only to a very small proportion of landless agricultural labour. Friends and others form a significant proportion among non-institutional sources.

It needs to be recognized that, though thrift society has emerged as an important loan agency for agricultural labour, a significant per cent of this group continue to rely on non-institutional sources. Comparatively, the reliance of artisans on non- institutions is much less.

Economic Impact: Reduced cost of Credit
High rates of interest as Cause of Poverty

The poor and the assetless pay high rates of interest on the loans they borrow. As a result, they are left with little surplus for reinvestment. The rates of interest paid on emergency needs of the poor are even much higher. Little access to credit combined with high rate of interest perpetuate conditions of poverty. Poor access to credit also serves as a constraint to shift of labour into self-employment, for, self-employment requires not only labour but also raw material. Access to credit should be preceded by access to raw materials. Further, those without property can neither offer a collateral, nor obtain raw material. Even if they manage to obtain credit from non-institutions, it is at an exorbitant rate of interest. Due to high rate of interest to be paid to a money lender, a self-employed person also becomes a wage labourers. A self-employed skilled weaver, sooner or later, turns into a wage labourer for a moneyed man, who owns about a dozen looms, as he cannot keep himself afloat as an independent weaver under adverse financial circumstances. As a labourer, he receives a wage only, whereas as a self-employed person, he could earn a little more than wage, as his wife and child also participate in the work. A poor woman who is traditionally hired by a farmer's family to dehusk paddy, receives a pound of broken rice and a meal of leftovers for a physically exhausting day's work. For the same work, if she had financial resources to buy and process paddy herself at reasonable rates of interest, she could earn more. Mohammed Yunus of Grameena Bank, Bangladesh writes, "If a woman who weaves bamboo baskets, jute mats and sleeping mats did not have to borrow from trade to buy inputs, she could sell outputs at fair price and perhaps double the income. If petty traders or petty producers, who have to borrow at 10% per month, per week or per day could borrow at community rates, they could earn a higher return on their investment. In each of the above cases, under existing circumstances, there is no chance for the poor to improve their economic base and thereby increase income, because the existing system makes it absolutely certain that the income is kept perpetually at such a low level and nothing can ever be saved and invested for economic base to expand." He continues, "If the control of financial resources can be loosened, the poor can, at the very least, enjoy fruits of their labour, expand the economic base, live their lives with dignity and look forward to building better lives for themselves."

Rates of interest on Institutional and Non- institutional loans in Cuddappah district

In the light of the need for access to credit at reasonable rate of interest, we examine the cost of credit for sample households in Cuddappah area. The non-institutional sources are professional money lender, village merchant, commission agent, agriculturist and friends and others. Of these sources, commission agent and agriculturist played a very small role. The single major source of finance among non- institutions is friends and others followed by village merchant and professional money lender. When borrowings are classified by rate of interest from non- institutional sources, they belong to four groups, a)Nil, b)24%, c)36% and d)40%. Around 60% of total loans borrowed from non-institutional sources are obtained at an interest rate of 24%. Around 14% of loans are borrowed at rate of 40%, while at the other end, 8% are borrowed interest-free. There were four cases of tied credit, all by agricultural labour with land. In all these cases, there was a linkage between product and credit market. The money was borrowed for working capital The explicit cost is 24% while the implicit cost, when lower price received under conditions of tied credit is considered, is much more.

Rate of Interest and size of Loan

Those who enter into smaller transactions of loan amount pay higher price. The negative relationship between the size of loan and the rate of interest also holds in respect of each group. But, the correlation coefficient between the two is not found to be significant.

Non-institutional loans by occupations and Rate of interest

Considering number of loans by occupational groups and rate of interest, 15 out of 16 loans borrowed by agricultural labour are at interest rate of 24% or more. Among artisans, 13 out of 15 loans, among petty traders, 2 out of 3 are at interest rate of 24% or more.

In terms of amount, 71.2% of amount borrowed by agricultural labour, 78% borrowed by artisans, around 80% by petty traders, 91% by salaried employees are at rate of 24%. Per loan amount is negatively associated with rate of interest not only in average but also under each occupational group.

Impact of Thrift Society on the cost of Credit

The weighted rate of interest charged by non- institutional sources for each occupational category is studied. The weighted rate of interest is arrived at by dividing total interest amount paid by each group by the total amount borrowed from non-institutional sources. The weighted interest ranges from 22% for artisans to 40% for others. The difference between rate of interest on non-institutional loans and thrift society ranges from 4% to 22%. The gain from thrift society is calculated by multiplying the amount lent by the society with the difference between and weighted rate of interest on the non-institutional sources and the interest rate charged by the thrift society. This is based on the assumption that, had there been no thrift society, the loanees would have to pay market rate of interest. The gain to loanee is related to the total cost on all borrowings.

The per cent gain thus estimated, varies from 8.32% in case of artisans to 37.75% in the case of others. Agricultural labour show a gain around 13% on the total cost. The extent of gain depends upon two factors: 1)the difference between market rate and rate of thrift society and 2)share of thrift society in total amount borrowed and cost thereof. If difference is large, the percent gain is large; if share is large and difference being same, the percent gain is large.

The gain from thrift society would appear smaller than the actual gain estimated by these procedures. One should expect a fall in market rate of interest with progress of thrift society and narrowing of difference. In fact, with progress of credit groups in Cuddappah area, market rate of interest appears to have come down. Therefore, the gain from thrift society, by way of reduction in cost of borrowing should be said to be larger than what is indicated in the table.

To examine this position, we looked at the rates of interest before members had access to thrift society. The weighted rate of interest on amount of loans outstanding before members joined thrift society was 36%, while for loans outstanding as on date of investigation, corresponding rate was 25%. As hypothesized, the improved access to credit resulted in reduction in rates of interest charged by the money lenders. A gain for borrowers is not the difference between the rate of interest currently obtaining from non-institutional sources and corresponding rate charged by thrift society, but the rate that would have prevailed in the absence of thrift society and the rate charged by thrift society. The gain for borrower for Rs.100/- borrowed from thrift society is not Rs.7/- but Rs.11/-.

The weighted rate of interest paid by each occupational group on loans outstanding before they had access to thrift society was examined. With the exception of salaried employees, who could get credit at 20% interest rate, in all other cases, range of rate of interest was from 35% to 48%. The artisans paid weighted interest rate of 40%, agricultural labour paid a weighted rate of 35%. If we assume that these interest rates would have continued in the absence of improved access to credit, the gain to agricultural labour from borrowings from thrift society is Rs.17/- per 100/- borrowed, while for artisans, the gain is Rs.22/- per 100/- borrowed. Given these wide differences, the gains to both the groups over the cost that would have been incurred in the absence of fall in interest rates would be much higher.

Lessons for Women's Economic Empowerment

Women's Thrift Credit Societies (WTCS), organised under the sponsorship of Cooperative Development Foundation (CDF), Hyderabad, have been functioning successfully for nearly a decade. These should be of interest to policy makers concerned with poverty alleviation since they emerged as the only credit organisations serving the needs of the poor women in rural areas. Their unique methods of operation, including democratic functioning, have contributed to their success.

In the dark environment of credit indiscipline, the WTCs have emerged as torch-bearers of credit discipline, thrift and self-reliance. Their progress may be slow and halting. But they offer the only hope that is available to the poorest of the poor in obtaining access to credit. In performing this function, they have also emerged as training grounds in economic democracy for women9Parthasarathy 1995).

The economic empowerment of women requires transfer of skills of management and control of the economic activities to the women's groups over a period of time, to enable women to feel confident and empowered. With women slowly gaining control and being involved in the decision making of various aspects affecting them directly, and as members of the society, real empowerment will emerge and a change in women's status will certainly take place. From the women's empowerment perspective, it is important that the women's economic activities are economically viable and the capacities and competencies of poor women, individually and collectively, are enhanced to organise and manage the economic activity. The real challenge is to be able to link and move beyond women's involvement and struggle through economic activities, where they are basically involved in trying to cope with the existing market systems in a better manner, to a process of being involved in the struggle against the exploitative forces. Empowerment in the real sense would be attained when women are actively involved in the larger struggle for social change.

CHAPTER VII
SUMMARY AND CONCLUSIONS

Women's empowerment is a global issue, and discussions on women's political rights are at the forefront of many formal and informal campaigns worldwide. The concept of women's empowerment appears to be the outcome of several important critiques and debates generated by the women's movement throughout the world, and particularly by Third World feminists. Its source can be traced to the interaction between feminism and the concept of "popular education" developed in Latin America in the 1970s.

Kamala Bhasin asks the question **why women need to be empowered?** They need to be empowered, she believes, because women have and will lead us in our search for a world free of violence and war. Women have led the peace and ecology movements in many parts of the world. She believes that sustainable development has to be woman centered. She does not say this because she is a women or a feminist. Historically and even today women take care of the basic needs of society like food, fodder, fuel, shelter, nurturing. They are also more in tune with nature. As child-bearers they have had to be more in tune with their own nature. They have also been creating and nurturing. She does not say that. It is because of women's socialization for centuries, and because of their pre-occupation with sustenance, nurturing, nursing.

Empowerment in its simplest form means the manifestation of redistribution of power that challenges patriarchal ideology and the male dominance. It is both a process and the result of the process. It is transformation of the structures or institutions that reinforces and perpetuates gender discrimination. It is a process that enables women to gain access to and control of, material as well as information resources. The concept of women's empowerment, throughout the world, has its roots in women's movement. It is since the mid 1980s that this term became popular in the field of development, especially in reference to women. In India, it is the Sixth Five Year Plan (1980-85) which can be taken as a landmark for the cause of women. It is here that the concept of women and development was introduced for the first time. It was realized that no more piecemeal strategies but an integrated approach would deliver the desired goods. The realistic and regenerative developmental efforts in the direction of progress, in terms of economic independence for women and educational advancement of them is what would answer the basic questions raised for empowering women.

Karl feels that, Empowerment is a word widely used, but seldom defined. Long before the world became popular, women were speaking about gaining control over their lives, and participating in the decisions that affect them in the home and community, in government and international development government and international development policies. The word 'empowerment' captures this sense of gaining control, of participating, of decision making. More recently, the word has entered the vocabulary of development agencies, including international organizations and the United Nations.

According to **Pillai** "Empowerment is an active, multi-dimensional process which enables women to realize their full identity and powers in all spheres of life. Power is not a commodity to be transacted; nor can it be given away as aims. "power has to be acquired and once acquired, it needs to be and once acquired, it needs to be exercised, sustained and preserved".

Empowerment is a process and is not, therefore, something that can be given to people. The process of empowerment is both individual and collective, since it is through involvement in groups that people most often begin to develop their awareness and the ability to organize to take action and bring about change. Women's empowerment can be viewed as a continuum of several interrelated and mutually reinforcing components:

- Awareness building about women's situation, discrimination, and rights and opportunities as a step towards gender equality. Collective awareness building provides a sense of group identify and the power of working as a group.
- Capacity building and skills development, especially the ability to plan, make decisions, organize, manage and carry out activities, to deal with people and institutions in the world around them.
- Participation and greater control and decision-making power in the home, community and society.
- Action to bring about greater equality between men and women.

In short, **empowerment is a process of awareness and capacity building leading to greater participation, to greater decision-making power and control, and to transformative action.**

The core of the **Women's Empowerment Framework** is its argument that women's development can be viewed in terms of five levels of equality, of which empowerment in an essential element at each level. The levels, according to **Longwe** are **welfare, access, conscientisation, participation** and **control**.

1. **WELFARE,** the first level, address only the basic needs of women, without recognizing or attempting to solve the underlying structural causes, which necessitate provision of welfare services. At this point, women are merely passive beneficiaries of welfare benefits.

2. **ACCESS,** the second level, is essential for women to make meaningful progress. The involves equality of access to resources, such as education opportunities, land and credit. The path of empowerment is initiated when women recognize their lack of access to resources as a barrier to their growth and overall well-being, and take action to address this.

3. **CONSCIENTIZATION** is a crucial point in the Empowerment Framework. For women to take appropriate action to dose gender gaps or gender inequalities, there must be recognition that their problems stem form inherent structural and institutional discrimination. They must also recognize the role they can often play in reinforcing the system that restricts their growth.

4. **PARTICIPATION** is the point where women are taking decisions alongside men equally. To reach this level, however, mobilization is necessary. By organising themselves and working collectively, women will be empowered aim increased representation, which will lead to increased empowerment and ultimately greater control.

5. **CONTROL** is the ultimate level of equality and empowerment. Here, the balance of power between men and women is equal: and neither party has dominance over the other. At this stage in the Empowerment Framework, women are able to make decisions over their lives, and the lives of their children, and play an active role in the development process. Further, the contributions of women are fully recognized and rewarded.

Since empowerment is a necessary part of any intervention to enhance women's income, it is essential, as given in the book 'Work and Empowerment' - Management of Women's Economic Activities: a Manual for Activists, New Delhi(1991), to understand some of the **critical tenets** of empowerment. These are :

Collectivization

Bringing a group of women together at a base to become an integral part of an economic activity is an important part of the strategy towards their empowerment. The coming together of poor women provides then an identity which is different from their other identities and helps highlight their worker role. It also provides them a sense of belonging in a totally different power equation - that is, of mutuality. Both of these are empowering experiences in themselves. For providing support to each other, the group of women can met periodically and there is a reference available for each group of women can meet periodically and there is reference available for each woman. For bargaining and negotiating activities, like bulk buying and selling, bulk acquisition, credit and other facilities, necessary for economic activities, collectivization can be there. This collectivization also brings in the possibility of pooling and sharing resources, skills, time-frames, space and other facilities. Pooling is an important way of strengthening the capacities of the poor women to work together and to develop a sense of strength.

Capacity Building

Once women start coming together, the next step is to enhance their capacity tot work as a group and play different roles, necessary for development and maintenance of the group. It is important from the point of view of empowerment that women are not only capable of functioning as a group but also are able to effectively participate in the process of economic activity undertaken by the group of women.

Capacity building of women in the areas of planning, executing and monitoring all aspects of the economic activity is equally desired in this context. This will include capacity to use legal framework to their advantage and the capacity to build as well as sustain a culture of the economic activity compatible with the realities of the women involved and to the nature of their activity.

Ownership and Control

Once women start acquiring the capacity to work as a group, planning, executing and monitoring the activities, the issue of taking control over the whole activity becomes critical. A sense of belonging and owing good and bad consequences of their own activity, is the first step in the direction. It implies that women being to consider the group and the group activity as their own activity, is the first step in that direction. It implies that women being to consider the group and the group activity as their own. Taking responsibility of more and more functions in the entire process of economic activity helps them gain control over their ventures. So, managing different components, apart from operational aspects of activity, like record-keeping, accounts-keeping, handling cash, being signatory to bank accounts, etc., are helpful in building this control.

Mediation

Another important aspect of empowerment of women is to strengthen their capacities to mediate with the external world, Mediation entails relating with the outside world, with the markets, with financial institutions, with competitors, with suppliers, with a host of policy-makers and other important segments of external environment, i.e., politicians, bureaucrats, officials, etc. Mediation also requires mediating with experts, with those who can provide some technical assistance in the conduct of the economic activity. Women's sense of empowerment gets a concrete base and mediation becomes an integral part of women's work in that economic activity.

Working towards the empowerment of a group of poor women is an ongoing and gradual process, which cannot be short-circuited under any circumstance. Therefore it is important that these different aspects are dealt with through a series of carefully planned and deliberately made interventions over a period of time, keeping specific requirements of a particular group and the economic venture it has undertaken, in mind.

No one magic formula or fail-safe design exists for empowerment. Nonetheless, experience clearly shows that empowerment strategies must intervene at the level of women's "condition" while also transforming their "position", thus simultaneously addressing both practical and strategic needs.

Several elements appear essential to challenge patriarchal ideology, and to enable poor women to gain greater access to and control over both material and informational resources. Although these elements are set out below in a particular sequence, they may be reversed or interchanged. Or several may be undertaken concurrently, depending on the context.

An organisation concerned with bringing about women's empowerment must begin by locating the geopolitical region (urban or rural) in which it wants to work, and identifying the poorest and most oppressed women in that area. Activists then have to be selected and trained. Intensive preparatory training is critical. It must impart to activists an awareness of the structures and sources of power, especially gender. It must equip them with skills needed to mobilize, while learning from, the women whose consciousness they plan to raise.

In general, female activists are preferable, since they are in a better position to initiate the empowerment process with other women, notwithstanding differences in class. Caste, or educational background. In the field, the activists encourage women to set aside a separate time and space for themselves as disempowered women rather than as passive observers.

Perhaps one of the clearest indicators of women's empowerment is an increase in women's capacities and willingness to support other women and to work diligently toward strengthening women in their efforts to survive or to gain equality .It is only through acknowledging women's and men's interdependency in constructive ways that women can enter into more powerful exchanges with men in society at large . Women's collective actions necessary to deal effectively with such important issues as violence against women ,and the persistence of patriarchy in welfare states.

The probability of realizing women's freedom is increased through their awareness of the plight and possibilities they share with other women . When women are able to organize their efforts around crucial goals, such as changing particular values (e.g., prejudice against nontraditional feminine values) or specific behavior (e.g., discriminatory practices against women) in wider society , women's empowerment will be realized more effectively.

It is impossible to even think of affecting the situation of the poor people in today's economy. The forces against the poor are so many and the social system so biased in favour of the rich that it will not respond to the demands of the individual poor woman. In the economy, the various forces that work against the poor are highly organised, It is so for the poor self employed workers, as well as the poor women workers, who are not organised as workers. To overcome the constraints and effectively use the space, that is, to be empowered, it is necessary for women to organise themselves.

The process of empowerment involves not just an improvement in physical and social conditions, but also equal participation in decision-making processes, control over resources and mechanisms for sustaining these gains.

In this context, **Longwe's** classification of the five levels of empowerment, namely, welfare, access, conscientisation, participation and control, and the need to move from the level of welfare to control, is a useful one. As one moves towards higher levels of empowerment, however, there is bound to be resistance and conflict, as exclusive male privileges are threatened . The enemy, in a sense, is not 'one' capitalist, but many landlords, trades, contractors, the police, law, municipal service and other state structures, that do not recognize the existence of these women as individuals and workers.

Organising is a slow and continuous process of enabling a group of people to perceive common interests and act collectively. The social activists and those working in the voluntary organisations, who are working with poor women, are organising them in some way or the other. When we are trying to affect the income levels, we are organising women around work issues directly. Organising around work has both occupational and locational aspects. Occupational aspects involve dealing with the specific problems of each occupation separately and focussing on specific occupations as the basis of organising people.. Locational aspects involve dealing with the issues of particular geographical locations and focussing on the specific needs of that area as the basis of organising people. We try to take into the variety of activities that poor women do to understand how we can organise them around work.

By understanding the various occupations in which poor women workers are engaged we are able to recognize the multiple occupational base of poor women workers as well . And this helps strengthen their positioning these occupations by organizing them around work. The problems they face in these occupation become issues for bringing them together. The problems of women in the same occupations across different locations become a focus when the numerical strength of women is necessary for collective action.

It is clear that positive change in the lives of poor women is not possible without organised pressure from the women themselves. Organisation with conscientisation then emerges as the key strategy to strength the hands of weak, vulnerable and isolated women, and prevent their continued subordination in society in the initial stages, however, poor womens organisations need support, or they can collapse. If they do collapse it is doubly difficult to motivate them to overcome all their constraints the second time round, as they also carry the weight of their previous experience with them. It is hence important to consciously develop leadership amongst the local women. Along with this there need to be structures to ensure democratic functioning, participation in decision-making and conflict resolution.

The gains, can, however, be sustained only by adopting a combination of strategies, ranging from policy reform to the elimination of discriminatory legislation in access and control over resources, more responsive state structures and services to provisions for relief and support in reproductive tasks.

A major implication for women workers organisation is the need to bridge the gap between micro insights and macro plans. The benefits of micro-organising are clear, but the issues raised need wider acceptance to bring about sustainable changes in economic and social relations. There is a need to link local struggles with large-scale political and economic processes. Sector- based organisation facilitates this process to an extent, by enabling common issues to be raised. Training, policy protection and building up a supportive social climate are also helpful steps.

In addition, there is a need for constant innovation, for strategies to be dynamic and responsive to changing local, national and international situations. They can range from legal battles to grassroots organisation, from providing alternative organizational forms such as cooperatives to building broad-based alliances, from conflict to cooperation, with a view to combining the practical and strategic interests of these womens groups.

What all this really points towards is that with a gradual shift in perspective from welfare to empowerment, the role of womens organisations is no longer restricted to influencing state policies, but encompasses handling cultural struggles, confronting the power structures in tradition, religion, class and gender as well. To be able to do so, members of the organisation need to have strong stakes and a deep commitment to it.

The disadvantages facing women are many. To confront them, a broad-based, large-scale movement of womens is required. If this broader political dimension is kept in mind, the direction for organizational strategies would necessarily be towards building a strong base at the grassroots, with women involved in the strategic decision-making processes, along with lobbying for recognition and positive policies at the local, national and international levels.

Literacy among women opens the possibility of unlimited exposure to new information and more importantly to new ways of thinking and new perspectives on existing information. Also literate women are able to constructively express their talents and give direction to their aptitudes. This enables them to lead a life which is mote fulfilling and satisfying.

Literacy among women leads to better hygiene improved nutrition practices an greater effectiveness in caring for family health and seeking timely medical intervention. This not only leads to better health status for the woman herself but improved maternal competence lowers infant morality. Better health status of the women makes her a more productive worker both at home and outside, leading the way to her **equality and empowerment.**

Female education also leads to later age of marriage and smaller desired family size by enabling women to take decisions to control their fertility. Further education can enhance their knowledge about contraception thus giving them choice in spacing and number of children and release them from continuous child-rearing and child-bearing. Women thus have more control over how their time is spent and are able to participate more freely in productive work outside the home. Studies have shown that an extra year of schooling for girls reduces fertility rates by about 5-10 per cent. A study on Gender and Poverty in India 1989, has found that the fertility of illiterate women in different age groups is between 30 to 50 per cent higher than that of literate women.

Infant mortality is less among children of educated women and their surviving children are healthier and better educated. The infant mortality rate of Indian children whose mothers are illiterate. Thus education of women emancipates them from wasteful child-bearing thus giving them more time to participate in market activities.

Educated women also make better use of their time. A study in urban south India found that higher education among women led to a reduction in the time they spend in non-market household activities which often go unrecognised. Thus education of women moves them from the non-monetized to the monetized sector, invisible to the visible and unpaid to paid activities thus allowing them to participate directly in household economy. This in turn enhances their status and decision making power within the family which is a major step towards their **equality and empowerment**.

Illiterate women and women with a minimal of education continue to be concentrated in low-paying low-end occupations mostly in the informal sector which not only offers little security but also makes them vulnerable to exploitation by being denied, for e.g., minimum wages; equal pay for equal work; leave benefits etc. Also for most such women there is almost no occupational mobility due to restricted choices in the type of work they can get. A majority of these women are found to be concentrated in domestic or personal service. According to the Census of India, the urban female work participation rate was abysmally low - a mere 7.29 per cent in 1981 which rose marginally and became 8.07 in 1991 census. This clearly indicates that women have not been able to increase their participation rate in formal, 'visible' or monetized sector of work. Conversely women are participating in the work force in the informal, 'invisible' or non-monetized sector and hence are not getting due recognition. Literacy is critical in enhancing women's economic choices by way of improved access to paid employment and higher earnings. Also literacy among women will help in drawing them away from the exploitative informal sector and give them more recognition for their work both at the household and national level.

Literacy levels of high school and above among women supported by vocational training can go a long way in helping women get out of low-skilled jobs which are extensions of domestic work and equip them to take up jobs requiring specific skills which would be better paying and less exploitative. A study of developing countries including India reveals that an additional year of schooling can increase a woman's future earnings by about 15 per cent compared with 11 per cent for a man. Further, low levels of literacy among women leads to their unequal situation in the labour market *vis-à-vis* men by way of reduced earnings and unequal pay for equal work; lack of access to credit which is a barrier to attaining independence and widening choices; and in absence of economic independence lack of status and power in the family. Literacy of women would lead to more and better economic opportunities and hence better income levels which in turn would lead to **equality and empowerment of women**.

If women are in labour force, then even a small amount of education greatly increases their earnings. In India studies have shown that even literacy without completed primary schooling results in higher earnings and that middle school qualifications double women's returns from labour. Education also helps women move out of agricultural labour into non-household manufacturing and service occupations in the modern sector. Just as literacy increases economic opportunities, school attendance familiarises girls with non-family social-settings and increases their skills and confidence to engage in productive work outside the home more competitively. They are better equipped to link into non-traditional work situations and compete with men in the fast paced labour market.

Self employment is a major sector of employment where poor women are concentrated. But in most cases the scale of operation is small and the consequent returns minuscule. If such poor women are educated, they would be in a position to take credit from banks or financial institutions which offer loans to this group of people. Such loans at present are not being fully utilised due to lack of knowledge among the women and insecurity felt by the lending institution(s) due to illiteracy of the borrower. if at all such loans are being taken, they are being awarded to the man inspire of the fact that experience in many countries has demonstrated that poor women invest money more wisely, make sound decisions to maximise returns and are more conscientious in returning the loans. Access to credit is one of the key elements in empowering women and in enabling them to participate in market opportunities.

Education of women will place them on an equal footing with men in decision-making positions in economic and political fields. **Empowerment of women through education** will lead to their greater participation in government and community institutions and better entrepreneurial opportunities. More women in parliament and cabinets, chief executive officers in major corporations, top administrators, managers and civil servants will quicken the pace of progress towards **equality and empowerment**. Having women in top decision making positions will also lead to a better integration of women's concerns into the formulation of national policies and development plans which in turn would result in developing the full potential of women.

Making women literate and educate them are pre-requisites not only for their **equality and empowerment** but for the development of the nation. Women should intimately be linked to the life of a nation because any delay in their education and advancement can only translate education into an impediment for the development of the country. Women are the educators of the next generation. It is through them that innovations that help the communities can be introduced in order to enable women to take part more effectively in modern life.

Literacy and education of women can go a long way in making changes not only in the image women have of themselves but also the roles that they play within the society. It will help change the stereo-typed ideas people hold about women's roles and make it clear that the development of a country is linked to women's welfare and productivity as it is to man's. From the psycho-sociological point of view, it is more through the education of women than through the education of men, that changes in attitudes and behaviour necessary for a better adaptation to the modern world are achieved.

Despite strong linkages between women's education and their **equality and empowerment,** female literacy remains very low in India. This is especially the case in rural areas where only about 20-25 per cent of the adult women are literate this is less than half the rural male literacy rate and roughly one third the urban female literacy rate.

Literacy makes the horizon of vision wider and, at a more mundane level, helps to disseminate knowledge of a host of women's issues. Within the context of sustained educational inputs for women, understanding the relationship between literacy and education becomes crucial. How do we define literacy? When does literacy end and education being? Or, should such a demarcation be made at all?

Over the years, the target of eradicating the 'curse of illiteracy' has been the most important consideration for planners and administrators Knowledge of the three R's is seen as an important stepping some towards reaching out to development process. While radical definitions of literacy - where literacy is seen as a tool or weapon to question existing structures of power - are increasingly invading policy documents, most literacy initiatives continue to be caught in the never- ending spiral of maintaining regular attendance, reducing drop-out rates and assessing the levels of the learners. Acquiring literacy skills becomes their primary focus of basic literacy programmes.

Usually, the basic literacy phase is followed by a post-literacy phase which concentrates on arresting replace, strengthening fragile literacy skills and visualizing how literacy may be applied by learners in their specific environments. The shift to development issues is seen as following the initial literacy inputs. The post-literacy phase in thus left to cope with questions of power, information and mainstreaming of marginalized groups.

The underlying assumption in this approach is that learning is a linear process akin to the manner in which learning is structured within the formal school system for children. It is a graded system where progress is recorded in a linear manner - technical acquisition of literacy and numeracy skills are taken care of in the lower classes, and acquiring competencies of self-expression, analytical abilities and independent learning are left for the higher classes.

Women, unlike children, have a rich indigenous information base, highly developed analytical abilities and an understanding of their lived realities. These considerations are ignored in most adult education programmes. Adopting this linear approach for adult women invariably results in their dropping-out from literacy classes in large numbers, after the first flush of enthusiasm. Further, the demands of survival related tasks and labour-intensive coping mechanisms make the sustained and prolonged acquisition of literacy skills a burden and a chore for the women. Since women are central and primarily responsible for these activities, they are most vulnerable to recording irregular attendance and high drop-out rates in literacy programmes. Thus, when the primary focus of adult education programmes limits itself to the acquisition of literacy skills, thereby delinking literacy and education, it decontextualises the meaning of education in their lives. Therefore, it is important to recognize that women's demand for education does not being or limit itself to literacy. Literacy is only one of the elements in the larger process of education, and not necessarily the first.

A strong impetus for promoting women's education comes from the link that has been made between female literacy and quality of life. Numerous empirical studies have brought our the positive correlation between women's literacy and certain indicators of women's status. The Kerala experience is a lucid example of how women's education has lowered child mortality and birth rates, besides improving the sex- ratio in the State. Indeed female literacy is 'so strongly associated with reduced fertility and decreased infant and child morality that it is accepted as a causal factor.' This was the conclusion reached in a recent WHO sponsored study on a comparative analysis of morality, per capita income and educational levels. Female participation in primary education corresponded closely to lowered morality rates.

However, this link between fertility and literacy for women holds within it the danger of women being bound within their reproductive role. It does not make visible the crucial productive work that hinges itself on women's labour. As we have argued in the beginning of this paper, given the centrality of women's role in performing survival tasks, literacy or education for women cannot by-pass this area of their lives.

It is evident, therefore, that strategies and structures that enable children or men to learn cannot be replicated for women. It is to this that review of the New Education Policy draws attention. As we know, education in itself is not necessarily liberating. It has also played a role in maintaining and reinforcing hierarchies. The review criticizes narrow attempts - like changes in training, redesigning curriculum and giving preference to female teachers - within formal and non-formal education efforts to bring about women's participation in education. The review states clearly that only through the process of empowering women can the objective of education be achieved.

However, over the years **empowerment** has now become a development buzzword. It is used by different sets of social actors - women, minority groups, academics, development agencies and even the government - who define it for themselves in a myriad ways. So the issue that must be addressed is - who define it for really mean when we talk about empowering education?

Bringing the concept of empowerment within the realm of education changes the definition and content of education. Empowerment, within a framework of women's education emerges from a live interaction between the Frierien model of people's participation and popular education, and deminist theory and praxis. In working out an alternative politics for daily life, the feminist movement in the 70s rejected the welfarist attitude of the State vis-à-vis education. They critiqued the existing education system as one that was promoting patriarchal systems of knowledge and reinforcing gender stereotypes. The growth of the movement saw women's groups constructing alternative systems of knowledge through an articulation of women's experiences, information systems and skills. Government run literacy programmes were thus suspect and were seen as a means of co-opting the poor and women into the existing hierarchical system. Women's literacy was therefore a non-priority area for the women's movement. Violence against women, dowry and rape related legislation, recognition of women's work and equal wages because the areas of struggle and contestation.

It was only in the mid-80s that conscientization and literacy found a link within adult education initiatives. Many experiments based on Friere's concept of the liberating potential of literacy were carried out. Within the women's movement the end of the women's decade (1975-85) brought a crystallization of theories, strategies and debates on gender as a category and as a means of protest and change. This process gave birth to the concept of **empowerment**.

Empowerment was defined as a process by which women gain greater control over resources (income, knowledge, information, technology, skill training), challenge the ideology of patriarchy and hence participate in leadership, decision making processes. Within the area of education a creative tension emerged between women's experiential knowledge and formal systems of knowledge. Access to information and literacy became part of women's attempt at redistributing power. Simultaneously, education got intion got infused with or broadened its objectives to one that would:

- enhance the self-image of women
- encourage women to become active participants in the process of change.
- build collective and alternative visions of their lived environment.
- question injustice and inequality.
- help women develop the skills to assert themselves.

One important criticism of the focus on **empowerment** is that it relegates the responsibility of initiating change, raising question and taking initiative on to the poor. What is the role of the State in this process- whether it is the local elite, the administration, the political parties and the social institutions and ideologies that define, bind and control the realities of the poor or women. What all the case studies point to is the role of different agencies in facilitating or in providing the time and space for the women to articulate their own need for learning and to move from a position of passive acceptance to active participation.

All the case studies also make this clear that irrespective of what the take off point is education and literacy becomes integral to sustaining and vitalizing these changes. Literacy at times becomes the by-product of other processes, such as organizing, agitating, skill building etc. These various processes may run parallel to each other, but they become self-sustaining and irreversible when they converge, and thereby alter the balance of power.

When we discuss the role of women, we emphasise on changing the equilibrium of social forces to treat them as equal partners in the society and to bring recognition to all their roles. When our concern is with the poor women, we are seized of changing both social and economic forces in favour of their worker-role in particular and other roles in general. Such a perception of poor women's work places, their empowerment as the central thrust of the desired goal, which is beyond increase in income levels, and , in financial terms. Empowerment entails struggle; it entails learning to deal with the forces of oppression; it entails having a vision of a new society; it also entails conscious and deliberate interventions and efforts to enhance the quality of life. Empowerment in this context entails gradually increasing control of poor women over the entire economic process and not merely as producers of some products and services which are otherwise controlled through other intermediaries. Transplanting alien activities which do not have the long-term regenerative and self-sustaining potential do not make the kind of activities that lead to empowerment. Thus, economic intervention is posited not only for enhanced income but also for increased empowerment of the poor women.

The economic empowerment of women requires transfer of skills of management and control of the economic activities to the women's groups over a period of time, to enable women to feel confident and empowered. With women slowly gaining control and being involved in the decision making of various aspects affecting them directly, and as members of the society, real empowerment will emerge and a change in women's status will certainly take place. From the women's empowerment perspective, it is important that the women's economic activities are economically viable and the capacities and competencies of poor women, individually and collectively, are enhanced to organise and manage the economic activity. The real challenge is to be able to link and move beyond women's involvement and struggle through economic activities, where they are basically involved in trying to cope with the existing market systems in a better manner, to a process of being involved in the struggle against the exploitative forces. Empowerment in the real sense would be attained when women are actively involved in the larger struggle for social change.

BIBLIOGRAPHY

Akhtar, F. 1992. (*UBINIG*, an NGO engaged in empowerment of rural women, Dhaka). Personal communication.

Andersen, M. L. 1988. *Thinking about women: Sociological and feminist Perspectives.* 2nd ed. New York: Macmillan.

Anveshi, 1993. *Reworking gender relations, redefining politics; Nellore village women against arrack*, Hyderabad.

Apte, J. S. 1995. Education and Women's empowerment: *Indian Journal or Adult Education* . Vol. 56, No.3, July - September.

Bam B.H. and Sarkar L. 1976. *New perspectives for Third World Women*, The E.V. Mathew Memorial Lectures..

Bandura, A. 1981. *Self - referent thought :* A developmental analysis of self-efficacy. In J.H. Flavell & L. Ross, (Eds), *Social Logative development: Frontiers and Possible futures*, Cambridge University Press.

Bandura, Albert. 1986. *Social Foundation of Thought.* Englewood cliffs, NJ. Prentice - Hall.

Banerjee, N. 1989. 'Fruits of Development: Prickly Pears for Women', In K. Young (eds.) *Serving Two Masters: Third World women in Development.*, pp. 129-47. New Delhi: allied Publishers.

Barker, R.L. 1991. The Politics of Empowerment: *Social Work.* Vol.4, No.2, March.

Barton, R. 1984. *Cognitive and developmental aspects of empowerment: An empirical comparison between citizen leaders and non-leaders.* Published doctoral dissertation university of Oregon.

Batliwala, Srilatha. 1994. The Meaning of women's empowerment : New concepts from Action in Population Policies Reconsidered Health, Empowerment, and Rights, March (Harvard series on Population and International Health).

Batliwala, Srilatha. 1995. The Meaning of women's empowerment . *Women's World. pp.23-34.*

Beck, B. 1983. *Empowerment: A future goal of social work.* CSS Working Papers in Social Policy.

Bell, R. R. 1981. Worlds of friendship. Beverly Hills; Sage.

Berger, M. and M. Buvinic. 1989. *Women and Women Ventures: Assistance to the informal Sector in Latin America.* Connecticut:. Kumarian Press.

Berlin, S. & Kravitz. D. 1981. Women as victims: A feminist social work perspective. *Social Work*, 26, 447- 448.

Bernard, J. 1971. *Women and the public interest*. Chicago: Aldine.

Bhasin, Kamla. 1992. Education for women's empowerment: Some reflections: Adult Educational Development, March, Number-38.

Bhatt, E. 1987.'The Invisibility of Home-based Work: The Case of Piece-rate Workers in India', In A.M. Singh and A. Viitanen(eds.) Invisible Hands, pp.29-33, New Delhi. Sage.Bhatt,E.1989."Towards Empowerment", *World Development*, 17(7):1059-65.

Biegal, D. E. 1984. Help seeking and receiving in urban ethnic neighborhoods: Strategies for empowerment. In J. Rappaport et.al (Eds.). *Studies in Empowerment : Steps toward understanding and Action*. New York. The Haworth Press.

Blau, P,M. 1967. *Exchange and power in social life*. New York: Wiley.

Blumberg, Race Lesser. 1978. *Stratification: Socio-Economic and sexual Inequality*. Iowa City: William C. Brown.

Bock, S. 1980. Conscientization: Paolo Friere and class - based practice. Catalyst 2 (2).5 - 25.

Bose, Joe AGR, 1997, Organizing Self-Help Groups: the CASA experience, *Participation and Governance*, vol. 4, No.10, July'97

Bott, E. 1957. *Family and social network: Roles, norms and external relationships in ordinary urban families*. London: Tavistock publications.

Bricker - Jenkins, M., & Hooyman, N. 1986. Not for women only, Social work practice for a feminist future silver sprint, M.D: National Associate of Social Workers.

Bricker - Jenkins, M. & Hooyman, N. 1991. Feminist social work practice in clinical setting Beverly Hills, CA: Sage Publications.

Brownmiller. S. 1975. *Against our will: Men, women and rape*. New York: Simon and Schuster.

Brydon. L., and S. Chant. 1989. *Women in the Third World: Gender issues in rural and urban areas*. New Brunswick, N.J., Rutgers University Press.

Burghardt, S. 1982. *The other side of organising* . Cambridge, MA: Shenkaman Public Co.Inc.

Cancian, F. M .1987. *Love in America: Gender and self-development*. New York: Cambridge University Press.

Chandra, Shanti Kohli. 1997.Women and Empowerment. Indian Journal of Public administration. July-September . VOL..XLIII. No.3

Chen, M. 1989. 'A Sectoral Approach to Promoting Women's Work: Lessons from India. *World Development*, 17(7): 1007-16.

Chodorow, Nancy. 1978 . *The Reproduction of Mothering*. Berkley: University of California Press.

Craig, Gray, and Mayo, Marjorie (eds.) Community Empowerment, London & New Jersey, Zed Books, 1995

Charlton, S.E.M., Everett, J., Staudt, K. (Eds.). 1989. *Women, the state, and development*, Albany: State University of New York Press.

Checkoway, B. & Norseman, A. 1986. Empowering citizens with disabilities. Community Development 21,270 -271.

Chernin, K. 1981. *The obsession: Reflections on the tyranny of slenderness.* New York: Harper and Row.

Clarke, Michael, Stewart, John 1992. Empowerment. A theme for the 1990s. Local Government Studies. Vol. 18. No.2 (Summer). Published by Frank Cass London.

Coppola, M & Rivas, R. 1985. The task-action group technique: A Case Study of empowering the elderly . In M. Parnes(ed.). *Innovations in social group work feedback from practice to theory*, New York: Haworth Press.

Diaz-Diocaretz, M., & Zavala, I. M. (Eds.). 1985. *Women, Feminist identity and society in the 1980's : selected papers.* Philadelphia: John Benjamins Publishing Company.

De Lauretis, Teresa. *Technologies of Gender.* Bloomington: University of Indiana Press. 1987.

Deve Gowda, H.D., 1997, Ushering in a New era of Women's Empowerment, *Gramin Vikas*, April'97

Dubey, Muchkund (ed.) Indian Society Today : Challenges of Equality, Integration and Empowerment, New Delhi Har-Anand Publications, 1995

Dodd, Pamela, Guitterez, Lorraine 1990, Preparing students for the future: A power perspective on community practice: Administration in social work, Vol. 14 (2).

Dowling, C. 1982. *The Cinderella complex: Women's hidden fear of independence.* New York : Pocket Books

Durkheim, E. 1966. *Suicide.* New York: Free Press. (Original work published 1987).

Durkheim, E 1984. *The division of labour in society.* New York: Free Press. (Original work published 1983).

Emerson, R.M. 1982. Power - dependence relations American Sociological Review 27,31 - 40.

England, Paula and Irene Brown. 1990. "Internalization and Constraints in Gender Inequality". Paper presented at the XXIIth World Congress of the International Sociological Association, Madrid, July.

Epstein, C.F. & Coser, R.L. (Eds.) .1981. *Access to power: Cross-national studies of women and elite's* Boston: Allen and Unwin.

Epstein, Cynthia F. 1988 *Deceptive distinctions: Sex, gender and the Social Order.* New Haven, CT: Yale University Press and The Russell Sage Foundation..

Fagan. H. 1979. *Empowerment : Skills for Parish social Action*. New York Pauline Press.

Fitzpatrick, E. 1990. *Endless crusade: Women social scientists and progressive reform*. New York; Oxford University Press.

Foner, A., & Kertzer, D. 1978. Transition over the life course: lessons from age-set societies. *American Journal to Sociology*, 83, 1081 -1104.

Forgacs, D.(ed.). 1988. *An Antonio Gramsci reader; selected writings*, 1916-1935. New York: Schocken Books.

Fox, J. 1984. Social work ethics and children: Protection Vs. empowerment. *Children and Youth Services Review*. 6, 351 -359.

Fredland, D.L.. 1992. 'Empowering women in rural India: a Model for Development' In J.M. Bystydzienski(ed.), *Women Transforming Politics: Worldwide Strategies for Empowerment*, pp. 192-213. Indianapolis: Indian University Press.

French, J.R.P.Jr. & Raven, B. 1959. The bases of social power. In D. Cartwrigh (Ed.), S*tudies in social power*. Annn Arbor: Institute for Social Research, University of Michigan.

Friere, P. 1973. *Education for critical consciousness*. New York: Continum. French, J.R.P. Jr. & Raven, B. 1959. The bases of social power. In D.Cortwrigh (Ed. J Studies in Social Power. An Arbor: Institute for Social Research. University of Michigan.

Freire, P. 1973. *Pedagogy of the oppressed*. New York: Seabury Press.

Garvin, C. 1985. Work with disadvantaged and oppressed groups. In M. Sundel. P.Glasser, R. Sarri & R. Vinter (Eds.). Individual change through small groups and edition. New York. The Free Press.

Gerson, K. 1985. *Hard choices: How women decide about work, career. and motherhood*. Berkeley: University of California Press.

Gilbert G.R, and Nelson, A.E. Beyond Participative Management /Toward Total Employee empowerment for Quality, Quorum Books, 1991

Glassner, B., & Freedman, J.A. .1979. *Clinical sociology*. New York: Longman.

Gopalan Sarala, Women's Development - Paradigm Shift from Welfare to Empowerment, Social Welfare, 43(5) August 19096, p.32-33

Government of India. 1963. *Report on Social Education*. New Delhi: Government of India. Committee of Plan Projects

——— 1979. *Report of the National Board of Adult Education Committee on post literacy and follow -up programmes*. New Delhi. Ministry of Education and Social Change.

——— 1980. *Report of the Review Committee on the NAEP*. New Delhi. Government of India, Ministry of Education and culture.

——— 1991. *Report of the Group on Post Literacy and Continuing Education*. New Delhi: Government of India. Ministry of Human Resource

Development. National Literacy Mission.

Griffen, Vanessa (ed.) 1987. Women Development and empowerment : A Pacific Feminist Perspective, Asian and Pacific Development Centre Kuala Lumper, pp. 117-118.

Grown, C and J, Sebstad. 1989."Towards a Wider Perspective on women's Employment', *World Development.* 17(7): 937-52

Gutierrez, L. 1988. *Coping with stressful life events*; An empowerment perspective. Ann Arbor, MI: Michigan, School of Social Work.

Gutierrez, L. 1990. Working with women of colour: An empowerment perspective. Social Work, 35, 149 - 154.

Gutierrez, L & Drtega, R. 1991. Developing methods to empower Latinds: The importance of groups. Social work with groups, 13(2), 23 - 24.

Gutierrez, Lorraine, Linnea Glenmayue and Kant Delois 1995. The organizational context of empowerment practice implication for social work Administration .*Social Work,* Vol. 40 No. 2 March.

Gupte, M and A. Bokar, 1987. Women's work, maternity and access to health care: Socioeconomic study of villages in Pune District, Bombay: Foundation for Research in Community Health.

Gugani, Hans Raj, 1994, Literacy, Liberation and Empowerment of women. *University News*, July 11, 1994

Haider Saraswati, Empowerment of Women a Misconstruct, *Mainstream* .Annual 1995, p 103-05

Hall, C.M. 1989. Triadic analysis : A conceptual tool for clinical sociologists. *Clinical Sociology Review*, 7, 97 - 110.

Hall, C,M., 1990a. *Women and identity - value choices in a changing world.* New York: Hemisphere.

Hall, C.M. 1990b. Identity empowerment through clinical sociology. *Clinical Sociology Review*, 8, 69 - 86.

Hall, C.M, 1992: *Women and Empowerment:* Hemisphere Publishing Corporation, London.

Hawkesworth, M.F. 1990. *Beyond oppression: Feminist theory and political strategy.* New York: Continuum.

Hess, R. 1984. Thoughts on Empowerment. In studies in empowerment. New York. The Haworth Press.

Hindberg, B.O. 1988. Violence against women. *Women and Health*, 13, 151 - 158.

Hirayama & Hirayama, K. 1985. Empowerment through group participation: process and goal. In M. Parenes (ed.) *Innovations in social group work: Feedback from practice to theory*, New York: The Haworth Press.

Hoffman, C. 1978. Empowerment movement and Mental Health: Locus of control and commitment of the united farm workers. Journal of Community Psychology, 6(3), 216 - 221.

Holter, H. (Ed.) 1984. *Patriarchy in a welfare society*. New York: Columbia University Press.

Horner, M. 1972. Toward an understanding of achievement related conflicts in women. *Journal of Social Issues*. 28, 157 - 175.

Iglitzin, L., & Ross, R. (Eds.). 1986. Women in the World, 1975 - 1985; *The women's decade* Oxford, England: Clio Press.

Ismail Razia, Empowerment or Power ? The Hidden Beijing Agenda, Mainstream, 33(40) 26 Aug, 1995, p.21-25

Jayalakshmi, K, 1997, Empowerment of women in Panchayats - Experiences of Andhra Pradesh, *Journal of Rural Development*, Vol. 16, No.2, April-June, 1997

Jesani Amar " Limits of Empowerment : Women in Rural Health Care", Economic and Political Weekly, 25(20), May 19, 1990, pp.1098-1103

Jethamalini, Rani (ed.). 1995. Kali's Yug - Empowerment, Law and Dowry-Deaths Warlaw, New Delhi Har-Anand Publications.

Joseph, A. 1993. Brewing trouble. *The Hindu*, March 7. Kahn, A & Bender, F.I. 1985. Self-help groups as a crucible for people empowerment in the context of social development. *Social Development Issues*, 9 (2).

Kannabiran, K. 1993 *(A feminist activist of ASMITA, a women's resource centre in Hyderabad, India)*. Personal communication.

Karl, Marilee. 1995: *Women and Empowerment Participation and Decision making*: Zed Books Ltd. London and New Jersey.

Keefe, T. 1980. Empathy skills and critical consciousness. *Social Casework* 61, 387 - 393.

Kessler-Harris, A. 1981. *Out of work: a History of wage-earning women in the United States*. New York: Oxford University Press.

Kieffer, C.H. 1981. The emergence of empowerment. The development of participatory competence among individuals in citizen organisations. Unpublished doctoral dissertation, University of Michigan.

Kieffer, C.H. 1984. Citizen empowerment: A Development perspective. In *Studies in empowerment*. New York : The Haworth Press.

Klandermans, B. 1993. ' A Theoretical Framework for Comparison of Social Movement Participation', *Sociological Forum*, 8(3): 383-402.

Lengermann, P.M., & Wallace, R.A. 1985. *Gender in America - social control and social change*. Englewood Cliffs, NJ: Prentice - Hall.

Lerner, M. 1980. Stress at the work place. *Catalyst*. 2 (4): 75 - 83.

Leslie J. Calman, Toward Empowerment : Women and Movement Politics in India, Bouldre, Westview Press 1992.

Levitt, Kari. 1990 "Debt, adjustment and Development: Looking to the 1990s". *Economic and Political Weekly*, vol. 25, no. 29 (July 21), pp. 1585-

1594.

Levy, M.J.. 1989. *Our mother-tempers.* Berkley: University of California Press

Lipman - Blumen, J. 1984. *Gender roles and power.* Englewood Cliffs, NJ: Prentice - Hall.

Longres, J & Mcleod, E. 1980. Consciousness-raising and social work practice. *Social Casework.* 61, 401 - 441.

Longwe, S. 1990. *"From Welfare to Empowerment: The Situation of Women in Development in Africa, a Post-UN Women's Decades Update and Future Directions' working Paper 204. Michigan State University.*

Lucy, T. V. 1995: Empowerment of women for sustainable development. *Social Action,* Vol. 45, April - June.

Marks, S. R. 1977. Multiple roles and role strain: Some notes on human energy, time and commitment, *American Sociological Review,* 42, 921 - 936.

Mason, K. O., & Bumpass, L. 1975. U.S. Women's sex-role ideology. *American Journal of Sociology,* 80, 1212 - 1219.

Mason, K. O., Czajka, J., & Arber, S. 1976. Change in U.S. Women's Sex-role attitudes, 1964 - 1974. *American Sociological Review,* 41, 573 - 596.

Maton, K & Rappaport, J. 1984. Empowerment in a religious setting. In J. Rappaport, C. Swift & R. Hess (Eds.), *Studies in empowerment: Towards understanding and action* (pp. 37 - 70). New York: Haworth Press.

Mathis, T. & Richan, W. 1986. Empowerment: Practice in search of a theory. Paper presented at the Annual programme Meeting of the council of social work education, Miami, Marsha.

Mayer, N. 1984, *Neighborhood organisation and community development.* Washington, DC. Urban institute.

Mckee, K. 1989. 'Microlevel Strategies for supporting Livelihoods, employment and income Generation of Poor women in the Third World: The challenge of significance', *World Development,* 1797): 993-1006.

Mills, C.W. 1967. *The Sociological imagination.* New York: Oxford University Press. (Original work published 1959).

Misra, A. 1978. *Chipko movement: Uttarkhand Women's bid to save forest wealth.* New Delhi: People's Action.

Mittal, Meenakshi, 1996, Literacy for women's Equality and Empowerment, *CREATIONS,* Directorate of Adult Education, New Delhi

Mitra, Jyoti, 1997. Women and Society - Equality and Empowerment, *Kanishka Publishers,* New Delhi.

Moghadam, Valentine M. 1990. WIDER Research for Action - Gender, Development, And Policy: Toward Equity and Empowerment, *World In-*

stitute for Development Research of the United nations University.

Mohanty, Bidyut, 1996, women and Political empowerment(ed.), Proceedings of the women's Political empowerment Day Celebrations 23-24, April, 1995, *Institute of Social Sciences*, New Delhi.

Molyneux, M. 1981. Women's Education Under Socialism: A model for the Third World? Brighton, IDS Publication.

Molyneux, M. 1985. *Mobilization without emancipation? Women's interests, the state, and revolution in Nicaragua, Feminist studies* 11:2

Mondros, J.B, 1981. *A study in neighborhood organisation: Issues resolution and empowerment.* Unpublished doctoral dissertation, University of Pennsylvania.

Moser, C. 1989. *Gender planning in the Third World: Meeting practical and strategic needs. World Development* 17:1799-1825.

Nelson, C. 1974. *Public and private and politics: Women in the Middle Eastern world. American Ethnologist* 1 (3):551-563.

Nelson, c. 1978. 'Women Must Help Each Other' in P. Caplan and J. Burja (eds.), *Women United, Women Divided*, pp. 77-98. London: Tavistock Publications

Nirantar, 1995, Beyond the 3 R's, *The Administrator*, July-September'95 Parul , Rishi, 1997, women and environment: from empowerment of women to sustainable development, *KURUKSHETRA*, Jan-Feb'97

O' Connel, B. 1978. From service delivery to advocacy to empowerment. *Social Casework*. 59, 195 - 202.

Oliker, S.J. 1989. *Best friends and marriage: Exchange among women.* Berkley: University of California Press

Omvedt, F. 1986. *Participation - Women in Popular Movements: India and Thailand during the Decade of Women.* Geneva: United Nations Research Institute for Social Development.

Parul , Rishi, 1997, women and environment: from empowerment of women to sustainable development, *KURUKSHETRA*, Jan-Feb'97

Papanek, Hanna. 1985. "Class and Gender in Education-Employment Linkages". *Comparative Education Review* 29, 3.

Papanek, Hanna. 1989. *"Socialization for Inequality: entitlements, the Value of Women, and Domestic Hierarchies."* Mimeo, centre for Asian Development Studies, Boston University.

Parenti, M. 1978 power and the Powerless .New York: *St. Martin's Press.*

Parsons, R. 1991. Empowerment: Purpose and practice in social work. *Social work with groups*, 14, (2), 7 - 22.

Parthasarathy, G, 1995, Economic Impact of women's thrift and Credit societies, *Institute of Development and Planning Studies*, Visakhapatnam.

Patnaik, B.K, 1996, Gender Justice, Women Empowerment and Maternal Health, *Yojona*, vol.40, No,11,Nov.'96

Patnaik, B.K., 1996, Political empowerment of women and village Development, *Yojona,* Dec'96

Pearce, J. 1993. ' NGOs and Social Change: Agents or Facilitators ? *Development In Practice*, 3(3), 222-27.

Prasad, Hemlatha, 1996, Economic Development of Rural Women: Case Studies of IFAD and DWCRA, *National Institute of Rural Development* (unpublished report), Hyderabad

Prasad, K. V.E. and C. Joseph. 1994. Organising Women in the Unorganised Sector: Some issues. Paper presented for the workshop on organising in the Unorganised Sector: Concerns, Priorities and Gender Sensitive Strategies, 22-24 February, New Delhi.

Pernell, R. 1985. Empowerment and social group work. In M. Parenes (ed.). *Innovations in social group work. Feedback from practice to theory*. New York, Howorth Press.

Pillai, J.K. 1995. Women and Empowerment: *Gyan Publishing House.* New Delhi.

Pinderhughes, E. B. 1983. Empowerment for our clients and for ourselves. *Social Case work*. 64 (6). 331 - 339.

Pinderhughes, E 1989. Understanding race, ethnicity, and power : The key to efficacy in clinical practice. New York: *Free Press.*

Rahman, M.A. 1990: Qualitative dimensions of social development evaluation: Thematic Paper. In *Evaluating Social Development Projects* ed. by David Marsden and Peter Okley: OXFAM.

Randour, M. L. 1987. *Women's psyche, women's spirit.* New York: Columbia University Press.

Rao, Nitya. 1996. Empowerment through Organisation: Women Workers in the Informal Sector, *Indian Journal of Gender Studies*, 3:2(1996), sage Publications, New Delhi.

Rappaport, J. 1981. In praise of paradox: A social policy of empowerment over prevention. *American Journal of Community Psychology*, 9 (1), 1 - 25.

Rappaport, J., Swift, C & Hess, R. (Eds.) 1984. *Studies in empowerment : Toward understanding and action*. New York: The Haworth Press.

Report of the UNESCO and National Literacy Mission. 1996. *Directorate of Adult Education,* New Delhi.

Report on Thrift and Credit Programme : *PODUPULAKSHMI* , Nellore district, Andhra Pradesh

Reskin, B., 1988. Bringing the men back in: sex differentiation and the devaluation of women's work. *Gender and Society*, 2, 58 - 81.

Resnick, R. 1976. Conscientization: An indigenous approach to international social work. *International Social Work*, 19, 21 - 29.

Rodda, A. 1991. *Women and the environment. London: Zed Books.*

Rogers, Everett M. et. al 1993. *Women's empowerment. Through Indian Dairy Cooperatives.* Paper Presented at the International Communication. Association, Sydney.

Roper. B. S., & Labeff, E. 1977. Sex roles and feminism revisited: An intergenerational attitude comparison. *Journal of Marriage and the family*, 39, 113 - 119.

Rose, S, Black, B. 1985. *Advocacy and empowerment: Mental Health care in the community.* Boston: Routledge & Kegan Paul.

Rowbotham, S. 1993. *Homeworkers Worldwide*. London: The Merlin Press.

Sanday. P.R. 1981. *Female power and male dominance*. Cambridge: Cambridge University Press.

Sarri, R. & duRivage, V. 1986. *Strategies for Self-help and empowerment of working low-income women who are heads of families.* Unpublished manuscript. Ann Arbor, MI University for Michigan, School of Social work.

Saxena, Kiran, Empowerment of Women : The Indian Context, *Indian Journal of Political Science*, 55(4) Oct-Dec, 1994, pp.391-400

Schaef, A.W. 1985. Women's reality: An emerging female system in a white male society. Minneapolis: *Winston Press.*

Schecter, S. et.al. 1985. *Violence against women. A curriculum for empowerment* (Facilitator's Manual). New York: Women's Education Institute.

Schuler, M.(ed.). 1986. Empowerment and the Law: Strategies of Third World Women. USA:OEF International.

Schuler, M., and Kadirgamar-Rajasingham. 1992. *Legal literacy: A tool for women's empowerment:* New York: UNIFEM.

Scott, H. 1982. *Sweden's "Right to be human" sex-role equality: The goal and the reality.* Armonk NY:M.E. Sharpe.

Sen, G, Germanain, A and Chen L.C (eds.). 1994 Population Policies Reconsidered - Health, Empowerment and Rights, Boston, Massachusetts, Harvard School of Public Health..

Sen, G., and C. Grown. 1985. *Development alternatives with women for a new era: Development crises and alternative visions.* London: *Earthscan.*

Sen, G and C. Crown. 1987. *Development, Crisis and Alternative Visions: Third World Women's Perspectives.* USA: Monthly Review Press.

Shah, C.Y. (ed.) .1989. *A Source Book on Adult Education.* New Delhi. Government of India. Directorate of Adult Education.

Shankar, Anuradha, B. 1996, Literacy for Women's Equality and Empowerment, *CREATIONS*, Directorate of Adult Education, New Delhi

Shapiro, J. 1984. Commitment to disenfranchised clients. In A. Rosenblatt & D. Waitfogel (Eds.) *Handbook of clinical social work.* San Francisco: Jossey Bros.

Sharma, Kumud 1991-92. Grassroot Organisations and Women Empowerment: Some issues in the contemporary Debate. *Samya Shakti: A Journal of Women's Studies*, 6, 28 - 44.

Sherman, W, & Wenocur, S. 1983. Empowering Public Welfare Workers through mutual support. *Social Work*, 28 (5), 375 - 379.

Shibutani, T, 1955. Reference groups as perspectives. *American Journal of Sociology*, 60, 562 - 569.

Simmons, C. & Parsons, R. 1983. Empowerment for role alternatives in adolescence. *Adolescence*, 18, 193 - 200.

Simmons, C. & Parsons, R. 1983. Developing internality and perceived competence: The empowerment of adolescent girls. *Adolescence*, 18, 917 - 922.

Simon, B. 1990. Rethinking empowerment. *Journal of Progressive Human Services* 1, 27 - 40.

Singh, Bhisma Narain, 1997. Education Empowerment for Women. Politics India. December'97

Smelser, N. J. 1962. *The theory of collective behavior.* New York: Free Press.

Solmon, B. 1976. *Black empowerment.* New York . *Columbia University Press.*

Srivastava, Ginny. Organising Poor Rural Women. UNICEF Report.

Stacey. M., M. Price 1981. *Women power and politics.* London and New York: Tavistock Publications.

Staples, Lee H, 1991. Powerful Ideas about Empowerment. *Administration in Social Work*, Vol. 14 (20).

Sudha, K, 1995, Training: an aid to empower rural women leaders, *Kurukshetra*, April'95.

Sujhata, Viswanthan 1997. Grouping Women for Economic Empowerment, *Yojana*, 41 (3), March , pp.37-42

Sujaya , Krishnan. 1997, EMPOWERMENT: the Mahila Samakhya Experience, *DPEP CALLING*, January'97

Swift, C. 1984. Empowerment: An antidote for folly: Foreword. In *Studies in empowerment*. New York. The Haworth Press.

Swift, C. & Levin, G. 1987. Empowerment: An emerging mental health technology. *Journal of Primary Prevention*, (1 - 2), 71 0 92.

Thomas, W. I. and Thomas, D. 1928. *The Child in America*, New York: Knopf Publishing.

Tilakratna, S. 1985. *The Animator in Participatory Rural Development. Some experience from Sri Lanka*, Geneva: International Labour Organisation.

Tripp, A.M. 1994.'Deindustrialisation and the Growth of Women's Economic Associations and Networks in Urban Tanzania, in S. Rowbotham and S Mitter (eds.), D*ignity and Daily Bread*, pp. 139-57. London: Routledge

Turner, R.H. 1981. The real self: from institution to impulse. *American Journal of Sociology,* 81, 989-1016.

UNICEF. 1989. The State of the worlds children 1989. London and NY: Oxford University Press.

UNICEF. 1993.'The Women's Empowerment Framework', Women and Girls Advance, Vol. 1, No. 1, , p. 5.

Young, K. 1988. Gender and Development: A relational Approach. *Oxford University Press.*

Walters, S.1991. Her words on his lips: Gender and popular education in South Africa. ASPBAE Courter 52:17

Wayanganker, Arun Rogers, Everettm, Rao Nagesh and Rogers, Shefner. 1995. Empowering Indian Women Dairy Farmers: *Journal of Rural Reconstruction.* 28 (1).

Weber, M. 1964. *The sociology of religion.* Boston: Beacon Press. (Original work Published 1922.).

Webster 1982. *New World Dictionary*: Second college Edition. New York Simon and Schuster.

Weeks, John R. 1988 "The Demography of Islamic Nations", *Population Bulletin* 43,4(Dec.).

Wieringa, Saskia. 1994 Women's Interests and Empowerment : Gender Planning Reconsidered", *Development and Change* 25(4), October, pp.839-48

Withorn, A. 1985, *Serving the people: Social services and social change.* New York, Columbia University Press.

Zimmerman, M. & Rapport. J. 1982. Citizen Participation, Perceived control and psychological empowerment. *American Journal of Community Psychology,* 16, 725 - 750.

Zippy, Allison, 1995. The Politics of Empowerment: S*ocial Work* Vol.4, No.2, March.

INDEX